INTERNATIONALIZATION, CORPORATE PREFERENCES AND COMMERCIAL POLICY IN JAPAN

Internationalization, Corporate Preferences and Commercial Policy in Japan

Hidetaka Yoshimatsu

First published in Great Britain 2000 by
MACMILLAN PRESS LTD
Houndmills, Basingstoke, Hampshire RG21 6XS and London
Companies and representatives throughout the world

A catalogue record for this book is available from the British
Library.

ISBN 0–333–80292–6 hardcover

First published in the United States of America 2000 by
ST. MARTIN'S PRESS, INC.,
Scholarly and Reference Division,
175 Fifth Avenue, New York, N.Y. 10010

ISBN 0–312–23124–5 (cloth)

Library of Congress Cataloging-in-Publication Data

Yoshimatsu, Hidetaka.
Internationalization, corporate preferences and commercial policy in Japan /
  Hidetaka Yoshimatsu.
    p. cm.
Includes bibliographical references and index.
ISBN 0–312–23124–5 (cloth)
1. International business enterprises – Japan. 2. Corporations, Japanese.
3. Japan – Foreign economic relations. 4. Japan – Commercial policy.
I. Title.
  HD2907.Y625 2000
  338.8′8952 – dc21
                                   99-054951

This book is printed on paper suitable for recycling and made from fully managed
and sustained forest sources.

10 9 8 7 6 5 4 3 2 1
09 08 07 06 05 04 03 02 01 00

Printed in Great Britain

Contents

List of Tables and Figures

Tables

Figure

Preface

This book is about the relationship between the internationalization of corporate activities and the evolving commercial policy preferences of Japanese corporations, and the impact of this relationship on policy processes in Japan. While Japan's trade relations with foreign countries have been critical issues since the mid-1960s, a major concern has shifted from constraints on Japan's exports to the opening of the Japanese market since the mid-1980s. At the same time, the internationalization of Japanese corporations accelerated with a massive outflow of foreign direct investment after the mid-1980s. This research thus links the increased internationalization of corporate activities with Japan's trade relations and commercial policy.

A critical element of the study of trade policy formulation is analysis of corporate preferences as an intervening variable in explaining changes in a state's trade policy. While most research in this field has had an interest of why and how industries and firms demand protection, some studies highlight political forces that favour anti-protectionist policy initiatives. These studies have founded that internationally oriented firms such as multinational corporations are the major actors who favour liberal commercial policy. However, previous research on anti-protectionist policy preferences has been confined to the western countries. This book seeks to fill the research gap by conducting similar research on Japan.

Using case studies of the automobile, electronics and textile industries, and of Keidanren – the most important federation of big business – I develop the argument that as firms strengthen international linkages in the form of multinational operations and international corporate alliances, they become more committed to trade liberalization of the global market, including the market at home. The study of anti-protectionist policy preferences in the Japanese context has special implications. Since it is often presumed that Japan has different institutional settings from those of other industrial countries and maintains close business–government relationships, an investigation of the argument developed on the basis of experiences in western countries is all the more interesting and provides valuable insight into the current study of Japanese politics and political economy.

Different versions of several chapters in this book have appeared in academic journals: 'Economic Interdependence and the Making of Trade Policy: Industrial Demand for an Open Market in Japan', *The Pacific Review*, vol.11, no.1 (1998) pp.28–50; 'Japan's Keidanren and Political Influence on Market Liberalization' (©1998 by The Regents of the University of California, *Asian Survey*, vol.38, no.3, pp.328–45.) Permission to use these materials is gratefully acknowledged to Taylor & Francis Ltd (11 New Fetter Lane, London EC4P 4EE, England) and the Regents of the University of California.

It is a pleasure to acknowledge my debt to those who have provided assistance through the preparation of this book which began as a PhD thesis at the Research School of Pacific and Asian Studies, Australian National University. I am indebted to Peter Drysdale and John Ravenhill for their intellectual guidance and constant encouragement. Professor Drysdale offered constant assistance, insight and advice over the course of this project. Professor Ravenhill gave me many valuable comments and criticisms that helped sharpen my thinking. I am also indebted to Aurelia George for her encouragement and assistance as well as helpful comments. Many others have offered valuable comments and suggestions, including Helen Milner, Ikuo Kabashima, Hayden Lesbirel, Keiko Tabusa, and William James.

I wish to express my deep gratitude to Makoto Sakurai and members of the Mitsui Marine Research Institute in Tokyo who generously supported my field research. I am also grateful to numerous interviewees who kindly shared with me their ideas and perspectives on this project. I also wish to thank Shinichi Ichimura and colleagues at the International Centre for the Study of East Asian Development (ICSEAD). ICSEAD has provided me with a valuable research environment. Lastly, my gratitude goes to my wife, Mutsumi, and my son, Satoshi. Their willing sacrifices and constant support encouraged me to complete this book.

HIDETAKA YOSHIMATSU

List of Abbreviations

ASEAN	Association of Southeast Asian Nations
CAP	Committee on Agricultural Policy
DRAM	Dynamic random access memory
EIAJ	Electronic Industries Association of Japan
EPROM	Erasable programmable read only memory
FDI	Foreign direct investment
FMVs	Fair market values
FTC	Fair Trade Commission
GATT	General Agreement on Tariffs and Trade
JAIC	Japan Apparel Industry Council
JAMA	Japan Automobile Manufacturers' Association
JCFA	Japan Chemical Fibres Association
JCSFWA	Japan Cotton and Staple Fibre Weavers' Association
JKIA	Japan Knitting Industry Association
JSA	Japan Spinners' Association
JSRFWA	Japan Silk and Rayon Fibre Weavers' Association
JTIA	Japan Textiles Importers' Association
JTIF	Japan Textile Industry Federation
JTMA	Japan Towel Manufacturers' Association
LDP	Liberal Democratic Party
MAFF	Ministry of Agriculture, Forestry and Fisheries
MFA	Multi-Fibre Arrangement
MITI	Ministry of International Trade and Industry
MNCs	Multinational corporations
MOF	Ministry of Finance
NIEs	Newly industrialized economies
NUMMI	New United Motor Manufacturing Inc.
OEM	Original equipment manufacturing
OTO	Office of Trade and Investment Ombudsman
PARC	Policy Affairs Research Council
R & D	Research and development
SIA	Semiconductor Industry Association
SII	Structural Impediments Initiative (talks)
TVs	Televisions
UCOM	Users Committee of Foreign Semiconductors
VER	Voluntary export restraint
VTRs	Video tape recorders

1 Introduction

Japan has become the second biggest economic power in the world. Its economic activities have an enormous influence on its major economic partners as well as on the world economy. In spite of Japan's huge economic power, the internationalization of Japanese corporations does not have a long history. Although Japanese corporations penetrated overseas markets through exports in the 1970s, multinational production on a large scale in manufacturing is a relatively recent development. Some sectors, such as textiles and electronics, commenced overseas production before the 1980s, but full-scale multinational production started in the mid-1980s, triggered by rapid appreciation of the yen, a desire to avoid trade friction with developed countries, and promotion of globalization strategies. Outward foreign direct investment (FDI) by Japanese manufacturing firms expanded sharply from US$2.6 billion in 1983 to US$16.3 billion in 1989 and has maintained a high level through the 1990s (Table 1.1). Expanding multinational operations created a network of trade flows within firms. The share of exports shipped to foreign affiliates in total exports by Japanese manufacturing parent companies grew from 29.9 per cent in 1983 to 49.5 per cent in 1992, while the share of imports shipped by overseas affiliates in total imports to Japanese manufacturing parent companies rose from 20.9 per cent to 37.4 per cent in the same period. Japanese manufacturing firms have also deepened their ties with foreign companies through the creation of various webs of international corporate alliances.

The central focus of this book is an exploration of the relationship between the enhanced internationalization of corporate activities and firms' preferences on commercial policy. International economic interdependence may not necessarily lead to the strengthening of firms' support for open trade. It often increases the incentives for some firms to demand protectionist measures by exposing them to further competition with foreign rivals. But heightened interdependence may make some internationally oriented firms represented by multinational corporations (MNCs) more interested in open trade and less tolerant of closed markets at home.[1] A closed home market may disadvantage these firms because it provokes retaliation against their overseas operations. Closure of the home market may also

1

Table 1.1   Internationalization of Japanese manufacturing firms, 1980–96

	1980	1983	1986	1989	1992	1995	1996
FDI (US$ billion)	1.7	2.6	3.8	16.3	10.1	18.6	20.3
Intra-firm exports (%)	16.4	29.9	39.2	41.1	49.5	48.5	55.6
Intra-firm imports (%)	32.5	20.9	23.4	30.9	37.4	32.2	41.3
Overseas production (%)	2.9	3.9	3.2	5.7	6.2	9.0	11.6

Note: The figures in intra-firm exports and intra-firm imports are a percentage proportion of exports to and imports by overseas affiliates in total exports to and imports by Japanese manufacturing parent companies. *Sources*:   Ministry of Finance, *Kokusai kinyukyoku nenpo* [Annual Report of International Finance Bureau], 1994; JETRO, *White Paper on Foreign Investment*, 1998; Ministry of International Trade and Industry, *Kaigai toshi tokei soran* [Statistical Report on Foreign Investment], No.1–No.6; Ministry of International Trade and Industry, *Dai 27 kai wagakuni kigyo no kaigai jigyo katsudo* [The 27th Survey on Overseas Activities of Japanese Firms], 1999.

disrupt trade flows between MNCs and their overseas subsidiaries. Hence, it is probable that internationally oriented firms have a preference for policies which promote the opening of their home markets. This generalization might be applied to the experience of Japanese industries and corporations.

This study hypothesizes that as Japanese corporations intensify international linkages in the form of multinational operations and international corporate alliances, they have more interest in the openness of the Japanese market. This hypothesis is tested through examination of Japanese corporations' preferences for liberalization of the Japanese market. This study seeks to address several questions on the relationship between the internationalization of Japanese corporations' activity and their preferences on trade policy. How have Japanese corporations changed their policy preferences as a result of their international activity? Have they strengthened their preference for open trade abroad and at home? What effects have changes in Japanese corporations' preferences had on Japan's trade policy and trade relations with foreign countries?

A study of the policy preferences of Japanese corporations and their effects on trade policy has theoretical implications. The formation of a nation's trade policy is an outcome of a struggle among domestic interest groups, the national government and the national conception of public interest, and foreign actors (Milner 1988, p.1). A study of trade policy formation thus needs to examine the activities of these actors and interactions between them in the policy-making process. Although the role and activities of bureaucrats and politicians in trade policy formation in Japan have been explored extensively, those of the private sector have not been thoroughly examined in previous studies.[2] So far, much of the research on corporate policy preferences has focused on American firms and their corporate demands on government.[3] Little attention has been paid to the case of Japan. The interest in Japanese corporations has been largely directed towards their corporate strategy and management skills. While quite a few studies have been undertaken of the interaction between business and government in Japan, most of them have tended to discuss the issue of how the government controls and administers the private sector. There are fewer studies that deal with the influence of corporate preferences on government policy or which examine the formation and evolution of the trade policy preferences of Japanese corporations. This study seeks to shed more light on these issues and fill the gap.

CAUSES OF MARKET OPENING IN JAPAN

The Japanese government has become more eager to promote market access for foreign firms and goods since the early 1980s, implementing various measures towards this end. In addition to successive market opening packages in the 1980s, several deregulation programmes have been announced in the 1990s.[4] New tax systems and loans programmes have sought to promote inward investment as well as imports.[5] The Japanese government has also adopted a relatively liberal stance, without taking protectionist measures in import competing industries such as textiles, steel and petro-chemicals. In the textile industry, for instance, the government has resisted the demand by textile circles to protect the industry under the umbrella of the Multi-Fibre Arrangement (MFA).

What factors have driven these open market policies? Sometimes these policy approaches are explained in terms of foreign pressure and strong government initiatives. Foreign pressure, *gaiatsu*, is broadly regarded as a major factor in changing commercial policies in Japan. While Calder refers to Japan as a 'reactive state' where 'the impetus to policy change is typically supplied by outside pressure', van Wolferen sees Japan as a nation lacking a political power centre (Calder 1988b, p.518; van Wolferen 1989). These views regard Japan as unlikely to formulate independent economic policies without external pressure.

Other scholars of the Japanese political economy presume that the bureaucracy has played a dominant role in shaping and implementing economic policy in Japan. Chalmers Johnson, one of the most celebrated scholars of this perspective, argues that Japanese policy making is controlled by the elite bureaucracy and all important policy initiatives derive from bureaucrats (Johnson 1982; 1995).[6] According to this view, the central bureaucracy has its own interests and policy preferences as well as the ability to devise public policy independently of societal actors. The private sector responsively follows bureaucrats' initiatives and guidance. In this conception, market liberalization in Japan is a consequence of bureaucratic leadership.

Quite a few policies designed to open up the Japanese market have been adopted as a consequence of pressure from foreign countries, especially the United States.[7] The Japanese government adopted various schemes to open up the Japanese market by accepting US demands.[8] But foreign pressure alone hardly seems sufficient to explain the whole picture of the trend towards market opening in Japan. As Tanaka (1989, pp.28–31) argues, the United States and China may have successfully exerted pressure on Japan, but other countries have rarely attained their objectives by such pressure. Japan has often modified the agenda of those external forces in directions more acceptable domestically. This result has been one of a blended response of concession and non-compliance (George 1991, p.16). For example, the Structural Impediments Initiative (SII) talks yielded mixed results in the various issue-areas.[9] In some areas, there were significant concessions (the savings–investment balances and the distribution system); in others, there was little or no concession (exclusionary business practices and *keiretsu* relationships), although the US interest was strong in the latter issues (Schoppa 1993).

Certainly bureaucratic initiatives have been vital in promoting market liberalization and overcoming domestic resistance. Yet bureaucratic leadership alone is insufficient to explain the recent tide towards market opening. Bureaucratic power is believed to have gradually declined because of the diversity of public policy objectives, a relative shift in power from bureaucrats to politicians, and rising foreign criticism of the government's interventionist policy. More fundamentally, recent studies of Japanese political economy challenge the view that the bureaucracy has dominated economic policy making. Many scholars who have undertaken detailed empirical research on the Japanese political economy show that there are quite a few instances where the government failed to realise its policy objectives against private business (Kitayama 1985; Friedman 1988; Noble 1989). The opponents of the bureaucracy-dominant view give more credence to the role of private business in policy making and policy implementation (Samuels 1987; Rosenbluth 1989; Calder 1993; Uriu 1996). They have shown that private actors retained control of the market or initiated government policy in various industrial areas. These studies imply that an understanding of business influence on policy making requires more detailed work on formal and informal interactions between business and government, taking into account changes over time and the direction of influence.

In addition, the main target of criticism of the closed Japanese market has shifted from official barriers to trade to non-official practices and institutions such as the Japanese economic structure and business organizations which limit access to the market. Control over these factors is significantly in the possession of the private sector. Even if the government urges the private sector to promote market access, the success of government initiatives is ultimately dependent on private actors able to provide foreign firms with opportunities for entering the market (ACCJ 1993, p.2). Hence, consideration of the stance and actions of private actors is necessary for adequate analyses of market access issues.

This study tries to explain the contribution of 'corporate policy preference' in the policy shift towards market liberalization. Among American scholars of trade politics who have examined the effects of corporate preferences on trade policy, Milner (1987; 1988) is the most prominent. In her case studies of US and French industries, Milner (1987, p.664) concludes that:

> [A]spects of increased international interdependence have wrought changes in the trade policy preferences of industries. Strengthened international economic ties in the form of exports, multinationality, and global intra-firm trade have raised the costs of protection for internationally oriented firms. These firms have thus resisted seeking protection even in times of serious import competition.

A crucial aspect of Milner's findings is that international economic interdependence has changed corporate policy preferences in advanced industrial economies in a similar way to that which she showed to be the case in the United States and France. Rising interdependence should have similar effects on Japanese corporations, if this is indeed the case. Rising international ties of Japanese corporations in the form of multinational operations, intra-firm trade, and various forms of international corporate alliances are likely to enhance the interest in the openness of the Japanese market. These altered corporate policy preferences are expected to facilitate the market access of foreign products and promote market liberalization in Japan.

This is somewhat at odds with the common perception of policy making in Japan. Some scholars doubt the influence of Japanese corporations in policy making. Lincoln (1986, p.166) contends that '[n]ot being truly international in outlook, Japanese multinationals do not seem to have put much pressure on the government to reduce investment barriers as a quid pro quo for their own advance overseas', in his argument objecting to the view that Japanese multinationals take a pragmatic stance in desiring fewer barriers. In the same vein, the Office of Technology Assessment (OTA) holds that although many multinational enterprises are increasingly 'multi' and less 'national' than in the past, this is less true of Japanese corporations because 'formal government policies and informal administrative guidance – as well as the signals effectively embedded in the structure of business networks – have encouraged companies to consider and act in the national interest' (OTA 1993, p.14).

These views are based on the conception that Japanese industries have developed in close collaboration with the home government and that Japanese firms maintain tight inter-corporate relationships among domestic firms. While there may be some truth in these assumptions, it is also true that Japanese corporations have only relatively recently embarked on overseas operations, and their overseas activities are expanding very rapidly. A new free-trade coalition consisting of general trading companies, large retail chains, business federations represented by Keidanren (a peak business federation), and internationally oriented bureaucracies like the Ministry of International Trade and Industry (MITI) has emerged and has an increasing influence on the policy-making process and policy outcomes on trade policy (Calder 1982; Yamamura 1994). These actors are committed to opposing protectionist trade policies and facilitating the access of foreign goods and firms to the Japanese market. It is likely, therefore, that Japanese MNCs with intensive links to the world economy have strengthened the orientation towards open trade, and represent this preference to the government through the activities of industrial associations and Keidanren.

RESEARCH APPROACH

This study argues that increased internationalization has modified Japanese firms' preferences in favour of open trade in world markets and liberalization of the domestic market. This argument will be tested through case studies at the national as well as sectoral levels. The degree and character of internationalization differ in each industry. The market structure and relationship to government agencies, which constitute important factors shaping firms' policy preferences, are also different across industries. Corporate preferences are often diverse within industries as well. These differences need to be examined carefully in case studies. There need to be sufficient case studies to allow cross-sectoral comparison and robust generalizations. As discussed in detail in Chapter 3, the peak business federations, especially Keidanren, play an important role in representing business interests to government and the community in Japan. The preferences of internationally oriented firms on overall trade policy are delivered to the government primarily through the activities of Keidanren. Accordingly, the representation of corporate preferences through Keidanren is examined.

The book does not aim to provide a complete account of the development of firms' trade policy preferences. It primarily focuses on the influence of internationalization on firms' preferences, although it considers other factors including those deriving from the character of each industry. The study seeks to demonstrate that corporate preferences have effects on the government's commercial policy formulation. But this does not mean that other factors such as domestic and foreign government pressures and a favourable exchange rate are insignificant, or that corporate policy preferences dominate.

It is hoped that this research will contribute to the study of Japanese political economy and comparative studies of business–government relations in several ways. The research aims to shed light on the black box of domestic politics influencing Japan's commercial policy. Detailed analysis of these issues will help to explain how domestic politics affect Japan's international relations. In addition, the study makes a contribution to the broader debate on business–

government relations in Japan. Examination of the influence of corporate preferences in trade policy formation involves exploring the relations between government agencies and major business actors. By focusing on this relationship in the formulation of market liberalization in an era when the Japanese economy has integrated more tightly into the global economy, the study should add new insights to the understanding of business–government relations in Japan.

OUTLINE OF THE BOOK

The aim of this study is to investigate the evolution of trade policy preferences of Japanese corporations and their effects on commercial policy. Chapter 2 introduces a hypothesis about corporate policy preferences. After explaining a rationale for anti-protectionist corporate preferences, it sets out the hypothesis that as Japanese corporations have intensified international activity in the form of multinational operations and international corporate alliances, they have had more interest in an open domestic market. The chapter also explains the research method – a case study method at the sectoral and national levels.

Chapter 3 explains the influence of business on Japanese policy making. As long as firms' trade policy preferences are embedded in policy making through the political process, it is necessary, before undertaking detailed case studies, to examine institutions through which business wields influence on the government. This chapter identifies two institutions, *zaikai* and *gyokai*, and explains their interface with bureaucrats and politicians.

Chapter 4 presents an initial sectoral case study – on the automobile industry. Two aspects are highlighted for testing the hypothesis linking internationalization of corporate activity to changing firms' trade policy preferences. One is the effect of internationalization on inter-corporate institutions, *keiretsu* groups. Supplier and distribution *keiretsu* have been criticised for impeding the market access of foreign products. This chapter considers how automakers, which have expanded their international operations, have shifted their stance on *keiretsu* groups and what actions they have undertaken to transform them. The other aspect this chapter looks at is the changes in the trade policy stance of the automakers by examining their reactions to the government's market-opening policies.

In Chapter 5, the electronics industry is studied. This industry, like the automobile industry, has undergone a thoroughgoing internationalization with complicated webs of corporate alliances in high-technology fields as well as extensive foreign investment. It examines what influence internationalization has had on the electronics firms' stance on import restrictions as well as market-opening policies. Special attention is paid to the US–Japan Semiconductor Arrangement, revealing how firms' stance on market access has evolved and what effect this has had on the implementation of the arrangement.

Unlike the previous two chapters, Chapter 6 tests the hypothesis by using the case of an import competing industry. The Japanese textile industry has suffered from a surge of imports since the mid-1980s, leading major industrial associations to call on the government to introduce import restriction measures. By investigating how various industrial associations with different international ties react to such a move, it explores the relations between the internationalization of corporate activities and its effect on firms' trade policy preferences. This chapter pays attention to the large textile producers' stance on import restrictions, analysing the complex motivations of these firms on import restrictions.

Keidanren, the peak federation of big business, is the focus of Chapter 7. Keidanren is the most influential business lobby. The influence of internationally oriented firms is most likely to be integrated into government policy through the activities of Keidanren. This chapter examines the development of Keidanren's views and activities on several trade policy issues. This analysis reveals how Keidanren's posture and commitment have evolved as Japanese industry has become interlinked with the international economy.

Chapter 8 evaluates the evidence on firms' policy preferences in the case studies, and asks whether Japanese corporations have strengthened their open trade stance as their international linkages have deepened. It also takes a look at the character of trade policy preferences specific to the Japanese case. The case of Japan is placed within the context of broader debate on international and comparative political economy in order to demonstrate its wider theoretical implications. The limitations of the study are discussed and suggestions are made regarding areas for further research.

2 The Rise of Multinational Corporations and Policy Preferences

What effect does international economic interdependence have on firms' trade policy preferences? Heightened interdependence has exposed firms to more competition with foreign rivals, and has often led domestically oriented firms to demand that the government introduce protectionist measures. At the same time, rising interdependence has produced firms whose global operations are deeply integrated into the world economy. Such internationally oriented firms, represented by multinational corporations (MNCs), have brought about quantitative and qualitative changes in international trade through foreign direct investment (FDI). FDI has promoted the industrialization of recipient countries through a transfer of capital and technology, creating additional trade. A large portion of this trade occurs in the manufacturing sector, and raises levels of intra-industry trade. FDI by MNCs has also promoted intra-firm trade.

Because of their tight linkages with the international economy, MNCs are said to have more interest in resisting the demand for protection and maintaining the stability and openness of the international trading system. They fear that protection at home will kindle retaliatory measures towards their operations abroad. In addition, closure of the home market puts internationally oriented firms in a disadvantageous position compared to domestically oriented firms. While internationally oriented firms may incur new costs of trade barriers, domestically oriented firms experience little or no effect. Furthermore, the increase in intra-firm trade means that closure of the home market is likely to hamper MNCs' trade ambitions.

This research seeks to examine whether the internationalization of corporate activities has changed the policy stance of Japanese corporations towards an open domestic market. As a prelude, this chapter provides the theoretical foundation of this study, which constitutes the basis for the analysis of detailed case studies in later chapters.

CORPORATE PREFERENCES ON TRADE POLICY

A voluminous theoretical and empirical literature has explored why industries and firms demand protection. It is generally held that demand for protection arises out of the rent-seeking behaviour of firms. Firms ask for protection if they believe that they can obtain excess rents from the imposition of quantitative restrictions and tariffs (Krueger 1974; Bhagwati and Srinivasan 1980; Bhagwati 1982). Other scholars argue that industries facing a comparative disadvantage – normally the labour-intensive industries in developed countries – seek to exert political pressure on government to adopt protectionist measures against foreign imports (Caves 1976; Ray 1981).

Other research on firms' preferences demonstrates the influence of industries' characteristics on firms' policy preferences and policy outcomes. It is generally accepted that the smaller the number of firms in an industry, the greater the industry gains in favourable policy outcomes. This is because small groups are more likely to overcome the free-rider problem and to maximize the benefits per firm arising from their influence on policy (Olson 1965). Other studies suggest that an industry's geographic concentration is positively related to its success in lobbying for protection (Pincus 1975). This is because greater geographic concentration improves the ability of an industry to communicate and coordinate the benefits of actions. Other industry characteristics which influence policy outcomes include the industry's size, the degree of industry concentration, the number of workers, and the average wage level.

Previous studies of firms' trade policy preferences tended to focus on why and how domestic societal actors demand protection. In recent years, some studies have focused on domestic political forces that oppose protection and favour pro-liberal trade policy initiatives (Ferguson 1984; Destler and Odell 1987; Milner 1987, 1988; Bhagwati 1988, chap. 4; Milner and Yoffie 1989). Milner, who explores the relationship between firms' pro-liberal policy preferences and domestic trade politics most intensively, argues that rising economic interdependence has strengthened the international ties of some firms in the form of exports, multinational operations, and intra-firm trade. This trend towards globalization has motivated internationally oriented firms to shift their preferences against protectionist measures in favour of more liberalized trade policies. Milner also suggests that trade policy preferences of industries have exerted a crucial influence on trade policy outcomes.[1]

Internationally oriented firms represented by MNCs are likely to resist appeals for protectionism and to favour open trade. This preference can be accounted for by several factors deriving from their characteristics as globally operating firms. First, MNCs generally gain more benefits from policies which reduce barriers to trade and investment flows. MNCs are basically trade-oriented, both because foreign production is impossible without some trade in intermediate products and because MNCs' value-added activities are directed to create or divert trade in goods and resources (Dunning 1993, p.402). Accordingly, lower trade barriers allow them to achieve higher profits resulting from more economic activities based on multinational corporate ties. In addition, not only do MNCs account for a large portion of exports but their imports tend to be concentrated on primary and intermediate products (Lavergne 1983, p.105). In 1993, for instance, MNC-associated trade accounted for 58 per cent of US merchandise exports.[2] As some studies suggest, firms that depend on extensive exports or imports of intermediate inputs are more likely to be in favour of free trade.[3]

Second, MNCs incur high costs from protection at home. MNCs fear that protection at home will promote retaliatory protection abroad or new restrictions on their operations and trade flows (Milner 1988, p.23). MNCs are vulnerable to foreign governments' measures against their operations. Retaliation may take the form of closing markets for their exports, causing disruption to MNCs' integrated world trade flows. Retaliatory measures may also take the form of disturbance to investment or strict application of performance requirements. In addition, costs and benefits derived from closure of the home market are distributed unequally between internationally oriented and domestically centred firms (Milner 1987, p.645). Domestically oriented firms gain substantial benefits from closing home markets because they experience little or no effect from trade barriers which impose new costs on internationally oriented firms. The closure of the home market strengthens MNCs' domestic rivals in relative terms by enhancing their profitability and market position.

Third, structural adjustment, a process whereby factors of production shift from declining sectors to those with future prospects, is relatively easy for MNCs (Grimwade 1989, pp.384–8). MNCs have more information about market trends and changes in international comparative advantage than uni-national firms. They are able to anticipate the need for adjustment and the emergence of new sources of supply for a particular product. In addition, they can maintain industrial competitiveness by relocating production bases to overseas countries because they possess mobile capital (Milner and Yoffie 1989, p.242). Furthermore, MNCs can move away relatively easily from declining sectors. They usually operate in multi-product areas, including sectors with better prospects. They can also easily develop new products because they possess the necessary funds as well as appropriate technology and marketing skills. Lower adjustment costs mean that MNCs are less worried about an upsurge of imports and therefore require less protection.

The fourth factor that has induced MNCs to resist the temptation for protectionist measures is the increase in intra-firm trade, defined as imports and exports involving firms related by ownership and operating in different countries. Intra-firm trade accounts for a large proportion of current international trade. In 1989, for example, 39.0 per cent of US merchandise exports and 43.5 per cent of imports were undertaken between US parent firms and their foreign affiliates (OECD 1993, pp.38–9). The rise in intra-firm trade strengthens the advocacy of free trade in goods and services. For a firm which exports to its home market, trade barriers at home may lead to the curtailment of its exports and act as an additional cost for internal transfers (Anderson and Baldwin 1987, p.24; Milner 1988, p.23). In addition, manufacturing MNCs often set up cross-national production networks in order to exploit profit opportunities by optimum location of the network bases. Each production base is given a particular specialization in the production chain. Closing a specific market including the home market and resultant disruptions to the flows of intra-firm transactions reduce the benefits that the production chain yields. Some empirical analyses support the tendency of firms involved in intra-firm trade to show a positive attitude to trade liberalization. Helleiner (1981, p.82) points out that import duties on primary and intermediate products are lower than average duties of final products, and these products are likely to be traded between MNCs and their foreign affiliates.

Although FDI still constitutes a crucial pillar in international corporate strategy, corporate alliances have emerged as an important strategy, along with FDI, in international business.[4] Alliances themselves are not necessarily new, and were widely used as a major corporate strategy in the past. But recent alliances, unlike those before, are characterized by a strategic character. Doz, Hamel and Prahalad (1986, cited in Young *et al.* 1989, pp.273–4) identify four features of current alliances: (1) they are composed of two or more partners from industrialised countries with comparable global strength and resources; (2) the partners of strategic alliances are often direct competitors in the same product/geographical market; (3) the contribution of partners regarding the production, marketing and technology is more balanced than in conventional alliances; and (4) the motivations underlying the formation of alliances are strategic and competitive in scope rather than such simple ones as the need for market access, economies of scales, or pooling of resources. Alliances with a strategic character are common in high-technology sectors like semiconductors and computers, although they can also be found in conventional industries such as steel, automobile, and machine tools.

Increased internationalization through corporate alliances has played a catalytic role in transforming corporate preferences towards resisting protectionist measures and promoting open trade policy. This change in preferences has sprung from several factors. First of all, corporate alliances contribute to making private firms less dependent on protectionist measures. Risk sharing through corporate linkages dissuades firms from demanding protection (Cowhey and Aronson 1993, p.225). Private firms incur huge costs in developing new products and establishing market bases. In the past, the need to pay these high costs motivated firms to call on governments to shut out foreign competitors. By sharing the costs of market development and R & D, corporate alliances undermine incentives to protect home markets. In addition, international alliances promote a division of labour enabling alliance parties to concentrate their management resources on their strengths while depending on their partners to cover weaknesses (Imai 1990, p.186).

Second, corporate alliances often encourage partners involved to resist protectionist claims against their partners. Alliance partners are expected to exert political pressure for the benefits of foreign counterparts. Even in a case when a partner firm does not take action but shows a passive attitude to protectionist measures against its foreign partner, this might be likely to divide the industry in the home country, weakening the industry's capability for protection. When the United Automobile Workers (UAW) pushed for quotas and domestic content legislation in the 1980s, GM (General Motors) opposed the move due to its arrangements for small car imports with Isuzu, Suzuki and Daewoo, and the joint venture of the New United Motor Manufacturing Inc. (NUMMI) with Toyota. Because of GM's disagreement, the industry's trade group, the Motor Vehicle Manufacturers' Association (MVMA) declined to support quotas and domestic content legislation (Kline 1985, p.64). Corporate alliances also promote mutual understanding of partners' institutions and customs, and thereby reduce the risk that disputes will become serious. Trade friction can spring from differences in institutions and social or economic customs between states.[5] In order to maintain alliances successfully, the parties seek to deepen their understanding of market conditions, and production and procurement methods prevailing in the countries of their partners.

Third, corporate alliances motivate firms to oppose protectionist measures by undermining the base for nationalistic trade and industrial policy. High-technology fields such as computers, information electronics and pharmaceuticals are viewed as critical for industrial competitiveness because of their spillover effects on other industries. Governments are increasingly trying to cooperate with private companies in these sectors and to sustain their activities through special tax treatment and the formation of research consortia which limit participation to national firms. In the high-technology sector, firms are so profoundly linked with foreign partners that it is almost impossible to find firms which are completely independent in their industrial activities. Even if a government seeks to support particular domestic firms, the benefits of such policies leak to foreign firms and countries through international alliances (Soete 1991, p.61; Stevens 1991, p.100). This is because firms which have cooperative R & D contracts with foreign partners often exchange new technological knowledge including that acquired from government-sponsored programmes. Hence, firms with international corporate alliances are generally less inclined to support nationalistic industrial and trade policies which lead to protection.

A MODEL OF CORPORATE POLICY PREFERENCE FOR JAPAN

The two internationalization variables, multinational operations and international corporate alliances, are likely to affect corporate preferences on trade policy. This connection suggests the hypothesis that as firms deepen international linkages in the form of multinational operations and international corporate alliances, they have less interest in protection and more interest in preserving the openness of the global market, including their home market. This study applies this hypothesis to Japan, seeking to examine how trade policy preferences of Japanese corporations have evolved with the expansion of their multinational operations and corporate alliances, and what effects such changes in policy preferences have had on Japan's trade policy.

In applying the hypothesis to Japanese industry, it is necessary to examine the degree of internationalization in Japanese industry. The hypothesis presupposes that intensive internationalization of corporate activity will change corporate preferences in favour of open trade. The most common indicator used to show the extent of internationalization of corporate activity is FDI. Since the mid-1980s, Japanese FDI has not only grown sharply but has also expanded its scope in terms of industries and recipient countries.[6] Japanese outward FDI increased from US$12 billion in 1985 to US$57 billion in 1990, and has maintained a high level through the 1990s (Table 2.1).[7] The share of overseas to domestic sales expanded from 3 per cent in 1985 to

Table 2.1   Japanese foreign direct investment by destination, 1981–96 (US$ million and per cent)

Year	Asia		North America		Europe		World
1981	3,338	37.4	2,522	28.2	768	8.9	8,931
1982	1,384	18.0	2,905	37.7	876	11.4	7,703
1983	1,847	22.7	2,701	33.2	990	12.2	8,145
1984	1,628	16.0	3,544	34.9	1,937	19.1	10,155
1985	1,435	11.7	5,495	45.0	1,930	15.8	12,217
1986	2,327	10.4	10,441	46.8	3,469	15.5	22,320
1987	4,868	14.6	15,357	46.0	6,576	19.7	33,364
1988	5,569	11.8	22,328	47.5	9,116	19.4	47,022
1989	8,238	12.2	33,902	50.2	14,808	21.9	67,540
1990	7,054	12.4	27,192	47.8	14,294	25.1	56,911
1991	5,936	14.3	18,823	45.3	9,371	22.5	41,584
1992	6,425	18.8	14,572	42.7	7,061	20.7	34,138
1993	6,637	18.4	15,287	42.4	7,940	22.0	36,025
1994	9,699	23.6	17,823	43.4	6,230	15.2	41,051
1995	12,264	24.2	22,761	44.9	8,470	16.7	50,694
1996	11,614	24.2	23,021	47.9	7,372	15.4	48,019
Total	100,094	17.8	248,473	44.2	105,709	18.8	562,320

Sources: Ministry of Finance, *Kokusai kinyukyoku nenpo* [Annual Report of International Finance Bureau] 1994, p.155; JETRO, *White Paper on Foreign Investment*, 1998, pp.527–8.

11.6 per cent in 1996.[8] In the late 1960s and 1970s, Japanese FDI was concentrated in resource extraction and import-substituting manufacturing sectors in East Asia. Since the mid-1980s, FDI has flowed into manufacturing parts and finished products, finance, insurance and real estate, and diversified geographically to North America and Western Europe.

Intra-firm trade, another vital indicator of firms' internationalization, is increasing in the major Japanese industrial sectors as well.[9] While the share of exports by Japanese manufacturers to their overseas affiliates grew from 29.9 per cent in 1983 to 48.5 per cent in 1995, the share of imports by their overseas affiliates rose from 20.9 per cent to 32.2 per cent in the same period.[10] Intra-firm trade is expected to rise more because some Japanese firms regard so-called 'reverse' imports – imports from overseas affiliates to Japan – as a pillar of corporate strategy. This propensity has been strengthened by two kinds of international division of labour (Ozawa 1991, pp.55–6). One is vertical division of labour. While Japanese firms export sophisticated components to Asian countries, they import final products from affiliates which use these components or under original equipment manufacturing (OEM) contracts. This is the case for calculators, standard colour televisions (TVs), and video tape recorders (VTRs). The other is horizontal specialization. Japanese firms are transferring production bases of low value-added products and models to overseas plants, and sending the products back to Japan. For example, Honda Motors is transferring the production of Civic and Accord models to the United States and Europe, while it concentrates at home on the production of luxury models such as Integra and Prelude. This leads to the import of the Accord model from the United States.[11] The increase in intra-firm trade and reverse imports is expected to be an important factor in changing firms' trade policy preferences.

Corporate alliances between Japanese and foreign companies have also become conspicuous. According to Nomura Research Institute data, the number of reports in *Nikkei Sangyo Shimbun* [Japan Industrial Newspaper] on corporate alliances increased from 4,700 between 1981 and 1983 to 8,417 between 1984 and 1986, and to 11,215 between 1987 to 1989 (Higashi and Ōkawa 1993, p.79). In the 1990s, quite a few alliances are transformed into those with strategic objectives. Table 2.2 shows the number of alliances between Japanese and US firms. While the number of alliances in equity relationships decreased from 497 in 1990 to 246 in 1994, that in manufacturing and technical alliances increased from 230 to 418 in the same period. This propen-

Table 2.2   Number of alliances between Japanese and US firms, 1990–94

Year	Equity relationships	Manufacturing technical alliance	Joint development	Technology grant	Total
1990	497	230	43	25	795
1991	370	215	50	59	694
1992	277	396	27	40	740
1993	183	469	9	42	703
1994	246	418	20	40	724

Source: *Soken chosa*, March 1995, p.73.

sity is seen at the firm level. For instance, the original aim of the alliance between Ford Motor and Mazda Motor was equity participation. However, this alliance now involves joint development of new models, mutual supply of vehicles and supply of Mazda's distribution channels.

The application of the corporate preference model to Japanese industry has at least two critical implications. The first is that study of the Japanese case enables an important research gap to be filled. Corporate preferences on trade policy have been studied intensively in the United States, but there has been little research on this issue outside the United States. Moreover, most of the literature focuses on protectionist pressures, and literature on anti-protectionist and pro-liberal domestic forces is an exception in the study of the political economy of international trade. Work on the anti-protectionist movement is very limited. As Milner (1988) suggests, the effects of international interdependence of corporate activity should be seen similarly in all industrial countries. The trend towards internationalization of Japanese industry might be expected to have made Japanese corporations more sensitive to the reactions of foreign governments and firms on trade policy, raising the likelihood that they would move to support an open market in Japan. Thus, undertaking research on Japan contributes to enriching the study of the anti-protectionist political pressure and to generalizing the influence of the pro-liberal corporate preference in policy formation in industrial countries.

Second, the application of the model to Japanese industry deepens our understanding of Japanese political economy. There has been a long and intensive debate over the cause of Japan's economic success. Some observers with a neo-classical perspective posit that Japan's economic success came from the vigorous activities of private firms in the market, and that the role of the government at best creates a supportive environment.[12] Others with a statist perspective argue that the critical and particular role of the government and effective industrial policy are the keys to Japan's economic success.[13] In recent years, some scholars, the so-called revisionists, have argued that Japan operates in a different political and economic system.[14] Although the revisionist thesis tends to exaggerate the different characteristics of Japanese political economy, it is a fact that some economic conditions in which Japanese industry operates are different from those in other industrial countries.

As examined in the next chapter, the relationship between business and government is closer in Japan than in the United States where business–government relations are frequently adversarial and at arm's length. The government has set up and utilized economic regulatory systems with particular policy objectives including rapid industrialization and equitable economic outcomes (Samuels 1996; Johnson 1995; Sakakibara 1996). The Japanese business community has distinctive features such as its powerful peak business federations and industrial associations, the dominance of long-term relational dealings, and the prevalence of financial *keiretsu* links. There is the possibility that even if conditions are developing in which internationally oriented Japanese corporations support an open domestic market, the characteristics which are peculiar to Japan may produce outcomes different from those in other countries. That is, long-term dealings based on *keiretsu* relations may affect Japanese firms' stance on liberalization of the domestic market, and the different institutional settings in Japanese business may provide different channels of influence on trade policy and different policy outcomes.

Given that Japan is presumed to have different policy orientations and institutional settings from other industrial countries, an investigation of the hypothesis developed on the basis of American experience is all the more interesting and will provide robust support for the assumption that the international interdependence of corporate activity has a similar influence on industrial countries. In order to test the hypothesis in the Japanese context carefully and sufficiently, detailed examination of how business interests affect the policy-making process in Japan, and the adoption of a methodology taking into account the particular institutional settings in Japan are required.

METHODOLOGY

Case studies at the sectoral and national levels

This study analyses whether rising economic interdependence has transformed Japanese firms' preferences on trade policy into promoting liberalization of the market, and what effects changing policy preferences have had on Japan's trade policy and trade relations. In order to accomplish this research objective, a case study approach is adopted. This study focuses on two sorts of case: one at the sectoral level and the other a national representation of Japanese industries' policy preferences. A particular interest is how firms and industrial associations in different sectors have responded, as well as how the peak business association has performed. Such factors as industrial structure, international operations, and relations with the government, which form the foundation of firms' policy preferences, differ across industry. Examination of industrial-level variables provides a clearer picture of the factors influencing firms' policy preferences. Policy preferences are frequently expressed by associations at the industrial level. Each industry has one or more industrial associations. These associations, as the representatives of firms in different industries, express their stance on public policy and conduct political activities such as lobbying, political donations, and submission of policy proposals. The activities of industrial associations provide clearer insights into the policy preferences of the different industrial sectors.

In the sectoral studies, firm-level variables are also examined. The real actors undertaking international operations, experiencing the costs and benefits of particular policies, and developing specific policy preferences are individual firms. Individual firms may have strong trade policy preferences even when the preferences of the industry are ambiguous. As Milner (1988, pp.36–7) points out, an industry's aggregate preferences may hide deep divisions among the firms within an industry. Individual firms, which have a different involvement in international operations or a different position in an industry, are affected in different ways by trade policies. These differences naturally create diverse preferences on trade policies. Heterogeneous policy preferences may have a crucial effect on the formation of an industry's policy position and the purposefulness with which it represents that position, a factor which needs to be taken into account in industry-level analysis.

In addition to case studies at the sectoral level, this study highlights the views and activities of Keidanren, a peak business federation, on trade policy at the national level. International linkages are formed by individual firms, and the characteristics of internationalization differ industry by industry, but the representation of firms' and industries' interests at the national level is important in some institutional settings. Two factors make it particularly useful to highlight the expression of corporate preferences at the national level.

The first factor is that Japanese peak business organizations have played a more politically influential role in policy making in Japan than their counterparts in some other industrial countries. US business has peak associations such as the National Association of Manufacturers and the Chamber of Commerce of the United States.[15] But because of their huge and heterogeneous membership and their history of development, these two associations cannot effectively coordinate the interests of their members, and their role in shaping policy is often overshadowed by issue-specific coalitions (Lynn and McKeown 1988, pp.81–3). The US business community also has more narrowly representative associations. The Business Roundtable, founded in 1973, comprises 175–200 chief business leaders. The Business Council, originally established in 1933 as a hybrid private–public organization, consists of some 150 business elites (Lynn and McKeown 1988, p.82). In spite of their small and homogeneous membership, these organizations have no strong common goals. Firms attempt to pursue their interests, acting individually instead of trying to coordinate their differences (Ouchi 1984, p.158).

Japanese business leadership – *zaikai* – organises at the national and local levels.[16] The national level *zaikai* operates through four business federations: the Japan Chamber of Commerce and Industry (Nissho); the Japan Federation of Employers' Associations (Nikkeiren); the Japan Association of Corporate Executives (Keizai Doyukai); and the Japan Federation of Economic Organizations (Keidanren). Although there is considerable overlap in the membership, the four business federations have different functions: Nissho is a forum for small and medium-scale business; Nikkeiren is a labour relations-focused organization; Keizai Doyukai is a forum for individual business leaders; and Keidanren is a representative of big business. Japanese *zaikai* takes positions that transcend narrow company- or industry-specific interests through its national-level associations. Although inter-industry disputes are also common in the

Japanese business community, their influence is less apparent than its US counterpart.

Zaikai is involved in the formation of government policy, as well. *Zaikai* is commonly consulted on important public policies.[17] *Zaikai* is also involved in policy formation through membership on advisory councils.[18] The mass media publish and represent the views and activities of *zaikai* as the collective opinion of business circles. *Zaikai* influences politicians directly through financial donations which were collected by Keidanren. Although the federation ceased channelling donations to political parties in 1994, it still maintains close relationships with politicians through unofficial gatherings between senior members of *zaikai* and leading politicians, and through the exchange of opinions between the secretariats of business federations and the deliberative organs of the political parties.

A second interest in Keidanren's national-level representation of business views derives from the division of policy concern between peak business federations and industrial associations. Unlike the peak associations in Europe, which often represent the interests of specific industries to governments, the activities of Japanese business federations have been directed to 'the issues on which there is consensus in the business community like the decrease in corporate tax and administrative reform, or issues which attracted meagre attention from individual firms like education, law and order, and defence' (Ōtake 1979, pp.96–100). In respect of trade issues, Keidanren deals with overall trade policy issues, non-tariff quotas and agricultural trade policy issues affecting the Japanese economy as a whole. Keidanren publishes position papers on specific industries, but these are often relevant to Japanese industry as a whole or economic relations with foreign countries. Industrial associations are more concerned with micro-level, industry-specific policy issues, and relay their opinions directly to the government through relevant bureaus and sections. Examining Keidanren's posture and activities enriches our understanding of firms' trade policy preferences in an institutional setting which is ostensibly very different from that of the United States, where most of the previous research has been carried out.

Selection of industrial sectors

Insofar as the internationalization of corporate activities is an independent variable, the industries selected for study need to reflect high degrees of integration into the international market or the large extent to which firms are tightly integrated into the world economy through FDI, global intra-firm trade and corporate alliances. At the same time, the selection of an industry which is facing high and rising level of imports and probably favours protectionist measures broadens the range of observation in a way that strengthens examination of the central hypothesis.

In order to select industries in the first category, the study highlights both firm-level and industry-level data. As long as the internationalization of corporate activity is a result of firms' strategies, the primary focus should be directed to data at the firm level. However, data at the firm level are meagre, while data at the industry level provide evidence about the degree and character of internationalization in the industry to which firms belong. Therefore, this study first highlights industry-level data in order to identify particular industries with advanced internationalization, prior to exploring firm-level data.

The study uses several measures of internationalization at the industry level: (1) the level of FDI; (2) the ratio of overseas production; (3) the extent of intra-firm trade; and (4) the number of corporate alliances. The first three provide an indication of the extent of multinational operations in each industry. The higher the relevant measures, the more the industry is involved in multinational activities. The last element provides a broader measure of internationalization.

All the manufacturing sectors increased FDI after 1985 (Table 2.3). Chemicals, electrical machinery and transport machinery are the leading sectors in FDI. Electrical machinery ranked first between 1986 and 1991, while chemicals and transport machinery ranked second or third.

The degree of internationalization of corporate activities is also usefully measured by the ratio of overseas to home production in each industry (Table 2.4). The more overseas operations grow, the higher the overseas production ratio. Although the overall overseas production ratio was almost unchanged between 1980 and 1985, it rose gradually after 1985, climbing from 3 per cent in 1985 to 11.6 per cent in 1996. The rise in electrical and transport machinery was the most remarkable. The ratio for electrical machinery exceeded 10 per cent in 1988 and the ratio for transport machinery jumped sharply above 15 per cent in 1992.

Global operations through FDI have also intensified international trade flows within firms. Tables 2.5 and 2.6 reveal trends in intra-firm trade for Japanese industry between 1980 and 1996.[19] The machinery

Table 2.3   Japanese foreign direct investment in manufacturing by sector, 1980–96 (US$ million)

Sector	1980	1985	1990	1993	1994	1995	1996	1951–96
Food	54	90	821	888	1,260	844	729	8,956
Textiles	91	28	796	498	641	1,043	606	7,831
Wood and pulp	78	15	314	346	140	357	619	5,173
Chemicals	314	133	2,292	1,742	2,601	2,114	2,059	23,074
Metals	493	385	1,047	754	1,038	1,555	2,446	17,833
General machinery	102	352	1,454	1,171	1,622	1,870	1,438	16,421
Electrical machinery	309	513	5,684	2,762	2,634	5,288	6,513	41,670
Transport machinery	176	627	1,872	942	2,021	1,989	3,873	22,890
Other manufacturing	89	208	1,207	2,029	1,826	3,564	1,974	23,929
Manufacturing total	1,706	2,352	15,486	11,132	13,784	18,623	20,258	167,777

Sources: Ministry of Finance, *Kokusai kinyukyoku nenpo* [Annual Report of International Finance Bureau] 1994, pp.420–21; JETRO, *White Paper on Foreign Investment*, 1998, p.529.

sectors have a high level of both intra-firm exports and imports. Three machinery sectors – electrical, transport, and precision machinery – exceeded 55 per cent in intra-firm exports in 1992. In intra-firm imports, general machinery and precision machinery maintained high levels of imports after the late 1980s.

It is not easy to determine the exact number of corporate alliances because the form of corporate alliances is nominal and they are often treated as confidential. However, those relating to large firms are announced publicly. One way to explore trends in corporate alliance formation is to examine newspaper reports of these activities. Table 2.7 shows the trend of corporate alliances in reports in *Nikkei Sangyo Shimbun*. The leading industry is electrical machinery, followed by metals and transport machinery. Though the number of corporate alliances in the metal sector has been increasing since the mid-1980s, alliances in the sector are mainly in high-technology fields such as semiconductors.

These industry-level data suggest that the transport and electrical

Table 2.4   Overseas production ratios in Japanese manufacturing sectors, 1980–96 (per cent)

Sector	1980	1985	1990	1991	1992	1993	1994	1995	1996
Food	0.7	0.9	1.2	1.2	1.3	2.4	3.2	2.6	4.0
Textiles	4.0	2.7	3.1	2.6	2.3	3.2	4.0	3.5	7.6
Wood and pulp	1.4	1.2	2.1	1.6	1.4	1.9	2.1	2.2	2.9
Chemicals	1.4	2.0	5.1	5.5	4.8	7.0	8.1	8.3	10.0
Iron and steel	3.4	5.3	5.6	4.9	5.0	6.3	5.4	9.2	12.1
Non-ferrous metals	4.1	2.7	5.2	5.2	7.8	6.5	8.8	6.7	11.1
General machinery	1.8	3.4	10.6	7.6	4.1	5.8	8.1	8.1	11.7
Electrical machinery	6.3	7.4	11.4	11.0	10.8	12.6	15.0	16.8	19.7
Transport machinery	2.2	5.6	12.6	13.7	17.5	17.3	20.3	20.6	24.9
Precision machinery	2.5	3.4	4.7	4.4	3.6	5.6	6.0	6.6	8.6
Oil and coal	–	0.0	0.2	1.2	5.2	7.1	5.6	3.7	2.8
Other manufacturing	1.0	0.8	3.1	2.6	2.3	2.8	3.0	3.0	4.3
Manufacturing total	2.9	3.0	6.4	6.0	6.2	7.4	8.6	9.0	11.6

Note: The figures are a percentage proportion of the sales of overseas affiliates to the domestic sales in Japan.
Sources: MITI, *Kaigai toshi tokei soran* [Statistical Report on Foreign Investment], No.3 (1988), p.10; *Dai 27 kai wagakuni kigyo no kaigai jigyo katsudo* [The 27th Survey on Overseas Activities of Japanese Firms] (1999), p.44.

machinery sectors are the most internationalized sectors within Japanese industry. Which industries appear the most internationalized from firm-level data? There are four kinds of firm-level data that can be used to address this question. The first is the Fortune Global 500 firm ranking. This ranking, confined to the manufacturing sector, is based on sales in world markets. Twenty Japanese MNCs were listed in the top 100 in 1992 (Table 2.8). These firms belonged to six sectors:

Table 2.5   Shares of intra-firm exports in Japanese manufacturing sectors, 1980–96 (per cent)

Sector	1980	1983	1986	1989	1992	1995	1996
Food	16.9	18.3	7.8	18.6	12.8	43.0	41.5
Textiles	3.2	2.7	7.2	3.3	11.0	16.9	19.2
Wood and pulp	0.2	0.4	0.0	5.2	5.7	2.8	5.5
Chemicals	17.5	19.5	9.4	21.9	25.9	30.4	34.3
Iron and steel	2.7	2.2	8.3	1.4	9.3	8.3	32.8
Non-ferrous metals	14.5	2.9	8.3	19.2	23.3	30.2	31.8
General machinery	19.5	12.8	32.2	43.8	43.3	43.1	44.4
Electrical machinery	23.8	24.8	43.3	50.9	57.1	71.1	57.2
Transport machinery	10.8	45.3	43.7	41.1	56.5	35.8	67.0
Precision machinery	39.4	38.7	59.6	52.8	55.5	55.9	53.5
Oil and coal	–	42.4	73.6	36.5	2.4	8.6	21.6
Other manufacturers	38.6	40.7	35.0	43.8	53.8	42.6	50.1
Manufacturing total	16.4	29.9	39.2	41.1	49.5	48.5	55.6

Note: The figures are a percentage proportion of exports shipped to foreign affiliates in total exports by Japanese parent companies.
Sources: MITI, *Kaigai toshi tokei soran* [Statistical Report on Foreign Investment], No.1–No.6; *Dai 27 kai wagakuni kigyo no kaigai jigyo katsudo* [The 27th Survey on Overseas Activities of Japanese Firms] 1999.

Table 2.6   Shares of intra-firm imports in Japanese manufacturing sectors, 1980–96 (per cent)

Sector	1980	1983	1986	1989	1992	1995	1996
Food	4.6	2.3	11.4	14.8	14.8	42.3	38.8
Textiles	5.2	5.2	27.9	14.8	27.2	47.4	45.9
Wood and pulp	14.4	22.0	25.7	22.9	32.1	24.2	17.6
Chemicals	6.8	8.0	17.1	9.9	17.4	15.9	25.9
Iron and steel	9.7	1.8	11.0	0.5	8.6	14.4	4.1
Non-ferrous metals	12.6	21.0	2.9	5.7	12.2	15.7	16.3
General machinery	7.7	20.0	12.0	34.2	52.4	68.3	62.4
Electrical machinery	46.1	41.9	49.2	35.8	33.3	34.8	49.1
Transport machinery	4.5	34.3	21.9	36.0	39.2	16.4	32.7
Precision machinery	49.2	32.1	36.4	38.1	57.7	80.3	74.8
Oil and coal	–	28.8	25.9	51.8	49.4	35.3	36.0
Other manufacturers	44.7	11.3	35.9	25.1	34.8	36.8	46.7
Manufacturing total	32.5	20.9	23.4	30.9	37.4	32.2	41.3

Note: The figures are a percentage proportion of imports shipped by foreign affiliates in total imports to Japanese parent companies.
Sources: MITI, *Kaigai toshi tokei soran* [Statistical Report on Foreign Investment], No.1–No.6; *Dai 27 kai wagakuni kigyo no kaigai jigyo katsudo* [The 27th Survey on Overseas Activities of Japanese Firms] 1999.

Table 2.7   Number of newspaper reports on corporate alliances

Sector	1981–83	1984–86	1987–89	1990–92	Total
Food	172	338	588	537	1,635
Textiles, wood, pulp	272	358	454	421	1,505
Chemicals	349	745	1,085	899	3,078
Pharmaceuticals	98	153	284	321	856
Metals	488	893	1,253	1,172	3,806
Machinery	505	623	755	661	2,544
Electrical machinery	826	1,586	1,946	1,877	6,235
Transport machinery	706	992	1,159	824	3,681
Other manufacturing	208	383	488	398	1,477
Total	3,624	6,071	8,012	7,110	24,817

Note: The figures are the number of articles that appeared in *Nikkei Sangyo Shimbun*. They were identified from the Nikkei Telecom database using the following key words: technical alliances, joint developments, production alliances, sales alliances, joint ventures, equity participation, and mergers.
Source: Higashi and Ōkawa (1993, p.79).

eight in electronics, five in automobiles, three in iron and steel, two in oil and coal, one in transport equipment, and one in rubber and plastics. The second set of data is the world's largest 100 MNCs identified in the United Nations' *World Investment Report*. This ranking, excluding firms in banking and finance, is based on foreign assets. Sixteen Japanese MNCs are ranked in this group (Table 2.8). Most of these firms belong to three sectors: five in trading, seven in electronics, and three in automobiles.

The third and fourth data sets are based on questionnaire surveys of firms' international operations (Table 2.9). The third set of data is a ranking of companies based on overseas sales. This ranking is dominated by the electronics and automobile sectors to which 14 out of the 15 top companies belong. The fourth data set is overseas sales ratios. Companies that have developed large overseas markets rank high in this list. Although this ranking incorporates companies in various sectors, the two major sectors are the automobile and electronics sectors. These data confirm the conclusion from industry-level data that the firms in the electronics and automobile sectors are the most internationalized of Japanese corporations.

Table 2.8   Ranking of Japanese multinational corporations (1)

Company	Industrial sector	Fortune ranking	UN ranking
Toyota Motor	Automobile	5	16
Hitachi	Electronics	10	5
Matsushita Electric Ind.	Electronics	12	6
Nissan Motor	Automobile	16	52
Toshiba	Electronics	25	38
Honda Motor	Automobile	30	45
Sony	Electronics	32	22
NEC	Electronics	40	67
Fujitsu	Electronics	42	–
Mitsubishi Electric	Electronics	44	–
Mitsubishi Motors	Automobile	47	–
Nippon Steel	Iron and steel	48	–
Mitsubishi Heavy Ind.	Transport equipment	49	–
Mazda Motor	Automobile	59	–
Nippon Oil	Oil and coal	62	–
Idemitsu Kosan	Oil and coal	83	–
Canon	Electronics	84	82
NKK	Iron and steel	88	–
Bridgestone	Rubber and plastics	96	47
Sumitomo Metal Ind.	Iron and steel	98	–
(Total)		(20)	(10)
Nissho Iwai	Trading	–	28
Itochu Corporation	Trading	–	54
Sharp	Electronics	(116)	55
Marubeni	Trading	–	57
Mitsui & Co.	Trading	–	75
Mitsubishi Corp.	Trading	–	90
(Total)	–	(20)	(16)

Sources: *Fortune*, 26 July 1993; United Nations, *World Investment Report 1994*, pp.6, 7.

The automobile and electronics industries are the 'soft' cases which are selected in terms of their high degree of internationalization. They have maintained relatively strong competitiveness and do not suffer significant import competition in the domestic market. Because a broader coverage is required in this study, a 'hard' case has also been selected, one facing rising imports and likely to favour protectionist measures.

Table 2.9   Ranking of Japanese multinational corporations (2)

Company	Industrial sector	Overseas sales (billion yen)	Overseas sales ratio	
Toyota Motor	Automobile	4,558	44.6	(9)
Matsushita Electric Ind.	Electronics	3,478	49.3	(6)
Sony	Electronics	2,965	74.2	(1)
Honda Motor	Automobile	2,753	66.6	(3)
Nissan Motor	Automobile	2,301	37.1	(12)
Hitachi	Electronics	1,800	23.9	(20)
Mitsubishi Motors	Automobile	1,515	47.6	(7)
Toshiba	Electronics	1,379	29.8	(15)
Canon	Electronics	1,342	70.1	(2)
Fujitsu	Electronics	1,149	33.2	(12)
NEC	Electronics	801	22.8	(21)
Sharp	Electronics	764	51.7	(5)
Mitsubishi Electric	Electronics	710	21.8	(23)
Mitsubishi Heavy Ind.	Transport equipment	639	22.6	(22)
Sanyo Electric	Electronics	630	41.0	(10)
Kyocera	Electronics	–	54.3	(4)
Dainippon Ink & Chemicals	Chemicals	–	46.9	(8)
Fuji Photo Film	Chemicals	–	39.3	(11)
Komatsu	Machinery	–	30.6	(14)

Note: Ranking is based on questionnaire survey on major 42
manufacturing companies.
Source: *Global Business* (15 January/1 February 1994, p.74).

The Japanese economy has sharply increased its imports since the second half of the 1980s. The increase in imports of manufacturing products is particularly salient, with the share of imports of manufacturing products in total imports rising from 27.2 per cent in 1983 to 52.0 per cent in 1993. The ratio of imports to domestic demand has gradually increased for a number of manufacturing products (Table 2.10).

Among these products, the increase in imports in woven outer garments and knitted outer garments is remarkable. In 1993, the share of imported products in total domestic demand was 61.1 per cent of woven outer garments and 45.8 per cent of knitted outer garments. In all textile products, the share of imports in total domestic demand rose from 26.1 per cent in 1985 to 50.8 per cent in 1993, as Japan became a net importer of textile products in 1987. This rise in imports has resulted in declining numbers of establishments, as well as stagnant employment and production in the industry. The number of employ-

Table 2.10   Import shares in major manufactured products, 1988–93
(per cent)

Product	1988	1989	1990	1991	1992	1993
Watches	14.6	12.9	9.0	7.6	8.6	11.0
Bicycles	11.1	10.1	7.9	11.5	14.0	18.8
Woven outer garments	38.9	45.1	45.5	48.5	55.0	61.1
Knitted outer garments	27.8	30.3	30.1	33.4	41.3	45.8
Copy machines	0.4	2.2	2.1	0.5	3.6	9.6
Electric calculators	38.2	38.8	36.2	37.7	39.3	52.9
Colour TVs	7.2	14.9	10.1	16.3	22.2	33.0
VTRs	5.5	8.5	11.3	6.5	20.2	39.9
Air-conditioners	3.0	3.6	2.6	8.8	10.1	13.0
Washing machines	1.3	1.5	1.2	2.7	3.2	3.7
Refrigerators	3.3	6.2	6.9	8.4	7.9	9.2
Microwave ovens	4.9	12.2	5.6	2.5	2.6	6.3
Fans	48.9	53.8	43.1	42.3	49.1	54.6

Note: The figures are a proportion of imports in total domestic demand.
Sources: JETRO, *Nihon no seihin yunyu doko* [Imports of Manufactured
Products in Japan] 1993; Electronic Industries Association of Japan, Facts &
Figures, 1995; Japan Electrical Manufacturers' Association, Electrical
Industries in Japan, 1995.

ees fell from 1.39 million in 1980 to 1.15 million 1993, and the number
of establishments declined from 147,500 to 117,300 in the same
period.[20] Production also declined, from 2.05 million tonnes in 1980
to 1.50 million tonnes in 1993.[21] In order to restrain a sharp rise in
imports, some textile producer associations filed anti-dumping and
countervailing suits. The major textile producer associations also
intensified their demands on the government to activate the Multi-
Fibre Arrangement. An examination of firms' preferences on trade
policy in the textile industry provides a valuable case to examine the
central hypothesis.

After the cases have been selected, the variables of this study need
to be identified. The independent variable is the internationalization
of corporate activities. In each sectoral case, the nature and extent of
internationalization are elaborated by using data on FDI, intra-firm
trade and international corporate alliances. This study also examines
the development and nature of international operations of individual
firms if these factors account for diverse trade policy stances among
firms. It is difficult to measure the independent variable in the aggregate Keidanren case because the federation comprises a wide range
of industrial associations and companies. However, it is possible to

measure the effects of internationalization by the rising influence of internationally oriented sectors on personnel and internal organization.

The dependent variable of this study is the preference of corporations for an open domestic market. Corporate preferences in the 'hard' case and the 'soft' case differ. In the hard case, industry is faced with high import pressure and rising levels of import penetration. Under such circumstances, the industry is likely to have a preference for demanding high levels of protection. In the soft case, the industry does not suffer from import pressure. However, firms and industries are expected to have a preference for promoting the opening of the home market and facilitating market access of foreign goods and firms because of rising costs resulting from their international operations. In particular, a perception by foreign firms and governments that the home market is closed is likely to lead to the interruption of their activities in foreign markets. The aggregate Keidanren case is more relevant to the opening of the market. The federation has been concerned with foreign criticism of a closed Japanese market and resultant deterioration of Japan's trade relations with its foreign partners.

In order to capture corporate preferences, I examined activities and views of firms and industries concerning the government's commercial policies. While the study is concerned with import protection policies in the textile case, it focuses on market-opening policies in the other two sectoral cases. In the textile case, I surveyed the stance and activities of firms and industrial associations over import restrictions. The survey covers views of industrial associations and company leaders in newspapers and industrial associations journals, opinions of industrial representatives at advisory councils, and lobbying of MITI and relevant politicians for introducing import restriction measures. In the automobile and electronics cases, I surveyed reports of companies and industrial associations, statements of company leaders, and firms' and industries' activities for expanding market access of foreign products. In the Keidanren case, its preferences can be measured by recommendations in formal position papers. At the same time, lobbying of politicians and government agencies are considered. In all cases, I conducted interviews with associations representatives, company managers, and government officials in order to supplement information on the stance and activities of firms and industries, and to obtain accurate information about corporate preferences.

CONCLUSION

This is a study of the relationship between rising economic inter-dependence and domestic trade politics. This chapter examined the theoretical underpinning of the argument that as firms have become increasingly interlinked with the world economy, they are more inclined to oppose protectionist measures in the home market. MNCs appear to have open trade preferences because they fear retaliation by foreign governments against protection in home markets, and are disadvantaged by the closure of home markets in relation to their domestically oriented rivals. The closure of home markets also disrupts the flow of the intra-firm trade that MNCs conduct. International corporate alliances are also a factor making firms' trade policy preferences more pro-liberal. Corporate alliances not only qualify interest in nationalistic trade policy but also make firms less dependent on protectionist measures.

From the literature review, the hypothesis that firms with intensive links to the international economy in the form of multinational operations and corporate alliances have more interest in maintaining open markets including their home markets is derived. This book examines this hypothesis and its application to the behaviour of Japanese industry. The links between Japanese industry and the world economy through multinational operations, intra-firm trade, and corporate alliances have clearly intensified remarkably. Examination of experience in Japan is of interest in understanding Japanese political economy, as well as enriching research on trade politics.

The particular institutional framework of the representation of corporate policy interest in Japan requires a review of the influence of business on Japanese policy making. This is undertaken in the next chapter. The discussion there is directed to the issue of how business interests influence the policy-making process and policy outcomes, as a prelude to examination of the hypothesis in detail in a case study through Keidanren, a peak business federation, as well as through sectoral case studies of the automobile, electronics, and textile industries.

3 The Influence of Business on Japanese Policy Making

As firms have become more interlinked with the world economy, it is hypothesized that they have increased their interest in open trade and liberal economic policies. This hypothesis, it is suggested, has a broad validity in the sense that economic interdependence has affected advanced market industrial economies similarly. This study tests the hypothesis in the Japanese context. In the study, corporate preferences are argued to be a pivotal factor affecting commercial policy. These preferences translate into policy through a political process in which various actors compete to achieve their policy objectives. Accordingly, it is necessary to understand the policy-making structures in which corporate preferences are transformed into policy outcomes. Close business–government relations in policy making and the existence of powerful peak business federations and industrial associations constitute distinctive features of the Japanese political economy. These features are likely to affect the formation of corporate preferences and their influence on commercial policy, and need to be spelt out.

In this chapter, I explore how business preferences are integrated into the policy-making process in Japan. This issue has been elaborated less extensively partly because previous studies of business–government relations in Japan have tended to focus on the issue of how the government has guided and directed private business. The answer to this question will show how the interests of business are aggregated and through what channels they are conveyed to government. An understanding of the aggregation of business preferences and their channels of influence on government offers a foundation on which detailed case studies in the book are developed.

INSTITUTIONS IN THE JAPANESE BUSINESS COMMUNITY

The business community is vertically organized in Japan. The top level is *zaikai*. The *zaikai* is often described in English as 'business world' or 'financial circles', but it could better be defined as a 'group of people who, apart from their identification with specific companies or industries, speak from the capitalist position and exert a strong influence on politics' (Tanaka 1979, p.64). *Zaikai* functions through four functionally differentiated peak federations. The oldest and broadest is the Japan Chamber of Commerce and Industry (Nissho). Nissho, originating from the *Tokyo Shoko Kaigisho* (Tokyo Chamber of Commerce) founded in 1878, consolidates some 500 local chambers of commerce and industry, covering 1.55 million small and medium-sized firms. It has served as a forum for small and medium-sized firms and represented their interests. In 1974 and 1983, for instance, Nissho played a central role in forcing legislation to arrest the expansion of supermarkets, thereby confronting big business (Calder 1988a, p.199). The Japan Federation of Employers' Associations (Nikkeiren) is an organization of employers and deals with labour–management relations. Nikkeiren coordinates wage negotiations with labour organizations at the annual *shunto* ('spring struggle'). The Japan Association of Corporate Executives (Keizai Doyukai) is a business forum where leading businessmen participate as individuals. The association, comprising approximately 1,500 senior corporate executives from some 900 firms, plays a unique role in submitting progressive recommendations on business, social and other issues beyond the interests of individual firms.

The Japan Federation of Economic Organizations (Keidanren) is the most influential peak business association.[1] This association, inaugurated in August 1946, is the principal power centre of *zaikai*. Its chairman has been labelled 'the prime minister of *zaikai*'. It is a federation of 123 major industrial associations, such as the Japan Iron and Steel Federation, the Japan Automobile Manufacturers Association (JAMA), the Electronic Industries Association of Japan (EIAJ), and so on. Membership also covers some 970 leading enterprises, encompassing trading companies, retailers, and banks, as well as a complete range of manufacturers.[2] The chief role of Keidanren is to collect opinions from the business community about domestic and external economic issues and to represent business interests to the Diet, the government, and the community.

The other institution through which private business exerts influence on the policy process is *gyokai*. *Gyokai* normally means a formal association (industrial association) which represents the interests of a specific industrial sector. Sone (1993, p.300) uses the term *gyokai* in a broader sense, referring to 'all of the entities (firms, enterprises, and trade associations) that fall under the legal jurisdiction of a particular ministry'. In evaluating the substantial function of *gyokai*, Sone's definition is appropriate. *Gyokai* comprises 'sub-governments' along with the Liberal Democratic Party's (LDP) Policy Affairs Research Council (PARC) or *zoku* with a special interest in a specific sector, and the bureaus or sections of ministries.[3] This sub-governmental triangle is an exclusive policy-making institution, which is insulated in large measure from other actors (Ōtake 1979, p.188). It has played a crucial role in formulating and implementing detailed sector-specific policies.

The substantial organization of *gyokai* is in industrial associations.[4] Industrial associations are organizations of firms with the objective of promoting the members' collective interests.[5] In 1995, there were 15,315 industrial associations in Japan, of which 4,416 were from manufacturing industries.[6] Japanese firms are broadly covered by industrial associations. According to a survey on industrial associations conducted by the Fair Trade Commission (FTC) in 1993, 32.5 per cent of the industrial associations surveyed accounted for 90 per cent of total sales, and 21.8 per cent accounted for 75 per cent to 90 per cent (FTC 1993c, p.5).[7]

The functions of industrial associations are divided into two categories. The first set of functions is related to administrative agencies. According to the FTC survey, 83.5 per cent of major industrial associations undertook the delivery of administrative information to its members, and 41.0 per cent implemented other cooperative functions relating to administrative agencies (FTC 1993c, p.10). The second set of functions is directed towards promoting the collective interests of their members such as market surveys, setting of industry standards, and the organization of seminars, symposia and study groups. The FTC survey shows that 67.5 per cent of major industrial associations conducted market surveys, and 43.5 per cent organized technical training seminars for their members (FTC 1993c, p.10). These functions include the promotion of long-term ties between firms, and the coordination of the interests of member firms involved in ferocious intra-industry competition. One source of Japanese economic success lies in the fierce competition among major firms in an oligopolistic market structure. Fierce competition may lead to excessive competition undermining the interests of the whole industry. Coordination through industrial associations has encouraged member firms to cooperate on matters perceived to be in their common interest (Okimoto 1989, p.166). The function of coordinating interests among firms is originally an internal one, but this is also helpful for the

Ministry of International Trade and Industry's (MITI) bureaus and sections that want the industry under their jurisdiction to be organized in an orderly manner (Komiya 1988, p.11).

Japanese industrial associations bring together the broad interests of firms in particular industries. All major firms join the primary industrial associations and play a role in the associations. It is usual in Japan for there to be several associations within an industry whose objectives or sub-sector interests are different from each other. For example, EIAJ has 14 associations as its relevant organizations in the electronics industry, while JAMA has as many as 22. But these associations play a supplementary role in realizing the broader interests of the industries. In addition, Japanese industrial associations enjoy a stable legal status because there are quite a few exempt cases in which the Antimonopoly Law provides exemption for actions of associations under its auspices (Lynn and McKeown 1988, chap. 3). For example, the amendment to the Antimonopoly Law in 1953 allowed industrial associations to organize depression and rationalization cartels.

POLITICAL INFLUENCE OF BUSINESS THROUGH *ZAIKAI*

How does *zaikai* exert influence on the policy-making process? This question can be examined by focusing mainly on the case of Keidanren. Keidanren is not only the most influential association representing the interests of private business to the government but three other business federations use similar methods to influence the policy process. *Zaikai* uses three common methods to influence the policy process. The first method is the submission of formal recommendations to relevant ministries and agencies. For this purpose, each business federation undertakes research on domestic and international issues. For example, Keidanren has 42 policy committees and 4 special committees chaired by leading businessmen. These committees conduct detailed research on a wide range of issues from small business and taxation to industrial policy and international trade.

Keidanren publishes some 30 policy recommendations every year. These recommendations identify problems in specific areas in the Japanese economy and industry, and suggest solutions to the problems. In quite a few cases, they have become the catalyst in creating and changing government policy. The most prominent instance is the promotion of administrative and financial reform. The low budgetary income after the first oil shock and the spending policies of the 1970s caused a large blowout in budgetary deficits. The government attempted to cope with the deficits by introducing tax increases. *Zaikai* orchestrated a chorus for 'fiscal reconstruction without tax increases', and Keidanren took the initiative in realising this slogan through a set of recommendations for policy and administrative reform. In September 1979, Keidanren made public a recommendation entitled *Opinions on the Future Tax System*, which urged the government to embrace reform and detailed policies for financial reconstruction, including simplification and rationalization of administration and finance, and extensive reform of budgetary expenditure. Then, Keidanren released a more detailed recommendation entitled *Hope for Decisive Implementation of Administrative and Financial Reform* in November. This was supplemented by another document the following month, *Proposals for the Urgent Issues of the Japanese Economy and the Tax Reform*. These recommendations led to the establishment of the Second Provisional Commission on Administrative Reform (*Daini Rincho*) in March 1981. Most issues discussed at *Rincho* were covered by Keidanren's recommendations (Heiwa Keizai Kenkyū Kaigi 1982, pp.85–6).

A more recent example of Keidanren's initiative in policy development is a comprehensive package of economic measures proposed in 1992 (Honjo 1993, pp.96–9). The Japanese economy plunged into a severe recession in 1992, and the average market share price index fell below 15,000 yen. After intensive discussions with the Ministry of Finance (MOF) and the three top-ranking officials of the LDP, Keidanren submitted a recommendation on 15 August which urged the government to introduce a massive public investment programme and decrease anxiety about the financial system by introducing public funding. On 28 August, the government announced the first round of comprehensive economic measures, which incorporated the requests from Keidanren. With exquisite timing, the average share market price recovered sharply to 18,000 yen.

The second channel of influence is through dispatching executive officials to advisory councils (*shingikai*). The advisory councils are attached to and appointed by ministries, and staffed by representatives from peak business, relevant industrial sectors, journalism and academia.[8] These councils function as intermediary vehicles reflecting the interests and opinions of various societal groups in the formulation of public policy.[9] Owing to the priority of economic growth in public policy and close ties with the bureaucracy, the business community has sent more representatives to the councils where their interests and opinions have tended to be adopted in the agenda and discussions. According to the 1992 data on advisory councils, 34 per cent of the members were from academia and journalism, and 25 per cent belonged to the business community. The ratio of business circle representation is higher in the advisory councils attached to economic ministries. In the councils attached to the Ministry of Posts and Telecommunications and MITI, 40 per cent and 38 per cent of the members came from the business community, respectively (Ryū 1995, pp.104–5). It is common for ministries and agencies to ask for Keidanren's recommendation about the membership of a council, where deliberations are relevant to the whole of the Japanese economy and industry (Heiwa Keizai Kenkyū Kaigi 1982, p.38).

The third method is policy coordination between the secretariats of business federations and relevant ministries through informal contacts. In the case of Keidanren, each division maintains constant communication and exchange of opinion with various bureaus and sections of ministries. When bureaus and sections formulate a new policy or bill, the officials responsible for this have prior consultations with the Secretariat of Keidanren. Once the policy or bill is drafted, chiefs of relevant bureaus explain the draft at the policy committee of Keidanren and collect the opinions and preferences of the business community (Heiwa Keizai Kenkyū Kaigi 1982, p.64). For example, in the process of the drafting of the Special Measures Law for the Promotion of Designated Industries (*Tokutei sangyo shinko rinji sochi ho*), Keidanren saw intensive interaction with MITI.[10] Between April 1962 and February 1963, consultation meetings between Keidanren and chiefs of the Enterprises Bureau of MITI were organized five times.[11]

The influence of *zaikai* has extended to the political world. *Zaikai* contributed massive financial donations to the LDP's running costs and huge election campaign costs. A large amount of money was collected by the National Political Association (*Kokumin Seiji Kyokai*), Keidanren's fund-raising institute.[12] In 1992, for instance, the LDP had an income of 25.5 billion yen, 12.7 billion yen of which were contributions from *Kokumin Seiji Kyokai*.[13] The financial contributions through *Kokumin Seiji Kyokai* were not necessarily designed to influence specific public policy, but rather to ensure that a party with a pro-business orientation stayed in power (Iwai 1990, pp.116–18). The contributions from big business were delivered through other channels: from individual business leaders, individual companies, and industrial associations to individual LDP representatives, faction leaders, and *zoku*. In addition, *zaikai* often supports the LDP in elections. For example, at the Upper House election of July 1989, the LDP's Secretary-General Ryutaro Hashimoto called on a managing director of Keidanren to list branches and factories in prefectures of major companies belonging to Keidanren, and asked them directly to support the party. Furthermore, it is reported that Keidanren's Secretary-General was asked to wield influence in the companies in the districts where the LDP was weak, and directors of Keidanren were engaged for days calling on heads of companies to support the LDP.[14]

Zaikai is also linked with the LDP through consultation meetings. The top four officials of the LDP – the Secretary-General, the chairman of the PARC, the chairman of the Executive Council and the chairman of the Upper House Diet members – and representatives of the four business federations have held a breakfast meeting once a month. Moreover, major *zaikai* members often organize unofficial gatherings which support senior LDP leaders who are prime ministers and candidates for prime minister. When Yasuhiro Nakasone was Prime Minister, he had at least six gatherings with *zaikai* members (Yamakawa 1984, p.114).

POLITICAL INFLUENCE OF BUSINESS THROUGH *GYOKAI*

Industrial associations wield influence on the policy process by sending members to advisory councils and submitting position papers with sectoral policy issues to the government. However, industrial associations exert a substantial influence through continuous give-and-take relationships with relevant bureaus and sections of ministries and agencies. Intimate relationships are formed through various channels and actions. Industrial associations and relevant sections and bureaus maintain close daily communication, through which industrial associations provide government officials with the latest and most precise information along with opportunities for simpler and more regular contacts with relevant firms. Industrial associations and relevant bureaus and sections are linked by personnel as well. Most executive directors of major industrial associations are retired bureaucrats from relevant ministries. The executive directors coordinate relations with relevant ministries by making use of the close communication ties with current bureaucrats.

Although MITI has expanded the mandate for Japanese industry, the increases in its budget and personnel have not been commensurate with the growth in Japanese industry. For instance, the total personnel of MITI decreased slightly between 1980 and 1995 from 10,670 to 9,078.[15] This is also the case with MITI's bureaus. For example, the number of personnel in the Machinery and Information Industries Bureau remained almost unchanged from 193 in 1980 to 200 in 1995, although the Bureau's jurisdiction covers fast-growing sectors including computers, semiconductors and automobiles.[16] MITI has sought to reduce the burden of its task by encouraging the private sector to organise industrial associations and by making use of their resources. Samuels (1983, p.499) describes this situation as follows:

> While it is frequently acknowledged that committees in Diet and the ruling Liberal Democratic Party (LDP), having limited expertise and staff, are dependent upon the bureaucracy for data and analysis, it is not as often recognized that the well-fabled Japanese bureaucracy is itself often dependent in the same way upon the industry associations and firms with which it works so closely.

Career bureaucrats experience frequent job rotation. When they know something about their jurisdictional sectors after two or three years, they are transferred to another division which has nothing to do with the previous division. 'As a consequence, staff in MITI bureaus frequently do not have personal expertise on any given industry, nor do they have a comprehensive memory of the history of policies applied to a specific case' (Friedman 1988, pp.84–5). Their inadequate expertise or specialized knowledge is made up for with instruction and cooperation from staff in the industrial associations and companies.

Based on close links to the bureaucracy, industrial associations are involved in the formation and implementation of government policy in various ways. First, industrial associations create an information-sharing system in which government policies are formulated and implemented effectively. The industrial associations conduct surveys on statistical data, supply and demand perspectives, and international markets. The results of these surveys become basic data for administrative operations. The associations also provide members with information that is necessary for implementing public policies. Thus, the industrial associations contribute to efficient policy by reducing asymmetry in information sharing between government agencies and firms

(Yonekura 1993). This involvement of industrial associations is particularly important in conducting administrative guidance.[17] Since administrative guidance is not based on law, there is no guarantee that it will be accepted by private actors or attain its objective. As a result, before deciding on administrative guidance, ministries and agencies have to conduct ample *nemawashi* or informal negotiations with industries as well as collect opinions at the formal advisory councils.[18] They talk extensively with relevant industries and firms about their requirements in order to prevent non-compliance after the guidance has been given (Muramatsu 1993, pp.14–15).

Second, some industrial associations engage in policy formation activities. Although MITI issues various reports for industry, some reports are drafted to a substantial degree by industrial associations. For example, the General Affairs Committee of the Industrial Policy Deliberation Council drew up *Vision of Trade and Industry Policy for the 1980s* in 1980. The Japan Industrial Robotics Association drafted a vision for the industrial robotics industry at a request from MITI (Lynn and McKeown 1988, p.77). Another example is *Vision for the 1990s in the Electronics Industry*. Although MITI finalized the report, the basic data were supplied and arranged by EIAJ. There are cases when sections of MITI and EIAJ jointly draft reports regarding industries, and the publisher of the reports is decided according to the conditions of the budget.[19]

Third, industrial associations play a role in implementing government policies, particularly administrative guidance. As explained before, the delivery of administrative information is one of the key functions of industrial associations. The role of industrial associations is not merely to deliver administrative information to its members. Formulated after adequate prior consultation with industrial associations, administrative guidance often reflects the consensual interests of the whole industry. Therefore, once administrative guidance is introduced, industrial associations play an intermediary role in supervising its implementation by member firms. More importantly, industrial associations, in some cases, call on the government to introduce administrative guidance in order to ensure coordination in the industry (Wada 1990, p.60). The conventional example is that when the private sector faces a problem in forming a recession cartel, a majority of the industry asks the government to use administrative guidance to encourage the formation of the cartel, and thereby restrains the opposition (Ōyama 1989, p.21). In 1966, for instance, the Petroleum Association of Japan asked MITI to use administrative guidance to force Idemitsu Kosan to comply with the association's efforts to curtail crude-petroleum production. In the same year, major spinning firms resorted to similar requests for help in order to make Nisshinbo continue a recession cartel (Lynn and McKeown 1988, p.93). In such circumstances, administrative guidance is a 'joint masterpiece' created both by administrative agencies and by industrial associations which serve as the 'confederate organization' of administrative agencies (Shindō 1992, p.112).

Industrial associations and bureaus and sections of ministries thus maintain intense communication networks and undertake intensive interactions. In general, government policies are formed and implemented with the cooperation of industrial associations. In some cases, industrial associations are deeply involved in the policy-making and policy-implementation process as joint organizers of government policies.

In the past, unlike industries in the United States that cultivate various channels with Congress, Japanese industries tended to have close relationships with the bureaucracy which drafts laws (Ueno and Atsuya 1977, p.24). Japanese industries had little incentive or necessity to lobby politicians because of their tight relationships with bureaucrats. The interests of industries were easily delivered to bureaucrats who willingly sought to realize them. However, the commitment of *gyokai* to politicians is gradually increasing. While donations through *Kokumin Seiji Kyokai* have been limited owing to the Political Donation Regulation Law, individual industrial associations and firms have gradually raised their donations to individual politicians. This is shown by the fact that the donations to individual politicians increased sharply against those to the party in the second half of the 1980s (Iwai 1990, p.119). In addition, *gyokai* has been more likely to cooperate with LDP's *zoku* in realising its policy objectives. A case in point is the revision of the Banking Law. In February 1981, MOF sent a proposal to the Joint Committee of the Committee on Financial Issues and the Budget Division of PARC to revise the Banking Law. MOF was facing the future liberalization of banking in Japan, and wished to strengthen its authority through the proposed revision which sought to put constraints on bank lending and make disclosures obligatory. The Federation of Bankers Associations of Japan, which made contributions to the LDP but not to individual politicians, pressured politicians by suggesting that it temporarily change the target of contributions from the party to individual politicians (Inoguchi and Iwai 1987, p.235). The discussions at the Joint Committee were delayed owing to detailed deliberation and numerous questions by the members supporting the bankers' position. In the LDP's redrafted law passed in the Diet in May 1981, the section regarding enforcement of the MOF's control over the banks was deleted and the section regarding disclosure was made advisory only.

Interaction between industries and the LDP also occurs through the Diet Members' Leagues (*giin renmei*), private groups of Diet members sharing specific policy objectives and interests in particular industrial sectors. While PARC committees and divisions function as supporting groups of bureaucrats, *giin renmei* tend to wield power by reflecting the interests of industrial sectors to government (Fukushima 1991, p.94).

On the firm level, major firms regularly send staff to the relevant divisions of ministries in order to obtain information from and consult with officials. The bureaucrats, on the other hand, receive visitors from companies in order to collect the latest information about their sectors. In addition, firms also accept *amakudari*, where bureaucrats 'descend' to high positions in companies. According to a survey by *Toyo Keizai Shimposha*, 629 out of 2,220 firms surveyed accepted 1,404 former bureaucrats as the executive members in July 1994.[20] *Amakudari* has been regarded as a means by which bureaucrats exert influence on industries as well as secure beneficial positions in retirement. Calder (1989) asserts, however, that firms hire retired bureaucrats in order to increase their influence on the policy process. Furthermore, quite a few business leaders have cultivated a web of personal connections with politicians and bureaucrats. A number of senior bureaucrats, companies' top executives and politicians who graduated from a small number of elite universities have maintained close contacts after graduation. This 'old-boy' network contributes to the facilitation of communication among them. Close relationships are also formed through participation in informal study groups and breakfast meetings. Government bureaucrats, politicians, and business leaders exchange valuable information in these informal networks, including information about sensitive issues which are not necessarily discussed in formal settings.

CHANGES IN THE INFLUENCE OF BUSINESS ON POLICY MAKING

There are *zaikai* and *gyokai* routes through which the business world represents its interests in policy making. These two business institu-

Business	Bureaucracy	Politicians
Zaikai ———	MOF, senior bureaucrats ———	LDP senior leaders
Gyokai ———	Bureaus and sections ———	LDP's *zoku*

Figure 3.1   Two-level relations among business, bureaucracy and politicians

tions have a different level of counterpart in the bureaucracy and among politicians. While *zaikai* interacts with high-level bureaucrats and LDP senior leaders, *gyokai* communicates with bureaus and sections of the ministries and *zoku* (Figure 3.1).

There have been two conspicuous changes to the relationship among business circles, the bureaucracy and politicians. The first change is the gradual decline in the influence of *zaikai* on political parties. In the 1970s, Curtis (1975) points to the declining role of Keidanren as a pressure group because of the pluralism within the business community, the internationalization of the Japanese economy, and the emergence of a new less cohesive generation in the business world. This decline has become evident in relations with the LDP. In the mid-1970s, Keidanren was the predominant pressure group whose financial contributions provided for some 80 per cent of officially disclosed political donations to the LDP. In 1977, for example, 7.6 billion yen of the donations from Keidanren accounted for 75 per cent of 10.1 billion yen of LDP's total income.[21] As many interest groups have been organized since the 1970s, the status of Keidanren as the foremost interest group has gradually waned.[22] Although Keidanren's financial contributions constituted vital financial resources to the LDP, the relative importance of Keidanren's donations declined in the late 1980s, accounting for some 50 per cent of the LDP's total income. Furthermore, as the financial contributions from Keidanren to the LDP became routine, the LDP took them for granted, while Keidanren considered them as a kind of necessary cost. This led to reverse power positions between a money provider and a receiver (Iwai 1990, p.118). This phenomenon escalated in 1990. Ichiro Ozawa, Secretary-General of the LDP, collected 16 billion yen directly from *gyokai* in the general election in February 1990, ignoring the route for donations through Keidanren. It was reported that the LDP gained 5 billion yen each from the automobile and electronics industries and 3 billion yen each from the finance and construction industries.[23]

Zaikai did not approve of the escalation of the LDP's money politics. Some *zaikai* leaders openly advocated financial and organizational reform in the LDP, and expressed their expectation of the emergence of a two-party system in Japan from the late 1980s. For example, Tokio Nagayama, a managing director of Nikkeiren as well as vice-chairman of Keidanren, irked LDP politicians by announcing that 'the historical mission of the conservative coalition is over. Two parties involving middle-of-the-road parties should compete on policies. It is desirable to return to the "two party system", a natural form of democracy' (Mainichi Shimbun 1991, p.32). Takuji Matsuzawa, a vice-chairman of Keidanren, also bowed towards the Japan Socialist Party, observing that 'the socialists join the government in ten out of 24 advanced nations joining the Organization for Economic Cooperation and Development (OECD). If the Japan Socialist Party pursues a western-style social democracy, we do not have to be hostile towards it.' It was reported that the LDP was shocked that the vice-chairmen of Keidanren endorsed restructuring the political world in this way (Mainichi Shimbun 1991, p.33).

The change in relations between *zaikai* and the LDP came to a head in September 1993 when Keidanren decided to cease funnelling donations from business circles to the LDP. This decision derived from the judgement that the rationale that donations should be given to support the capitalist system was less valid after the waning of the Cold War. The need to take action to redress turbid relations between *zaikai* and politicians was also felt (Matsumoto 1993, p.78). After the collapse of the LDP's single-party dominance in August 1993, it became difficult for *zaikai* to support any one party. More than one conservative coalition had emerged as a potential government. The relations between *zaikai* and politicians began to fragment inexorably.

The second change is that the internationalization of the Japanese economy has transformed the role of *gyokai*. As explained before, *gyokai* has a strong influence on policy making, and this influence stems largely from the cohesion of member firms. However, dynamic internationalization of the Japanese economy and industry after the mid-1980s has undermined this cohesion. Many foreign firms have joined industrial associations in Japan.[24] For instance, the Trust Companies Association of Japan, which had long been composed of eight Japanese bankers, accepted nine foreign-affiliated firms in 1986.[25] The increase in foreign firms as members makes it difficult for industrial associations to conduct their activities on the basis of implicit practice among members with homogeneous interests, and this weakens the cohesion of the associations. In addition, dependence on overseas markets by some Japanese firms has undermined the role of *gyokai*. Firms have become less interested in preserving order in the industries, and industrial associations have difficulty in coordinating members' activities and interests outside Japan. The declining cohesion of *gyokai* and the diminished role of the industrial association has contributed to the weakening influence of administrative agencies whose operations were facilitated by industrial associations.

On the firm level, global corporate activities have made Japanese firms less dependent on the government. Firms operating in international markets gain ready access to foreign sources of capital, making them less dependent on MOF and the Bank of Japan, which controls bank loans (Fukui 1987, p.163). Large firms with widespread international corporate networks have more information regarding their industries and rival firms in the world than do bureaucrats. As the internationalization of corporate activities has proceeded, it has become extremely difficult for government officials to project a clear vision of future trends in the macro-economy and industries. As far as R & D is concerned, big firms rely less on government laboratories. Even now they acknowledge the advantage of government-financed high-risk research programmes, but they spend an increasingly large portion of their profits on R & D as they recognise the importance of basic research. Besides, Japanese firms that operate in overseas markets cannot depend on the home government with respect to the risks involved in their overseas operations. They no longer live in a risk-free society where private citizens and enterprises are supposed to be protected from damage or failure by a paternalistic and benevolent government (Fukui 1987, p.163). Japanese firms are more sensitive to reactions from foreign governments and firms, and have less interest in maintaining a close relationship with the home government.

CONCLUSION

This chapter examined how the policy-making structure in Japan has allowed business interests to influence the policy-making process and policy outcomes. The Japanese business community retains well-organized vertical institutions. *Zaikai*, at the top, influences policy making through the submission of policy recommendations, dispatch of members to advisory councils and informal policy coordination between the secretariats of business federations and the bureaucrats. *Zaikai* has also been linked to the ruling LDP through financial donations, active cooperation at the national elections, and participation in the gatherings which support the senior leaders of the LDP.

While *zaikai* exerts influence on macroeconomic policy and national issues, *gyokai* is influential in sector-specific policies. Although industrial associations are linked with government policy in a similar way to *zaikai*, their influence on the relevant bureaus and sections is exerted in more informal forms. In addition to an exchange of information and opinions, major industrial associations accept former bureaucrats as executive directors. Furthermore, in some cases, industrial associations initiate the formation and implementation of government policies. This can be seen when industrial associations take the initiative in forming recession cartels by calling on the government to exert administrative guidance. As the LDP's *zoku* enhanced their influence in policy making, *gyokai* became more dependent on them to achieve their policy objectives. In Japan, individual business leaders also have some influence on the policy-making process using various communication channels with bureaucrats and politicians.

Relations among business, bureaucrats and politicians have changed significantly in recent years. *Zaikai* and the LDP no longer have such close relations owing to the cessation of financial contributions through Keidanren to the LDP and the end of the single party dominance of the LDP. The internationalization of the Japanese economy has also undermined the influence of *gyokai*. While the participation of foreign-affiliated firms in industrial associations has weakened the cohesion of industry, more dependence on foreign markets makes some firms less interested in seeking cohesion. The declining influence of *gyokai* has been associated with the decreasing influence of the bureaucracy.

The review of the role of business in Japanese policy making and the exploration of business channels of influence on the government set the context in which detailed case studies are explored. This is particularly significant for investigating Keidanren's stance and activities on commercial policy. Corporate preferences and their effects on trade policy in specific sectors are examined through Chapter 4 to 6. In Chapter 7, the representation of Japanese firms' attitudes to trade policy is examined through an analysis of the stance and actions of Keidanren.

4 The Japanese Automobile Industry and Market Liberalization

The automobile industry has developed the most fully-fledged international operations of all Japanese manufacturing sectors. Japanese automakers have actively strengthened local production in North America and Europe since the early 1980s. Corporate alliances with foreign auto-producers have also evolved from equity participation to joint ventures and joint vehicle development. This chapter examines whether major Japanese auto producers have supported market-opening policies in Japan as they have deepened multinational operations and corporate tie-ups. This question is addressed from two directions. One examines the transformation of *keiretsu* groupings in the automobile industry, and the other looks at the reactions of automakers to market-opening policies.

Keiretsu groupings impinge on Japan's trade relations in the sense that they are regarded as an initial barrier to the Japanese market. In the automobile sector, supplier and distribution *keiretsu* are widely prevalent. More commitment to multinational production is likely to have induced Japanese automakers to open up these *keiretsu* groupings.

The Japanese government has become more inclined to promote the access of foreign goods to the Japanese market since the mid-1980s. In addition, the US government has requested that the Japanese government and auto industry purchase more US-made auto parts and vehicles. This study explores how the Japanese automobile industry has reacted to such policies and demands, with the hypothesis that as multinational production and international corporate alliances expanded, the industry assisted the government's market-opening policies and its attempts at resolving the auto issue with the United States.

The chapter is organized as follows. The first section examines the internationalization of corporate activity in the Japanese automobile industry. The second section investigates the effects of internationalization on the transformation of supplier and distribution *keiretsu* groups. In the third and fourth sections, automakers' reactions to government policies for import promotion and their stance on market opening are examined. The third section highlights international cooperation programmes that major automakers announced in 1989. The fourth section examines the interaction between the government and industry over the Action Plan in January 1992, and the automakers' stance on market access as revealed by this event.

CHARACTER OF INDUSTRY AND INTERNATIONALIZATION

The automobile industry is one of the major manufacturing sectors in Japan. In 1994, the value of domestic output of motor vehicles was estimated at 39.7 trillion yen, representing 13.3 per cent of Japan's total manufacturing output. Automobile-related industries accounted for roughly 10 per cent of the total workforce in Japan.[1] The industry is highly concentrated, reflecting its highly capital-intensive character. There are 11 auto assemblers, including two makers producing only trucks and buses. This number is large compared with other auto manufacturing countries. For example, there are three makers in the United States and eight in Germany. In 1994, Toyota, the leading company, accounted for 33.2 per cent of total domestic output. The second maker, Nissan, accounted for 14.8 per cent in the same year, falling from 23.9 per cent in 1980.[2] Under the assemblers, there is a great number of parts suppliers, most of which are small and medium-sized firms. The auto assemblers make up the Japan Automobile Manufacturers Association (JAMA), one of the most representative industrial associations in Japan. The chairmanship of JAMA has been assumed by Toyota and Nissan alternatively. Parts suppliers form the Japan Auto Parts Industries Association, while auto dealers are represented by the Japan Automobile Dealers Association.

How, then, have Japanese automakers developed the internationalization of their corporate activities? The multinational operations of the Japanese automobile industry commenced in the early 1980s, mainly in order to circumvent trade friction with western countries. This movement started in the United States. Honda, which had begun business as a manufacturer of motor cycles, developed the automobile business mainly through targeting the US market. It decided to make inroads into the United States in 1978, before a voluntary export restraint (VER) on Japanese car exports was announced. Honda led the Japanese automakers in production and sales in the United States, developing local production to exceed exports from Japan. In 1990, Honda's export volume from Japan to the United States was 391,000, whereas local production was 435,000. Owing to steady growth in local production and success in sales of the Accord model, Honda's sales surpassed those of Chrysler, the third US passenger car producer, in 1991, obtaining a 9.8 per cent share in the US market.

Honda was followed by Nissan, which opened assembly plants for pickup trucks in June 1983 and for passenger cars in 1985. Although Nissan's local production in the United States has not experienced steady growth because of limited production capacity and failure to introduce competitive compact car models, Nissan did expand production capacity to nearly 400,000 in 1993 after the introduction of compact cars in 1992. Toyota was behind Honda and Nissan in local production in the United States. Toyota, in spite of its dominant status in the domestic market, was extremely cautious about local production because it doubted whether its efficient Japan-based production system would work outside Japan. However, the sharp growth of Honda in the US market compelled Toyota to decide on local production in the United States. Unlike its forerunners, Toyota selected a joint venture with General Motors (GM), establishing the New United Motor Manufacturing Inc. (NUMMI) in California. NUMMI, which started production in December 1984, was regarded as an experiment aimed at examining whether Toyota's production and management styles were applicable in the United States (Fourin 1991, p.19). NUMMI took over the Fremont plant of GM, which had been closed owing to unsuccessful management. Toyota revitalized the plant by creating cooperative management–labour relations and developing close relations with selected parts suppliers. Confidence built on the success of this joint venture led Toyota to set up a wholly-owned plant in Kentucky in 1988. Five other Japanese automakers launched locally based production in North America in quick succession.[3] Total production in 11 plants owned by Japanese automakers amounted to 2.36 million in the United States in 1995 (Table 4.1).

Multinational production by Japanese automakers also grew in other regions. In Europe, production was initiated by Nissan in July 1986, and mainly limited in the United Kingdom. Isuzu followed Nissan, establishing a joint venture with GM in September 1987. In order to prepare for the integration of the European Community in 1992, Honda, then Toyota began local production in the United

Table 4.1   Local production by Japanese automakers in the United States, 1985–95 (units)

Company	1985	1990	1991	1992	1993	1994	1995
Honda	145,337	435,437	451,199	458,254	403,775	498,710	552,995
Nissan	151,232	235,248	265,024	300,328	385,973	444,608	523,821
NUMMI	64,601	205,604	208,601	256,136	321,445	363,040	353,308
Toyota	–	218,215	187,708	240,382	234,060	275,678	381,445
AAI	–	184,428	165,314	168,859	219,096	247,004	149,562
DSM	–	148,379	153,936	139,783	136,035	169,829	218,161
SIA	–	66,960	116,297	124,491	126,558	153,883	181,459
Total	361,170	1,494,271	1,548,079	1,688,233	1,826,942	2,152,752	2,360,751

Source: JAMA, The Motor Industry in Japan 1996, p.25.

Table 4.2   Reverse import of passenger cars, 1988–95 (units)

Company	1988	1989	1990	1991	1992	1993	1994	1995
Toyota	10	146	2,109	862	2,363	7,955	9,918	32,899
Nissan	4	31	69	1,062	2,264	944	11,587	15,103
Honda	5,395	4,697	7,534	14,302	19,835	26,880	47,296	50,694
Mitsubishi	84	279	3,095	1,183	586	1,214	1,304	3,295
Total	5,493	5,153	12,807	17,409	25,048	36,993	70,105	101,991

Source: Japan Automobile Importers' Association, Imported Car Market of Japan 1993, pp.22–3; 1996, pp.24–5.

Kingdom in 1992. The feature of local production in Europe is that Nissan led the move. By 1993, Toyota, Nissan and Honda respectively had 28, 13, and 26 plants outside Japan manufacturing auto vehicles and parts.[4] The proportion of overseas production relative to total production in 1993 was 24.9 per cent for Toyota, 35.7 per cent for Nissan, and 35.8 per cent for Honda.[5]

As a consequence of extended multinational production, intra-firm trade has increased rapidly in the automobile industry. Intra-firm trade mainly takes the form of reverse imports of finished cars from overseas plants to Japan. Reverse imports climbed from almost zero in 1986 to more than 100,000 cars in 1995 (Table 4.2). The share of reverse import cars in total imported vehicles rose to 26.3 per cent in 1995. In particular, Honda has boosted the export sales of the Accord coupe made at its Ohio plant since 1991. The sales volume of Honda has been larger than that of the total sales of the Big Three US auto producers since 1991, and Honda became the primary importer of cars into Japan in 1994, surpassing the Volkswagen-Audi group and Mercedes-Benz.

Table 4.3   OEM supply from Japanese to US automakers, 1986–92 (units)

Recipient	Supplier	1986	1988	1990	1991	1992
GM	Toyota (NUMMI)	170,507	96,868	109,631	98,433	74,346
	Isuzu (CI)	101,384	70,690	88,215	79,392	72,251
	Suzuki (CAMI)	–	–	85,995	107,165	115,839
	Suzuki (CI)	60,993	50,233	43,260	13,917	11,822
Ford	Mazda (AAI)	–	77,763	103,062	76,295	63,659
Chrysler	Mitsubishi (DSM)	–	–	69,441	66,334	61,290
	Mitsubishi (CI)	219,002	174,944	74,896	69,118	67,474
Total	Local production	170,507	174,631	368,129	348,227	315,134
	CI	381,379	295,867	206,371	162,427	151,547
		551,886	470,498	574,500	510,654	466,681

Note: CI denotes captive imports.
Source: Fourin (1993, p.177).

The other pillar of the internationalization of Japanese automakers is corporate alliances. These alliances commenced in the 1970s as equity participation by US automakers in Japanese auto manufacturers: Chrysler and Mitsubishi in June 1971, GM and Isuzu in September 1971, and Ford and Mazda in November 1979. Ford has a 33.4 per cent stake in Mazda; GM holds 49 per cent of Isuzu and 9.99 per cent of Suzuki. Chrysler also owned 6 per cent of Mitsubishi Motors until July 1993. Corporate alliances deepened in the 1980s through the undertaking of joint ventures. As explained before, Toyota and GM started production at a joint venture NUMMI in December 1984, while Mazda and Ford did the same at AutoAlliance International (AAI) in September 1987. In Canada, Suzuki and GM established a joint venture called CAMI Automotive and began production in April 1989. Corporate tie-ups are also seen in the supply of vehicles. The Big Three sell vehicles manufactured by the joint ventures (Table 4.3). Captive imports from Japanese makers to the Big Three are continuing, although their scale is decreasing in the 1990s.[6] In addition to the supply of finished cars, the provision of engines and transmissions is also undertaken. While Mitsubishi Motors provides engines for Chrysler, Chrysler offers engines and transmissions to Diamond-Star Motors (DSM). Mitsubishi also decided to procure transmissions from Chrysler for a high rank model manufactured in the US plant.[7]

The cooperative relationship between Japanese and US automakers further evolved to include joint development of vehicles. Nissan and Ford worked jointly in the development of minivans. Mitsubishi also developed models for Chrysler at DSM.[8] It is often believed that relations between the Japanese and the US auto industry have been characterized by constant disputations since the late 1970s, but cooperative relationships on the business level have progressed steadily. Some scholars observe that cooperative relationships have contributed to mitigating the friction between Japanese and US automakers in the US market (Sei 1987). As described later, alliances play a crucial role in facilitating access for foreign vehicles to the Japanese market.

INTERNATIONALIZATION AND OPENING OF *KEIRETSU* RELATIONS

Japanese automakers have developed multinational production and international corporate alliances since the early 1980s. What influence has growing internationalization had on the stance of Japanese automakers on trade policy? Has it changed their preferences for an open domestic market, as our argument predicts? One way of answering this question is to examine automakers' stance on detailed trade issues. However, it is also useful to investigate how Japanese automakers have sought to transform *keiretsu* groupings.[9] The formation of *keiretsu* groupings stems from business practices, not government policy, but they have been alleged to be one of the barriers to the Japanese market.[10] This allegation has intensified as the basis of the closed Japanese market has shifted from official barriers and non-tariff barriers such as customs procedures and testing and certification requirements to non-official business practices. The transformation of *keiretsu* links has had a great impact on Japan's trade relations as well as on the opening of the Japanese market.

The opening of *keiretsu* supplier groups

Supplier *keiretsu* in the automobile industry is characterized by a multiple chain of suppliers. In the case of Toyota, for example, there are 230 primary, 4,000 secondary and more than 30,000 tertiary suppliers.[11] The assembly makers and parts suppliers maintain tight links through equity participation, personnel, and cooperation in technology improvement. In addition, assemblers and *keiretsu* parts suppliers forge long-term contracts. Survey data by the Fair Trade Commission (FTC) confirm the above characteristics (FTC 1993a, pp.23–30). The auto manufacturers have, on average, an equity of 58.7 per cent in the leading 30 parts suppliers. In addition, auto manufacturers send their employees to 38.7 per cent of the leading 30 parts suppliers where they serve as executives. In terms of the trade period, 82.2 per cent of the deals between assemblers and parts suppliers are for more than five years, and in the case of the primary 30 parts suppliers, 91.7 per cent of deals are for more than 20 years. Insofar as *keiretsu* groups are formed on the basis of long-term relationships, they tend to be fixed and to impede the entry of newcomers. Even the Japanese parts makers admit this nature of *keiretsu* groups. According to a survey by *Nihon Keizai Shimbunsha* of 101 auto parts companies, 61.3 per cent of respondents considered that 'Japanese *keiretsu* deals are rational but not open' against 19.8 per cent supporting them as 'rational and open'.[12]

Foreign criticism of supplier *keiretsu* derives from the small number of deals made between Japanese assemblers and foreign parts suppliers. The small number of contracts negotiated with foreign suppliers is largely due to differences in production and procurement systems between Japanese and foreign automakers. Japanese and US parts manufacturers used different methods of quality control until recently. Japanese parts manufacturers seek to attain no defects by building quality assurance into each part of the production process. They design equipment and train employees so that defects and problems are resolved as soon as they occur. In the US automobile industry, many parts manufacturers accepted a minimal level of defects as a trade-off for increased efficiencies in mass production. They gave up weeding out defective items somewhere down the line in the production sequence (JAMA 1993, p.6). In addition, there is a difference in design methods between Japan and the United States. There are two methods in auto parts design. One is the design provision method. Under this method, automakers mostly design parts in-house, and suppliers manufacture the parts by referring to the automakers' drawings. The other is the design approval method, in which suppliers receive approval for the design that they draw themselves using their own information and technical ability, and make the parts according to the approved design (Asanuma 1989a, p.69). Even though the share of in-house parts production is decreasing in the Big Three, the shares are higher than in the Japanese companies: 70 per cent in GM, 50 per cent in Ford and 30 per cent in Chrysler. They are also dependent on the design provision method in ordering parts and components. Therefore, US parts makers have little experience in design. The average share of in-house parts production in Japanese producers is 30 per cent. The major method adopted in Japan is the design approval method, under which Japanese parts makers have sufficient experience in designing. Because of these differences, Japanese automakers tended to depend on Japanese parts suppliers, especially their *keiretsu* members.

Japanese automakers seek to break through these bottlenecks by two means. The first method is the promotion of design-in.[13] Design-in functions are an effective method of exchanging techniques between automakers and parts suppliers as well as rationalizing design costs and time. At the same time, design-in has been regarded as a serious impediment to market access for foreign companies. Foreign companies which had little or no experience in design-in, a precondition for deals with Japanese automakers, were therefore unable to participate in this method of parts supply.

Japanese automakers and JAMA have implemented activities to accustom foreign suppliers to design-in. JAMA has organized conferences for design-in. In addition to the conferences in April 1991, a conference held in Detroit in June 1993 drew 145 participants from Japanese automakers and parts manufacturers and 360 from US parts manufacturers. At these conferences, they discussed the problems and detailed methods of design-in. Toyota established a design-in office within the technical division at its headquarters. The company also holds design-in teaching seminars for foreign suppliers. Five groups of foreign suppliers were accepted to the seminars between October 1992 and March 1993. As of January 1991, nearly 300 US parts suppliers had engineers who had been trained in design-in development by Japanese automakers, and more than 300 other companies had engineers in training.[14] Reflecting these efforts, the number of design-in contracts is steadily increasing. In the case of Toyota, the number of finished design-in contracts grew from 119 in September 1991 to 697 in February 1994, with an additional 404 under development.[15]

The other method to eliminate the bottleneck is through direct assistance to foreign parts suppliers. The Big Three, which had kept short-term contracts with independent parts suppliers, had little incentive to assist them to improve their technical skills because they feared that inside information might be leaked to competitors through them (Dertouzos *et al.* 1989, p.177). Japanese automakers seek to support US parts manufacturers in order to ensure reliable parts procurement. Toyota established a Supplier Support Centre in Kentucky in September 1992. The centre holds seminars where the engineers explain

Toyota's quality assurance philosophy. The centre also dispatches production engineers to the factories of suppliers, including those which do not have any business with Toyota. These engineers provide detailed advice on quality improvement and cost reduction. The centre represents 'a voluntary effort by Toyota to support American suppliers, indeed [the] American manufacturing industry in general, to become more efficient through rationalization of their operations' (Shimokawa 1993, pp.35–6).

Nissan has also implemented measures to buttress foreign parts suppliers. For instance, Nissan organised the Supplier Development Team, which encouraged suppliers' own efforts to improve factory floor operations. The Team advises suppliers to use various techniques for improving productivity and abating costs, such as value analysis (VA) and value evaluation (VE).[16] Nissan also established the Nissan Logistics Corporation in the United States in October 1993. Many foreign suppliers have little experience in exports and have to spend time and money becoming accustomed to the export business. The Corporation centralizes control of parts exports from North America to Nissan's plants in Japan, and removes the burden of complicated export business for local suppliers.

Some observers dismiss these efforts as token gestures, directed merely to pacify the dissatisfaction of foreign automakers. However, design-in is a core characteristic of the *keiretsu* supplier groups. Supplier companies capable of developing parts from the early stage of vehicle development were accepted as members of *keiretsu* groups. In addition, since design-in incorporates the offer of inside information about new models, automakers cannot help forging long-term relationships with design-in participants. The Japanese automakers' efforts to expand design-in to foreign suppliers indicate their willingness to expand *keiretsu* groups to foreign suppliers. The assistance to foreign suppliers also illustrates willingness of Japanese auto producers to become truly international companies in each market.

These efforts contributed to the breakup of *keiretsu*-based parts procurement. Although there are a number of cases in which Japanese automakers selected foreign suppliers instead of Japanese suppliers, there are few direct data to indicate the change in *keiretsu* deals.[17] It is possible to guess at the change from the trends in trade with foreign suppliers. The number of US suppliers doing business with Japanese automakers quadrupled from 298 in 1986 to 1,245 in 1993. The number of business contracts has also increased substantially from 807 to 2,726 during the same period (Table 4.4). As a con-

Table 4.4   Number of US suppliers and business contracts, 1986–93

	1986	1987	1988	1989	1990	1991	1992	1993
Suppliers	298	408	527	657	816	906	1,179	1,245
Contracts	807	1,046	1,225	1,523	1,805	2,087	2,387	2,726

Source: JAMA, internal documents.

Table 4.5   Value of US parts purchases, 1986–95 (US$ billion)

	1986	1987	1988	1989	1990	1991	1992	1993	1994	1995
Imports	0.40	0.65	1.05	1.49	1.95	2.08	2.44	2.61	3.23	3.38
Local use	2.09	2.49	3.86	5.63	7.12	8.45	11.18	12.93	16.63	17.65
Total	2.49	3.14	4.91	7.12	9.07	10.53	13.62	15.54	19.86	21.03

Source: JAMA, internal documents.

sequence, the total value of deals between Japanese automakers and US parts suppliers has expanded sharply. Japanese automakers' purchases of US-made parts and materials increased eightfold from US$2.49 billion to US$21.03 billion between 1986 and 1995 (Table 4.5). The content of purchased parts has gradually changed from commodity parts at the start of local production to high-quality parts such as engines, chassis, and electric/electronics parts.

The value of the purchase of foreign parts by individual automakers has also steadily increased. The total value of Toyota's imports and local purchases from foreign suppliers grew from US$4.1 billion in 1990 to US$ 6.3 billion in 1992.[18] Nissan experienced a steady increase in imports, the value expanding from US$374 million in 1988 to US$976 million in 1992.[19] Although domestic vehicle output declined in the early 1990s, the value of total imports remained at the level of US$900 million. Imports therefore have expanded as a proportion of Nissan's total procurement.

Critics often say that even if Japanese automakers increase their deals with parts suppliers in the United States, most are allocated to *keiretsu* Japanese parts makers. Indeed, Japanese parts makers have expanded overseas investment since the mid-1980s (Table 4.6). There are no data which show the breakdown in the number of deals with local US parts suppliers compared with Japanese local plants because Japanese automakers regard all suppliers manufacturing in the United States as US parts suppliers. However, if the trend of an automaker's total deals with parts suppliers in compared with the number of Japa-

Table 4.6   Number of overseas plants established by Japanese parts makers, 1986–92

Region	1986*	1987	1988	1989	1990	1991	1992	Total
North America	44	32	49	27	32	13	4	201
Asia	144	21	40	28	21	13	12	279
Europe	15	5	6	7	8	5	9	55
Other	26	2	2	2	0	3	2	37
Total	229	60	97	64	61	34	27	572

Note: *Up to 1986.
Source: JAPIA (1992, p.20).

Table 4.7   Number of parts suppliers dealing with Honda in the United States, 1985–92

	1985	1986	1987	1988	1989	1990	1991	1992
Total suppliers	40	–	60	110	180	194	240	250
Of which Japanese	–	–	–	28	–	76	–	–

Source: Mair (1994, p.100).

nese local plants, we can estimate whether Japanese automakers are dealing mainly with their *keiretsu* parts suppliers. In the case of Honda, the number of suppliers was small in the early 1980s, but has risen sharply in the late 1980s from 60 in 1987 to 194 in 1990 (Table 4.7). This resulted partly from the high appreciation of the yen and partly from the doubling of production in Honda's manufacturing plant in 1985–6 (Mair 1994, p.100). Japanese parts suppliers also expanded from 28 in 1988 to 76 in 1990. This was a boom period in FDI for Japanese parts makers. Even after the boom, the number of local suppliers increased from 194 in 1990 to 250 in 1992. Toyota also experienced a sharp increase in business with local suppliers. Toyota's local suppliers sharply increased from 204 to 296 between 1991 and 1992 (Table 4.8). These figures suggest that Japanese automakers do not necessarily stick to the trade with their *keiretsu* parts suppliers.

The opening of supplier *keiretsu* groups has impacted on supplier associations, the representative bodies of *keiretsu* groups. Supplier associations are organized by parts suppliers which have deals with the Japanese automakers, except for Honda.[20] Associations play a crucial role in organizing seminars and cooperative research and

Table 4.8   Number of US parts suppliers dealing with Toyota, 1990–93

	1990	*1991*	*1992*	*1993*
Imports	83	94	119	131
Local procurement	194	204	296	301
Total	277	298	415	432

Source: Toyota, internal documents.

development (R & D) as well as in coordinating relations between suppliers and the assembly maker, and among suppliers. In the past, participation in supplier associations was limited by the trade period or transaction amount (Tsuruta 1992, p.8). However, these qualifications were excluded, and foreign companies have been invited to become members. Toyota's first-tier suppliers organize *kyoho-kai*, consisting of some 230 members divided into *Tokai* (the area around Nagoya), *Kanto* (the area around Tokyo) and *Kansai* (the area around Osaka and Kyoto). *Kanto kyoho-kai* admitted the participation of three parts divisions of GM in April 1994. Although several foreign parts suppliers had joined Toyota's supplier association, the parts divisions of the US Big Three automakers participated in it for the first time.[21] Restructuring of the supplier associations was also seen in the Nissan group. This group had set up the two supplier associations, *takara-kai* composed of suppliers which started deals at the Nissan's establishment, and *shoho-kai* composed of suppliers which entered the trade afterwards. They were dissolved in June 1991 and a new combined association, *nissho-kai* was established. The new association included 22 new parts makers, including such foreign firms as Garrett Turbo and Texas Instruments Japan.[22]

Why have Japanese automakers extended parts contracts to non-*keiretsu* foreign suppliers? Foreign pressure for raising local content in overseas markets and for expanding imports in the Japanese market has been one critical factor explaining this change. The appreciation of the yen also forced Japanese automakers to use more foreign parts. Yet, as Japanese automakers have expanded their international operations, they themselves have a stronger incentive to expand procurement from foreign suppliers beyond *keiretsu* groups.

The key feature of supplier *keiretsu* lies in the nature of its long-term transactions (Yaginuma 1992, p.32). Long-term transactions have considerable economic advantages compared with spot market transactions. First, long-term transactions reduce transaction costs. Long-term relationships enable contracting parties to accumulate information about product development, product quality, technological innovation, and so on. The accumulation of information reduces the cost of maintaining contractual relationships (Tsuruta 1992, pp.6–7). Second, long-term contracts ensure stable supply channels. This provides incentives to make valuable, specific investments based on a long-term perspective (Sheard 1993, p.37). Third, long-term contracts enable parts suppliers to develop 'relation-specific skills'.[23] On the basis of these skills, parts suppliers and assembly makers undertake steady improvement in part quality, rationalization of production methods, and cost reduction. It is reasonable for firms to enter into long-term contracts given such economic benefits.[24]

Why, then, have Japanese automakers sought to transform *keiretsu* links with economic advantages? Division of long-term contracts into the first contracting stage and the contract renewal stage helps to address this question (Sheard 1993, pp.33–6). While Japanese automakers have little incentive to transform the practice in the contract renewal stage, consideration of foreign parts suppliers at the first contracting stage is indispensable for successful multinational operations. For Japanese automakers which, on average, outsource 70 per cent of parts and materials, identification of parts suppliers that provide products of the highest quality, at the lowest prices, and with the most reliable delivery is critical. In the past, Japanese automakers concentrated on domestic production, and developed efficient production and procurement systems with domestic parts suppliers. They had little incentive to negotiate contracts with foreign suppliers. However, as Japanese automakers extended multinational production, they recognized that it was not feasible to rely heavily on Japanese parts suppliers. They also sought to enhance their international competitiveness by fostering relationships with leading supplier companies in specific product sectors on an international scale. Furthermore, as Japanese automakers strengthened local production, they had to manufacture differentiated models that took into account local preferences and tastes. The participation of local parts suppliers contributes to the development of locally oriented vehicles. Japanese automakers seek to expand parts transactions at the first contracting stage to foreign suppliers, and to make use of the advantages deriving from long-term contracts.

The cultivation of trustworthy relationships with local suppliers led to an increase in imports of foreign parts to Japan. Previously Japanese producers had little information about excellent foreign parts suppliers, and it was difficult to increase imports. Import from the parts suppliers with which overseas subsidiaries have already dealt is reliable and efficient.[25]

Reflecting the changes in firms' stance on parts procurement, Japanese automakers are inclined to pursue an open procurement policy, targeting overseas suppliers. For instance, Tatsuro Toyoda, President of Toyota, shocked the *keiretsu* parts suppliers by announcing that Toyota would make efforts to attain the most appropriate procurement anywhere in the world at the new year conference of its supplier association in 1994.[26] Toyota started to accumulate an international data base on parts suppliers in 1994 in order to realize a worldwide parts procurement system.[27] Nissan announced that any firm having dealings worth more than 1 billion yen annually could automatically join its supplier association.[28] This indicates Nissan's intention to establish cooperative relations with any parts makers, irrespective of nationality.

The opening of *keiretsu* distribution groups

Japan's car distribution system, based on *keiretsu* dealer networks, has been a source of trade friction in the automobile industry.[29] For example, several agenda items at the Structural Impediments Initiative (SII) talks such as the distribution system, exclusionary business practices, and *keiretsu* relations were relevant to the car distribution system (Shioji 1991, pp.189–90). A collaborative survey by MITI and the US Department of Commerce announced in February 1994 also concluded that tight linkages between makers and dealers through finance and personnel created environments where foreign automakers found it difficult to penetrate the Japanese market.[30] The criticism of Japan's car distribution system by foreign car makers has also been severe. For instance, Robert A. Lutz, President and chief executive officer of Chrysler, in October 1993, criticized the entry barriers to the Japanese market such as manufacturer-mandated 'exclusivity clauses' for dealers, high distributor margins, and extremely high costs associated with meeting safety and other regulatory requirements.[31]

The major Japanese automakers have several sales channels (Table 4.9). Sales channels are generally determined by the terms of franchise agreements. Under these agreements, dealers are allocated specific car models, so it is difficult for them to handle models that have been allocated to other sales channels in the same company, as well

Table 4.9 Distribution channels of major Japanese automakers, 1994

Company	Channel	Dealer	Outlet	Model	Imported car
Toyota	Toyota	50	1,264	12	GM
	Toyopet	52	1,081	10	
	Corolla	76	1,497	11	
	Auto	66	1,065	10	
	Vista	66	693	10	
Nissan	Nissan	57	1,140	20	
	Motor	37	683	15	
	Sunny	57	993	14	
	Cherry	4	50	10	
	Prince	51	1,037	16	
Honda	Clio	94	479	9	Chrysler
	Primo	986	1,426	10	Chrysler
	Verno	94	399	8	Chrysler
Mitsubishi	Galant	129	729	24	Mercedes-Benz
	Car Plaza	129	360	16	
	Fuso	47	297	8	
Mazda	Mazda	54	662	21	
	Infini	55	605	16	
	Ford	115	300	15	Ford
	Autozam	807	876	8	Fiat
	Euros	143	250	11	Citroen

Source: Nikkan Jidosha Shimbunsha, *Jidosha Nenkan 1995*, pp.71–85.

as models from other automakers, including imported models. In addition, the prefecture-based territory system is adopted as the basis for sales in Japan. Automakers seek to contract at least one dealership for each of the sales channels in 47 prefectures, and the prefectures where a dealership is located constitute the dealers' areas of prime responsibility for sales (JAMA 1990, p.2). This broad territory system has led dealers to compete for outlets, and has strengthened their dependence on the automakers.[32] Furthermore, Japanese auto producers intervene in the management of car dealers. They not only hold equity in dealer companies and dispatch their employees to them, but they also support them by offering loans and rebates.[33]

Japanese automakers have taken measures to open dealership networks in recent years. The opening of the distribution system has been implemented from two directions: one is to revise the dealer contracts, and the other is to handle foreign vehicles in automakers' dealer channels. The most problematic custom between automakers and dealers was the prior consultation requirement clause in franchise agreements. Under this clause, dealers were required to consult with automakers about any plans to sell cars distributed to other sales channels or to sell other makers' cars. However, according to the managers of the automakers, what was required was that they should be informed when dealers made decisions which had a 'serious' effect on management. To handle foreign cars was not necessarily 'serious'. Therefore, dealers were free to deal in foreign cars on their own initiative.[34] Yet, because the clause was apt to generate misunderstanding, Japanese automakers eliminated the prior consultation requirement clause in dealership contracts, and made it clear that dealers could freely sell cars from other manufacturers. Toyota sent its dealers a document in November 1991 which explained that dealers could handle any kind of car they wished.[35] Mitsubishi, Nissan, and Mazda also revised dealership contracts in order to clarify that dealer companies could deal in other makers' vehicles.[36] However, some dealers did not understand that they could handle any kind of car including imported vehicles. Japanese automakers therefore undertook further measures to provide a better environment for dealers to trade in foreign cars. In May 1994, for instance, Toyota, Nissan, and Mitsubishi rectified the payment method of rebates and the limitation of sales territory.[37]

As Japanese automakers have strengthened corporate alliances with foreign partners, they have forged tie-ups for distribution and sales of imported cars, especially in the late 1980s. Mazda formed the Autorama channel as single-franchise outlets for Ford brand cars in 1982.[38] Mazda has also handled Fiat of Italy since June 1989, and Citroen of France since September 1989. Isuzu has handled GM since 1973 and Adam Opel of Germany since December 1988, while Suzuki has traded in GM and Peugeot-SA of France since April 1988. These moves have expanded to leading producers in the 1990s. Honda started to sell Chrysler's Cherokee in September 1990 based on a sales agreement with Chrysler. Toyota also commenced the sales of foreign cars. The company started to sell Volkswagen and Audi in its Duo dealer channel in April 1992. Toyota agreed with GM in November 1993 to sell 20,000 right-hand drive Chevrolet Cavaliers annually through its sales channels in 1996.

The deals regarding foreign car sales mentioned above were determined by auto manufacturers, and dealers continued to handle foreign cars according to manufacturers' policies. However, US automakers demanded the right to negotiate dealership contracts directly with individual Japanese dealers. It is generally believed that there are few cases where dealers themselves negotiated contracts with foreign manufacturers or their Japanese subsidiaries. However, there are quite a few cases.[39] But these dealers sell German, not American vehicles.

This trend has expanded to US cars in the 1990s. Four Nissan dealers decided to establish sales outlets for Ford cars. This resulted from Ford's asking Nissan to introduce dealers who had an interest in handling Ford's cars. Toyota dealers are also embarking on direct sales contracts with the Big Three. Chiba Toyopet, one of the major Toyota dealers, decided independently to begin the sales of Ford cars in November 1994.[40] This decision had significant implications. Toyota dealers were regarded as the least likely to deal in foreign cars because they were the most profitable dealers in Japan. The Chiba Toyopet case reveals that this is not the case.

The critical factor which led Japanese automakers to trade in more US vehicles was their commitment to corporate alliances and their interest in the US market. Honda started to handle Chrysler's Cherokee in 1990. One reason for this action was that Honda did not have any Jeep type car such as the Cherokee. The other reason was relevant to Honda's local production in the United States. Honda had steadily expanded local production in the United States in the late 1980s, and took the status of the third US passenger car producer from Chrysler in 1991. Honda recognized the necessity for promoting cooperation with Chrysler, leading to an agreement to sell Chrysler's Jeep in Japan. Reflecting this consideration, Honda has made serious efforts to sell the Cherokee. After importation from the United States, the Cherokees had several defects such as hollows and paint spots. Although Chrysler maintained that such trifling defects were not problems, Honda spent money and time to correct them through predelivery inspections.[41] Honda also expanded the number of dealers from 430 in 1990 to 694 in 1993. This led to an exceptional success for US vehicles in Japan with the sales volume increasing from 807 in 1992 to 3,747 in 1993.

Toyota's handling of foreign cars in its dealer network can be explained by its commitment to corporate alliances and multinational production. Toyota started the sales of Volkswagen and Audi in April 1992. The two giants had already commenced joint production of small trucks in Germany in 1989. Toyota aimed to strengthen the relations with Volkswagen through the sales agreement. In addition, the sales agreement had much to do with Toyota's plan to begin local production in Europe. Toyota planned to start the production of passenger cars in the United Kingdom in 1992. However, following a move to restrain the total volume of Japanese cars which included imported and locally produced cars, Toyota sought to ensure its sales in Europe by showing its commitment to expanding the access of European vehicles to the Japanese market.[42]

Toyota's decision to handle GM cars can be understood in this context, as well. Before announcing that Toyota would sell GM cars, Toyota examined the possibility of selling GM cars in 1989 and 1990. However, the plan was not realized due to Toyota's consideration for GM's importer Yanase & Co., which had sold GM cars since 1915. The relations between Toyota and GM had steadily been strengthened after they started a joint venture, NUMMI, in 1984. In May 1988, the two companies established a joint venture, the United Australian Automotive Industries Ltd. (UAAI) in Australia. This company became the parent company of Toyota's subsidiary, Toyota Motor Corporation Australia Ltd. and General Motors-Holden's Automotive Ltd. in May 1991.[43] Furthermore, NUMMI expanded its business in spring 1991 by starting the production of small trucks. Therefore, the handling of GM cars resulted partly from Toyota's intention to strengthen the relations with GM by selling its vehicles in Japan. This intention was reflected on Toyota's decision to sell GM Cavaliers through the Toyota channel, the most powerful and profitable dealer channel.[44]

What is important is that Toyota has changed its stance on opening its dealer network. There were, however, several episodes reflecting Toyota's managers' opposition to its dealers handling foreign cars. For example, when the president of Chiba Toyopet asked a direct sales manager of Toyota to handle Ford, he agreed. But the president was not convinced that the agreement was his real intention.[45] In summer 1994, Tatsuro Toyoda proclaimed that Toyota's dealers would be able to handle other makers' cars if they wished. Within hours of this announcement, Toyota's managers sent dealers faxes advising that if they did so they could expect to lose their connection with Toyota.[46] These episodes do not necessarily reflect the views of Toyota's senior executives. Sales managers tend to make efforts to ensure stable sales of Toyota's vehicles. However, the senior executive appreciated the necessity of opening the dealer network to foreign vehicles in order to tighten relationships with foreign alliance partners as well as to promote reciprocal relationships with foreign automakers.

MARKET-OPENING POLICIES AND
INDUSTRY REACTION IN 1989

Nissan's international cooperation programme

After the early 1980s, the Japanese government became more eager to promote market access of foreign goods, and implemented various measures towards this end.[47] The government has held import expansion meetings since the mid-1980s. At the first meeting in April 1985, senior executives of 60 export-oriented companies, and trading and retail companies were requested to establish a division for import expansion, to submit an import expansion programme, and to report periodically on the implementation of the programme. The next year, the target number increased greatly, to 302 companies.

The response by the automobile industry to government requests for expanding imports was similar to other industries until 1989. In 1989, however, automakers announced international cooperation programmes that included import expansion plans. The most challenging programme was announced by Nissan. The second largest auto producer in Japan outlined its international cooperation programme on 20 September 1989. This programme consisted of three pillars. First, the firm would double the value of its imports worth US$370 million in 1988 by 1992, and would double this again by the second half of the 1990s. To expand imports, Nissan would sell the Volkswagen Passat in its dealer network in 1990, and import cars from its overseas factories in North America and Australia. Second, Nissan would expand local production and reverse the ratio of exported vehicles to locally built vehicles in Nissan's unit sales overseas. The ratio would be changed from 2 to 1 in 1989 to 1 to 1 in 1992 and to 1 to 2 by the end of the 1990s. For this purpose, Nissan would increase local content and promote the localization of management through recruiting local persons to senior executive posts of each subsidiary. Third, the programme included a plan to whittle down exports. The peak export volume of Nissan was 1.41 million in 1985. The volume would be reduced to 1 million by 1992 and to around half a million by the end of the 1990s. In order to promote the programme, Nissan established an international procurement division at its headquarters in January 1990. The division was set up on the model of the domestic procurement division. Procurement divisions were also established in Nissan North America and Nissan Europe, the regional headquarters.

Motivation of Nissan's programme

Why did Nissan announce this international cooperation programme in 1989? Did this programme have anything to do with the internationalization of Nissan's corporate activity? It may be thought that Nissan's programme did not stem from the change in corporate preferences but from the encouragement by MITI which was keen to expand imports. However, there are at least two factors which suggest otherwise. The first factor relates to Nissan's response to MITI's guidance on a capital investment plan. In October 1989, the Minister of MITI requested automakers to refrain from making large capital investments. Nissan ignored this request on the grounds that the capital spending would not lead to a further export drive.[48] The second factor is that other automakers resisted MITI's guidance to formulate a similar programme to Nissan's. MITI expected Toyota, Honda and Mazda to draw up the programme. Though all these firms eventually announced programmes, the contents of these programmes did not meet MITI's expectations. Toyota's programme only included an import expansion plan. Honda did not abide by MITI's guidance for some time. After some resistance, Honda announced a programme which summarized an existing import–export plan.[49]

Nissan's programme sprang from several factors. First of all, trade relations with the United States had entered a serious phase. Japan's trade surplus with the United States remained high, in spite of a rapid increase in imports in the second half of the 1980s.[50] The US government launched new measures to rectify trade imbalances. In May 1989, the government identified Japan as a country carrying out unfair trade practices under Super 301, and listed supercomputers, satellites, and wood products as items subject to unfair trade practices.[51] At the same time, the US government proposed the Structural Impediments Initiative (SII) talks to discuss measures to reduce structural impediments to trade between the two countries. These moves motivated Nissan, which was dependent on the US market for exports and local production, to take measures to reduce trade friction with the United States.

Second, the programme was influenced by domestic political factors. The Liberal Democratic Party (LDP) experienced an historical setback in the Upper House election of July 1989. The automobile industry was accused of bearing a large responsibility for the defeat. The Confederation of Japan Automobile Workers' Unions was one of the major constituents of the Japanese Private Sector

Trade Union Confederation (*Rengo*) whose remarkable advance was largely responsible for the loss of LDP's seats. On 25 July, two days after the Upper House election, Seiroku Kajiyama, the Minister of MITI, and top ranking officials of MITI met senior executives of the automobile industry such as Shoichiro Toyoda (President of Toyota), Yutaka Kume (President of Nissan), and Satoshi Okubo (Chairman of Honda). Kajiyama argued that although the industry enjoyed benefits from the introduction of the consumer tax, it did not contribute support to the LDP government (Mainichi Shimbun 1991, pp.19–21).[52]

Besides, the LDP had a specific quarrel with Nissan. Takashi Ishihara, Chairman of Keizai Doyukai as well as Chairman of Nissan, had had a great impact on business and political circles by pushing for the resignation of the Takeshita administration in April 1989 (Mainichi Shimbun 1991, p.20). In June 1989, he also criticized the reaction of the government towards the Tiananmen Incident in China as being lukewarm compared with other countries which severely censured the military actions of the Chinese government. His remarks irritated LDP politicians. Senior executives of Nissan probably felt the need to announce some measures that would appease the anger of the LDP government.

Third, the programme was set up as a result of changes in the policy stance of Nissan on market access. Japanese auto producers became more sensitive to market access issues in the late 1980s. This change was seen in the attitude of major automakers to the purchase of foreign semiconductors. Automakers had previously shown little interest in expanding the purchase of foreign semiconductors on the grounds that the semiconductor disputes were caused by electronics firms. The share of foreign semiconductors in the total purchases for Toyota, Honda, and Nissan was only 2 per cent in 1988, when the average share of foreign semiconductors in the Japanese market was more than 10 per cent. However, these firms announced plans to increase the purchase of foreign semiconductors in 1989. In May 1989, Nissan announced a plan to begin imports of memory chips from Intel for use in the electronic-control units of engines.[53] In the same month, Honda also published an action programme, in which the value of semiconductor purchases would be expanded tenfold, and the ratio of foreign semiconductors in the total purchase would be raised from 1.8 per cent to more than 10 per cent by 1992.[54] Toyota also decided to purchase micro controllers and memory chips from Motorola, a US company.[55]

Why, then, did Nissan change its stance on market access issues? This question is relevant to the issue of why Nissan announced its bold programme. The programme had a great bearing on Nissan's multinational operations. Nissan's expansive international operations made it possible for Nissan to draw up concrete plans including adjustment of the ratio of imported vehicles to locally built vehicles and the reduction of exports (Tsuchiya 1989, p.53). Nissan's international activities date back to 1957 when it agreed to offer technical assistance to Yulon Motors of Taiwan. In 1961, Nissan established Nissan Mexicana, its first offshore production plant. Nissan extended local production to the United States in June 1983, half a year behind its forerunner, Honda. Its globalization was swift in Europe as well. After the equity participation in Nissan Motor Iberica in Spain in January 1980, local operations started in the United Kingdom in July 1986. Nissan was the first Japanese automaker to manufacture vehicles in Europe.

Nissan's multinational operations were extended in the late 1980s. Nissan had proceeded with globalization in a four-step process: first, creation and development of local production; second, strengthening of local R & D capabilities; third, localization in management functions; and fourth, localization of decision-making process.[56] Unlike other Japanese automakers, Nissan has made efforts to localize management. Not only were three out of four overseas manufacturing plants managed by local chief executive officers but the ratio of Japanese in employment at overseas plants was extremely low.[57] With the opening of regional headquarters, Nissan Europe in April 1989 and Nissan North America in January 1990, the company has arrived at the final step.

The advanced stage of Nissan's internationalization encouraged it to pay attention to developments in the international market. In 1989, a corporate planning office was organized under the direct control of the president. The office drew up the first long-term plan which envizaged that the automobile industry in Japan and the world would promote multinational production and a globalization strategy. The top executives of Nissan considered that since Japanese cars have penetrated the world market and Japanese automakers have actively promoted multinational operations, they would have to take into account more seriously international cooperation with foreign makers.[58] This consideration led to the plans for a curtailment of exports as well as to the doubling of imports in the programme. At the same time, by announcing that the company would take measures to promote access of foreign products to the Japanese market and did not intend to disrupt the world market, Nissan hoped that its local production facilities in the United States and Europe would be accepted as insiders.[59]

What is crucial about Nissan's programme was that it suggested a change in stance on free trade. Japanese automakers supported free-trade principles in the early 1980s. When the Japanese government sought to introduce a VER in 1981, automakers were strongly opposed to it, arguing that the VER contradicted free-trade principles. The primary reason why they adhered to free-trade principles was that these provided conditions for keeping export markets open. The automakers showed little interest in opening up their own home market and in rectifying high export dependence. However, they gradually recognised that other methods were necessary to sustain the free-trade system. For this reason, Nissan's voluntary programme included concrete measures to reduce exports for the first time. Nissan's President Yutaka Kume stressed the importance of this point, arguing that 'we thought the import expansion alone would not be effective in correcting Japan–U.S. trade imbalances. Judging from the seriousness of Japan–U.S. commercial relations, we concluded it would be best to cut down exports instead of just denouncing the U.S.'[60]

Although it is a matter of debate as to whether Nissan's internationalization has been successful, Nissan was the leading company in the Japanese auto industry in terms of internationalization through the 1980s. This enabled Nissan to take a lead in announcing programmes designed to expand market access for foreign products and to abandon an export-dependent corporate strategy.

Influence of Nissan's programme

The international cooperation programme that Nissan announced in September 1989 impinged not only on the behaviour of other auto companies, but also the government's policies for expanding market access. Even when the programme was announced, other automakers paid scant attention to it, asserting that every auto producer was reducing exports as they expanded local production in North America and Europe.[61] However, after Nissan announced the programme, other industries and the overseas press asked why other automakers were not announcing similar programmes.[62] In succession, other firms eventually announced similar programmes. Mazda announced a programme on 20 October 1989 to quadruple the value of imports in 1988 to 200 billion yen by 1992: to increase car imports from 7,200 in 1988 to 60,000 in 1992; and to expand the international procurement of semiconductors and electronics equipment.[63] Toyota's programme was announced on 30 October. The programme, which aimed to raise the import value to 300 billion yen in 1992, included reverse imports of Camry from its Kentucky plant in the United States as well as imports of other foreign-made cars.[64] Honda followed on 24 November and Mitsubishi on 17 January 1990.[65] Automakers other than Nissan were forced to draw up cooperation programmes by the unintentionally associated moves by MITI and Nissan.[66] It is doubtful whether other producers would have made their plans so early, if Nissan had not initiated its programme.

Nissan's programme also contributed to creating a new impetus in the government's import expansion policy. The programme considered import expansion from a rather long-term perspective, three years or more. MITI had previously considered short-term plans, within one year, but recognized that import expansion was important in the longer term. Around one month after Nissan's announcement, MITI requested some 50 export-oriented firms in automobiles, electronics, general machinery, which accounted for 60 per cent of Japan's exports, to double their 1988 import value by 1993, and to add the same value of imports as exports if they expand exports by 1993.[67] MITI expected these firms to draw up a medium-range programme like that which Nissan had announced. This request was exceptional because MITI had already held regular import expansion meetings in June. The import-doubling programme launched by Nissan motivated MITI to take this additional action. The efforts by private firms indirectly affected government policy. MITI sought to introduce an import promotion tax system in 1989. Although this idea was resisted by the Ministry of Finance (MOF), MITI succeeded in including the import promotion tax arrangements in the 1990 tax reform plan. The import expansion efforts by firms provided MITI with the pretext for the introduction of this tax reform system.

Nissan's programme was epoch-making in its effect on the relations between MITI and the automobile industry. The automobile industry was regarded as less cooperative with MITI's policy compared with other industries such as iron and steel. Relations between MITI and the automobile industry were marked by a history of disputes. MITI drew up the 'people's car' concept in 1955, but this concept failed, owing to the objections of automakers. MITI also advocated the two-group concept in 1968, designed to reinforce the oligopoly position of Toyota and Nissan. This concept again failed because of strong opposition from smaller manufacturers. Before a VER was introduced in the US market in 1981, MITI encouraged automakers to invest in the US market to mitigate trade tension. However, the major automakers turned a deaf ear to MITI (Chung 1993, chap. 6). When a VER was introduced in 1981, Naohiro Amaya, MITI's negotiator with the United States, implored the top executives of auto producers to accept the VER (Amaya 1981; Kotani 1982). The crucial factor in MITI's voluntarily extension of VER in 1985 was that MITI could not draw on cooperation from the automobile industry.[68] In the case of import promotion in 1989, however, a company in the automobile industry offered a sample plan that MITI could use as a pretext to persuade other companies and industries. Nissan's programme functioned as a catalyst promoting momentum for market access.

THE ACTION PLAN IN 1992

Background

Market access in the automobile industry became an issue and the stance of Japanese automakers on market access was revealed in the Action Plan announced in January 1992. The automobile sector became the main target when US President George Bush visited Japan, and the Japanese government and automobile industry clashed over the import expansion of auto parts and vehicles before and during Bush's visit. On 9 January 1992, Prime Minister Miyazawa and US President Bush announced the Tokyo Declaration, which confirmed the Japan–US global partnership after the Cold War. In the Action Plan attached to the Tokyo Declaration, the Japanese government announced assistance with design-in training for engineers of US parts manufacturers, sales missions to Japan and other measures to assist the US parts manufacturing industry. The government also promulgated further improvements in tax and financial incentives to promote imports to and investments in Japan, such as tax incentives for the establishment of foreign firms, low interest rate loans, and debt guarantee facilities. With respect to imports of finished vehicles, the government proclaimed its intention to increase opportunities for the sales of foreign vehicles through budgetary allocations, holding

Table 4.10   Japanese automakers' goals for US-made auto parts purchases
(US$ billion)

Company	Target for 1994			Purchases in 1990			(a/b)
	Local content	Imports	Total (a)	Local content	Imports	Total (b)	
Toyota	3.82	1.46	5.28	1.90	0.70	2.60	203.1
Nissan	2.90	0.80	3.70	0.90	0.40	1.30	284.6
Honda	4.38	0.56	4.94	2.52	0.28	2.80	176.4
Mitsubishi	1.20	0.40	1.60	0.52	0.16	0.68	235.3
Mazda	1.90	0.40	2.30	0.97	0.22	1.19	193.3
Others	0.80	0.38	1.18	0.12	0.03	0.15	786.7
Total	15.00	4.00	19.00	6.93	1.79	8.72	217.9

Source: *JAMA Report*, No.45, p.4.

foreign automobile shows in Japan, and JETRO (Japan External Trade Organization) activities.

The Japanese auto manufacturers and related industrial associations also suggested measures to increase the purchase of US auto parts and vehicles. The automakers set purchase goals of US$19 billion for US-made auto parts in 1994, up US$10 billion from 1990 (Table 4.10). Parts procurement from US suppliers by Japanese affiliates in the United States was expected to more than double, from US$6.9 billion in 1990 to US$15 billion in 1994. As a consequence, the percentage of local procurement in the total purchase of parts was expected to increase from some 50 per cent in 1990 to 70 per cent in 1994. By contrast, the percentage of imports from Japan would decrease from 50 per cent to 30 per cent. Imports of US-made parts were expected to double, from US$1.8 billion in 1990 to US$4 billion in 1994. Japanese automakers also suggested that they continue further efforts to encourage design-in, expand R & D facilities in the United States and assist US parts suppliers to develop long-term business relationships.

In terms of complete cars, the Japan Automobile Dealers Association reconfirmed their willingness to undertake dual dealerships to sell US automobiles. This statement was a response to US criticism that Japanese dealers avoided dealing with US cars under a single dealership contract with manufacturing companies. Major Japanese automakers also announced their target figures to support imports of US cars (Table 4.11). The total number of 19,700 units attained within

Table 4.11   Japanese automakers' goals for US
vehicles sales (unit)

Importer	Supplier	Volume	Target year
Toyota	GM	5,000	Not specified
Nissan	Ford	3,000	Not specified
Honda	Chrysler	1,200	1994
Mitsubishi	Chrysler	6,000	1995
Mazda	Ford	4,500	1992
Total		19,700	

Source: *Yomiuri Shimbun* (10 January 1992).

a few years was roughly 6,000 units more than in 1990. In line with these objectives, they expressed their willingness to cooperate in expanding sales opportunities for US cars in Japan and to provide space to exhibit the Big Three's cars at seven showrooms in the Metropolitan Tokyo area.

Interactions between MITI and the automakers

Before Japanese automakers announced their voluntary plans in the Action Plan in January 1992, there was tough bargaining between the government and the automobile industry. Bush's tour included exceptional features for a top US–Japan meeting. The schedule of the tour was suddenly changed. Bush was originally expected to visit Japan in early December. The tour was postponed because of rising economic problems in the United States. The objective of the tour was also altered. The original objective of the meeting was to strengthen the friendly ties between the United States and Japan on the 50-year anniversary of the Pearl Harbour attack. But the objective was transformed into a detailed discussion of trade issues affecting automobiles and other areas in order that Bush could demonstrate to the American people his serious interest in economic matters in an election year. The Bush delegation was accompanied by 21 leading business executives, including eight business leaders from the auto sector. The tour that Bush hailed as 'a mission to create jobs and restore prosperity for all Americans' was thus changed into Bush's campaign for presidential re-election in November 1992.

The Japanese government was forced to take urgent measures to promote the summit's success and to cope with the changes in tour's schedule and objectives. On 11 December, Vice-Minister of MITI, Yuji

Tanahashi, requested the top executives of automakers to make maximum efforts to respond to the US request, including providing assistance to US car sales.[69] Two days later, MITI suddenly called in Shoichiro Toyoda, President of Toyota, and requested him to redress the trade imbalance with the United States through expanding the purchase of US auto parts and vehicles.[70] The government's focus on the auto industry accelerated after Robert Zoellick, US Undersecretary of State, arrived in Japan on 20 December for consultation prior to Bush's visit. He was dissatisfied with the voluntary programmes which Japanese automakers had announced in November and persuaded the Japanese government to make concessions on trade issues so as to arrest the protectionist movement in the US Congress. Prime Minister Kiichi Miyazawa requested the automobile industry on 25 December to consider lifting the purchase of US auto parts.[71] MITI invited the top executives of major automakers to a breakfast meeting on 26 December, and persuaded them to draw up new programmes which would boost the purchase of US-made parts and targeted goals for US car sales.[72] MITI fixed the deadline for the new programmes on 6 January of the next year.

MITI faced strong resistance from the automakers. Toyota, the leading automaker, was the main target of MITI's guidance, shown in the special commitment by MITI on 13 December. Toyota rejected successive MITI's requests, asserting that the purchase of parts should not be implemented according to the government's request. Yuji Tanahashi, Vice-Minister of MITI, was impatient with this attitude.[73] The top executives of Toyota, who maintained a close connection with the *kochi-kai* (Miyazawa faction), hoped that if they asked Prime Minister Miyazawa, they would obtain his support for their stance.[74] Although they met Miyazawa twice, this commitment was not forthcoming. Miyazawa had his own reasons for wanting a successful summit. Miyazawa, who had become Prime Minister a few months earlier, did not enjoy sufficient support within the LDP. In addition, he had just failed to pass the bill allowing the dispatch of Self Defence Forces overseas for United Nations peace keeping. There was strong pressure on Miyazawa to make substantial concessions to Bush.

After failing to persuade Miyazawa, Toyota showed a more flexible attitude. The figure for purchases of US parts which Toyota announced in November 1991 was US$4.6 billion. The procurement division concluded that additional purchases of US$0.3–0.4 billion were the best that could be achieved. This figure was boosted to US$5.28 billion. This new target was set by the external relations division and the decision of top executives (Watanabe 1992, pp.12–13). Toyota had earlier rejected the idea of selling GM cars on the grounds that it was non-sense to proceed unless GM asked Toyota to sell cars. However, Toyota eventually accepted a target for annual sales of 5,000 GM cars on several conditions.

The decision to increase purchases of US-made auto parts and sales of US cars was difficult for Nissan as well. Yutaka Kume, Nissan's President, summoned the firm's executives on 5 January in order to discuss countermeasures to MITI's request to boost the voluntary programme in November 1991 and to assist the sales of US vehicles. Some executives asserted that it was nonsense to propose that Nissan sell US cars as long as US automakers themselves did not put this pro-posal to Nissan.[75] Kume decided to accept MITI's request. Nissan agreed to increase purchases of parts and announced a plan to coop-erate in sales of US cars. The value of parts purchases was raised from US\$3.3 billion to US\$3.7 billion. The company also decided to provide showrooms for US cars and to sell Ford's minivan, Quest, and Taurus in its dealer networks.

Japanese automakers gathered on 6 January in order to make a final decision on the purchase of US-made cars and auto parts. At the meeting, all auto producers except Toyota decided to accept targets for purchases of parts and vehicles. Toyota followed other companies after the top executives met Miyazawa in the afternoon of 7 January. Nissan announced its cooperation programme on 7 January and the other four major auto firms the next day.

The actions of automakers were characterized by strong resistance to the requirements of MITI and the Prime Minister's Office to increase the purchase of US-made parts and to assist the sales of US vehicles. They did not keep the original deadline for new pro-grammes which MITI had determined, and the negotiations between automakers and MITI continued until 8 January, the day before the second Miyazawa–Bush meeting. Further, MITI's goal of boosting purchases of auto parts by 50 per cent from November plans was not realised.

The actions of automakers superficially indicated a reluctance to promote market access of foreign products. However, there were plausible reasons for their resistance. They had already announced voluntary programmes for expanding imports twice in late 1991. The first programmes were forged in November. The programmes, based on the Market Oriented Sector Specific (MOSS) agreement in Sep-tember 1991, involved a purchase plan for US-made auto parts.

Although some firms were dissatisfied with the managed trade method, the automobile industry by and large cooperated in implementing the government agreement.[76] Under these programmes, the total value of imports and local procurement was expected to increase to US$16.4 billion in 1994, 91 per cent up from 1990.[77]

One month later, the automakers announced a second voluntary programme which targeted imports worldwide under the Business Global Partnership (BGP) Project.[78] Under these programmes, the five leading auto producers would increase annual imports from US$4.4 billion in 1990 to US$7.4 billion in 1994, and expand purchases by overseas subsidiaries from US$12.8 billion to US$24.6 billion in the same period.[79] The two programmes were announced after consultation with MITI as gifts for Bush's visit. However, MITI forced automakers to revise the November figures after a short time. The automakers asserted, quite plausibly, that if they revised the figures that had been announced only two months earlier, these figures would seem to have been calculated irresponsibly. Furthermore, the industry feared that the figures would be regarded as a pledge when they were included in the governmental document, and might be used as a pretext for retaliation if the targets were not achieved.[80] The automakers sought to settle with figures that were attainable.

Japanese automakers did not necessarily wish to promote the purchase of US auto parts and vehicles. Their real intention lay in the two programmes that they announced in 1991 in order to promote market access of foreign products. What Japanese automakers resisted was MITI's unreasonable demands to revise the plans within a short time frame and MITI's intervention which might lead to managed trade.

Motivation of the automakers

If automakers regarded MITI's demands unreasonable, why did they agree to boost the purchase of US auto parts and to sell US vehicles? It seemed that the automakers' actions were a result of MITI's strong pressure. Indeed, at that time, MITI was greatly worried about the auto trade issue with the United States. In addition to statistical data suggesting that the share of Japanese automakers combining imports and local production exceeded 30 per cent in the US market, and that three-quarters of the US$40 billion US trade deficit with Japan in 1990 was attributable to the automobile industry, another factor forced MITI to respond positively to the US demand. GM announced on 18 December that it would close down six assembly plants and 15 parts plants, and slash its North American workforce by 74,000 by 1995.

Reflecting this concern, MITI's request to boost the earlier plans was persistent and strong. It is reported that at the meeting with automakers' executives in late December, MITI suggested banning the exports of cars and auto parts under the Export Trade Control Ordinance.[81] MITI asked automakers to announce increased figures for the purchase of US auto parts regardless of whether these figures could be achieved. In addition, the volume of US car sales allocated to each firm was based on the number of dealer shops, not on a feasible calculation of how many cars automakers could sell.[82] The fact that MITI asked major companies to purchase US cars in the event that Japanese consumers would not purchase them also revealed MITI's desperation.[83]

To explain the automakers' actions in terms of MITI's pressure alone seems implausible because the influence of MITI on the automobile industry was limited. MITI had implored the top executives of auto producers to accept a VER in 1981. MITI also failed to coordinate views among automakers when the extension of the VER became an issue in 1985. It is also said that the director of the Automobile Division in MITI only learned of the plan through a newspaper report of Toyota and GM to establish a joint venture.[84] Although MITI's influence had gradually increased as the automobile sector had become the source of the Japan–US trade friction, major automakers could have rejected MITI's request, if they had wished to do so.

What, then, were the other factors encouraging automakers to expand the purchase of US auto parts and vehicles? One factor was that all major actors supported the idea that the Japan–US summit should be successful at any cost. A successful summit was important to Prime Minister Miyazawa's strengthening his stance in the LDP. There was consensus within the LDP on the need for a successful summit. Originally, LDP members were hostile towards the automobile industry. Party members were disappointed that because of continuous trade imbalances with Japan, most of which were attributable to the industry, the US government had strengthened its demand for market-opening measures in agriculture, construction and small retail business, which constituted major constituencies for funding and support for the LDP (Nihon Keizai Shimbunsha (ed.) 1990, p.201).

Accordingly, the Diet Members' League on Automobiles (*Jidosha giin renmei*), composed of 212 members of the House of Representatives and 52 from the House of Councillors, showed little interest in trade issues concerning auto and auto parts.[85] The LDP not only regarded the summit as a crucial turning point in the Japan–US relationship but also hoped that President Bush, a free-trade advocate, would be re-elected.[86] The four business federations also advocated the need to promote cooperation with the United States through substantial measures in the auto and rice issues.[87]

More importantly, Japanese automakers had their own incentives to expand market access and to promote cooperation with US automakers. These incentives stemmed largely from the expansion of international operations. First, Japanese automakers feared that the US auto industry would strengthen demands for restraints on local operations of Japanese automakers. In 1991, there were several developments which indicated moves to restrain the total volume of Japanese cars (both exports and local production) distributed to the US market. In January 1991, the United Automobile Workers (UAW) sent a letter to the Japanese government, demanding that the government restrain the share of Japanese imports and locally produced cars in the US market.[88] On 6 March, Lee Iacocca, Chairman of Chrysler, sent a letter to US President Bush, urging him to regulate the volume of Japanese cars. The Big Three filed an anti-dumping petition against the Japanese minivan on 31 May 1991.[89] Japanese automakers feared that the demand for volume controls would gain momentum as a result of this suit.[90] On 20 December 1991, the House of Representatives majority leader, Richard Gephardt, proposed the Trade Enhancement Act which would request Japan to curtail its trade surplus with the United States by 20 per cent each year over the next five years, otherwise Japanese car sales (including imports and locally produced vehicles) in the United States would be reduced by 250,000 each year.[91]

Local production by Japanese automakers in the US market reached some 1.5 million units in 1990. Japanese automakers regarded local production as a key strategy in reducing exports from Japan, and also as a contribution to the US economy by creating job opportunities. Consequently, they were keen to avoid any restrictions on local production. The fear that the United States might adopt volume controls partly explains why Japanese automakers accepted US demands.[92] This fear also motivated Japanese automakers to make

concessions with an eye to sustaining the re-election of Bush and preventing a change in government to the more protectionist Liberal
Party.[93]

Second, the Action Plan stemmed from Japanese automakers'
intention to tighten linkages with foreign suppliers on a global scale
(Ishizawa 1992, p.260). In the process of negotiations with the government over the Action Plan, Japanese automakers announced substantial measures to improve relations with US auto parts suppliers.
In order to help US parts suppliers improve production efficiency and
reduce costs, Toyota announced the establishment of a Supplier
Support Centre in the United States. Honda had maintained a list of
priorities in sourcing parts. The first place on the list went to local parts
suppliers. The second place went to joint ventures or technical licensing arrangements between local manufacturers and established Japanese parts makers, and the third to established Japanese parts makers
that construct local plants or in-house production (Mair 1994, p.101).
Other automakers announced that they would adopt similar procurement methods.[94] These plans were not merely temporary means
for appeasing US pressure. Japanese automakers had already become
more willing to sustain the US auto parts industry by their own efforts.
These measures were to their own benefit as well as a contribution to
the US automobile industry because the establishment of cooperative
relationships with local suppliers was indispensable for successful
local production.

Third, Japanese automakers changed their stance on market access
as they intensified international operations. As explained before,
Nissan changed its policy stance, announcing its international cooperation programme in 1989. In the 1990s, Toyota also gradually
changed its stance. Toyota had made pursuit of market share a fundamental corporate strategy until the late 1980s. Toyota's key strategy
in the 1980s was the 'Global 10', which aimed to attain 10 per cent of
the global production share.[95] Toyota's expansionist policy was supported by the maxim: 'What is wrong with selling quality cars at a low
price? It makes the consumers happy.' In pursuing market share,
Toyota paid little attention to the criticism that Japan was a closed
market.

Toyota's stance on the pursuit of market share and the opening of
the Japanese market changed in the 1990s. This change was incorporated into Toyota's new guiding principles, which were revised for the
first time in 57 years. The new principles, set up in January 1992,
embodied Toyota's new stance. Article 1 is 'Be a company of the

world'. Although the English version is very simple, a literal translation of the Japanese version is 'Be a trustworthy corporate citizen in the international community, based on open and fair corporate activity.' The phrase 'open and fair corporate activity' was excluded in the English version because this is taken as given in foreign business custom. Article 7 is 'Building lasting relationships with business partners around the world' in the English version. The Japanese version literally translated is 'Realise long-term and stable growth and co-existence and co-prosperity through mutual enlightenment and development based on open trade relationships.' Thus, the new guiding principles paid attention to being accepted as a trustworthy company in the world.

The changes in stance were also demonstrated in Toyota's actions on market access. Toyota announced in September 1991 that it agreed with six US semiconductor producers to undertake joint development of 28 semiconductor devices. The share of foreign semiconductors in total use jumped from 5 per cent in 1990 to 20 per cent in 1993.[96] Toyota also reacted swiftly to the guidelines for the Antimonopoly Law that the FTC announced in July 1991. One month after the announcement, Toyota drew up a manual on observing the Antimonopoly Law. Toyota was the first company to draw up this kind of corporate manual.[97]

Toyota's changed strategy saw it accepting a boost of the sales of US auto parts and vehicles. Public statements by Toyota's senior executives showed this change. Shoichiro Toyoda, President of Toyota, explains the voluntary plan of January 1992 as follows: 'The United States is the most important country for Japan. The prosperity of today's Japan depends on its guidance. It is quite natural to offer any assistance to the US automobile industry in a critical situation. This is the more so because Toyota raises "co-existence and co-prosperity" as an ideal corporate policy.'[98] He also answered the question of whether sales of foreign cars in Toyota's dealer networks would lead to a reduction in home sales: 'We have to pay such costs in order to maintain "co-existence and co-prosperity" in the world. We sell a lot in the overseas markets.'[99]

One of the critical reasons why Toyota changed its stance on market access lay in its growing commitment to overseas markets. As explained before, Toyota was reluctant to make inroads into overseas markets. Toyota decided on local production in America in 1984, six years after Honda and four years after Nissan. In spite of the late start, Toyota caught up with Honda by 1989 in its production volume in the

United States after it started production in its own plant in May 1988. Toyota also decided in January 1989 to start local production in the United Kingdom in 1992. In June 1991, Toyota decided to establish two head divisions for administrating operations in North America and Europe.[100] Thus, Toyota's multinational operations were fully developed in the 1990s. This growing presence in overseas markets made Toyota vulnerable to reactions from foreign competitors and governments. Toyota also sought to become a true insider in each local market rather than an exporter, and had a strong incentive to develop and increase local production for maintaining steady growth. In order to attain these objectives, it had to cease its aggressive expansionist strategies as well as to promote cooperation with local competitors and parts manufacturers and to re-invest profits to the local community.

In particular, the minivan dumping suit by the Big Three in May 1991 motivated Toyota to reconsider its expansionist policy. Although the suit was directed at Toyota and Mazda, the main target was Toyota's Previa. GM, Toyota's partner in NUMMI, participated in the suit. Toyota was shocked at the fact that GM, which had long adhered to free-trade principles, took the same stance as Ford and Chrysler because Toyota considered NUMMI as making a contribution to GM as well as the US automobile industry.[101] Through the incident, Toyota was reminded of the need to promote cooperation with the Big Three as well as to contribute to the US auto industry.

In brief, Japanese automakers became willing to expand market access as they intensified their international operations. Not only did they fear retaliatory treatment in overseas markets, but they saw more deals with local suppliers and the resultant expansion in imports as increasingly necessary and inevitable. These political and economic pressures played a crucial role in motivating Japanese automakers to boost the purchases of US auto parts and to sell US vehicles in the Action Plan.

CONCLUSION

The Japanese automobile industry has rapidly expanded its multinational operations and international corporate alliances since the 1980s. Japanese automakers came to exhibit more commitment to opening the Japanese market as they strengthened their international linkages. They also sought to open up their *keiretsu* groups. They attempted to increase deals with local parts suppliers both by offering guidance in respect of the Japanese procurement and production systems and by accepting local parts suppliers as design-in partners. The car distribution *keiretsu* has also been opened up by thorough elimination of exclusive clauses in dealership contracts and by handling foreign vehicles in automakers' distribution channels. These actions were driven largely by the internationalization of corporate activity. As Japanese automakers intensified overseas operations, they regarded it as indispensable to successful localization to increase deals with local suppliers. In addition, they considered international procurement policies as indispensable to realize the most appropriate procurement in each local market, irrespective of the suppliers' nationality. In distribution *keiretsu*, corporate alliances are critically tied to the handling of foreign vehicles. Japanese automakers deal in vehicles that their alliance partners manufacture.

The shift in the automakers' stance was also evident in their commitment to market access expansion. The major automakers displayed a passive attitude towards facilitating the market access of foreign products to Japan until the mid 1980s. However, they became more eager to expand market access in the late 1980s. When market access became a critical policy issue in 1989, automakers responded by announcing voluntary international cooperation programmes. This response was closely linked with the internationalization of corporate activity. This was clearly shown in international cooperation programme of Nissan, which took the lead in the move among the automakers. This programme stemmed from several factors including the need to mitigate trade friction with the United States and to appease criticism from the LDP government towards the automobile industry. However, internationalization also constituted a critical pillar. Expanding multinational operations induced Nissan to take more cooperative action towards market access than other Japanese automakers, and enabled it to announce challenging and comprehensive plans.

In 1992, the major automakers announced voluntary plans to increase the purchase of US auto parts and vehicles. In the process of drawing up these plans, they strongly resisted MITI's entreaties to purchase more US auto parts and vehicles. Superficially, they appeared reluctant to assist in the expansion of access for foreign products to the Japanese market. However, what they resisted was MITI's aggressive demand to appease the US government and auto industry as an expedient, rather than a genuine opening of the Japanese market. Their desire to cooperate in the expansion of market access was shown by the two programmes announced in the previous year. In these programmes, there was a willingness to boost the purchase of auto parts from the United States and from all over the world.

Japanese automakers had reason to promote market access of foreign parts and vehicles. There was, at that time, a possibility that the US government might adopt policies to regulate production in America by Japanese automakers as well as exports from Japan. The likelihood that local production would suffer from restrictions induced them to promote market access of foreign auto parts more seriously. They also had to make more deals with local suppliers in order to deepen their own local production operations. The shift in the stance of major automakers on free trade and market access also had much to do with the expansion of foreign parts purchases. In the past, they had aggressively pursued market share, and considered that free trade was necessary to realize this strategy. As operations expanded to the global market, more commitment to local markets and to sustaining local auto producers followed inevitably. The expansion of market access to Japan was necessary to achieve these objectives. Thus, internationalization of corporate activity played a critical role in changing the stance of Japanese automakers in favour of open trade. This led to action to expand the access of foreign products to the Japanese automobile market.

5 The Japanese Electronics Industry and Trade Policy

The electronics industry is similar to the automobile industry in that it is one of the most internationally oriented sectors of Japanese industry. Japanese electronics firms have strengthened international linkages through foreign direct investment (FDI) since 1985 and the creation of a web of corporate alliances in the high-technology subsectors since the late 1980s. The objective of this chapter is to examine what influence growing international linkages have had on the stance of Japanese electronics firms towards market liberalization.

This chapter focuses on two aspects of trade policy. The first is the effect of internationalization on the stance of electronics firms over rising imports. Imports of electronic products have been rapidly increasing since the mid-1980s. Just how internationalization affects electronics firms' reaction to this import surge is a subject of particular interest in this context.

The second aspect concerns market liberalization. The Japanese government has been willing to promote the market access of foreign products to Japan since the mid-1980s. How has the Japanese electronics industry responded to this policy, and how has its response been influenced by growing international activities? The reaction of electronics firms to market opening policies is examined further with respect to the semiconductor sector. The US and Japanese governments concluded the US–Japan Semiconductor Arrangement in 1986. This arrangement was controversial because both governments and the two industries were in serious conflict over its implementation, to the point where US sanctions were imposed against Japan's alleged non-compliance in April 1987. The stance of Japanese electronics firms and its influence on the implementation of the arrangement are examined. This is a case in which internationalization changed the stance of Japanese electronics firms on market access.

In the next section, the character of the Japanese electronics industry and its internationalization are outlined, followed by an examination of the issue of rising imports and the response of electronics firms. The influence of internationalization of corporate activity on the stance on electronics firms' market-opening activities is then analysed.

The final section sheds light on changes in corporate preferences and government policy through an analysis of the US–Japan Semiconductor Arrangement. It sketches how corporate preferences evolved in this process of influencing the arrangement.

CHARACTER OF INDUSTRY AND INTERNATIONALIZATION

Character of the industry

Although the electronics industry manufactures a wide variety of products, they are normally divided into three groups. The first group is consumer electronic equipment which covers audio-visual products and electrical appliances. The second is industrial electronic equipment which incorporates radio communication systems, broadcasting equipment, and applied electronic equipment. The third group, electronic components, includes electronic tubes, integrated circuits, and liquid crystal devices. These product categories are related to the three classifications of Japanese electronics producers. The first group is comprehensive electronics makers which manufacture various products, ranging from heavy electrical apparatus to semiconductors. Hitachi, Toshiba and Mitsubishi Electric are in this category. The second group is computer and communications equipment makers. NEC, Fujitsu, and Oki Electric belong to this category. The third group is consumer electronics makers. The representatives of this category are Matsushita Electric Industrial, Sony, Sharp and Sanyo Electric. Although these classifications are still useful in understanding differences in corporate strategies among firms, the borders between them are becoming more blurred. Not only do NEC and Fujitsu produce consumer electronic products, but all the companies mentioned above manufacture semiconductors.

The policy preferences of the electronics firms are normally expressed through industrial associations, represented by the Electronic Industries Association of Japan (EIAJ). The association, with a membership of roughly 600 companies, including some 50 foreign-affiliated firms, covers consumer and industrial electronic equipment and electronic components and devices. NEC, Sony, Toshiba, Hitachi, Matsushita, and Mitsubishi Electric have played a pivotal role in decision making in EIAJ. All the past chairmen of EIAJ have been selected from these companies.[1]

Table 5.1   Production of the Japanese electronics industry, 1960–95
(billion yen; per cent)

	1960	1970	1980	1985	1990	1992	1994	1995
Consumer	241	1,473	2,932	4,912	4,436	3,563	2,772	2,435
electronics	(49.0)	(43.4)	(32.6)	(26.3)	(18.4)	(16.2)	(12.9)	(10.7)
Industrial	108	1,030	3,396	7,614	11,342	10,527	10,106	10,679
electronics	(21.9)	(30.3)	(37.7)	(40.7)	(46.9)	(47.7)	(47.1)	(47.1)
Electronic	143	893	2,677	6,162	8,373	7,966	8,530	9,565
components	(29.1)	(26.3)	(29.7)	(33.0)	(34.7)	(36.1)	(40.0)	(42.2)
Total	491	3,397	9,005	18,688	24,151	22,057	21,408	22,679

Note: The figures in parentheses are percentage share in total.
Sources: Urata (1993, p.54); EIAJ, *Nihon no denshi kogyo* [The electronics industry in Japan] 1997/98, p.9.

Several distinctive features of the Japanese electronics industry need to be noted because they affect the formation of policy preferences of the electronics firms. The first feature is a traditionally high dependence on consumer electronic products. The share of consumer electronics in total electronics production decreased significantly from 49.0 per cent in 1960 to 10.7 per cent in 1995 (Table 5.1). However, the share in Japan at 16.2 per cent in 1992 was still high compared with 4.0 per cent in the United States and 8.0 per cent in Europe.[2]

The second feature is that Japanese electronics producers are vertically integrated producers engaging in various sub-sector businesses.[3] Major Japanese electronics firms manufacture various products ranging from electrical appliances such as air-conditioners and refrigerators to industrial electronic equipment including facsimiles and computers, and semiconductors. Therefore, a considerable quantity of electronic components are used for internal consumption.[4] In addition, Japanese electronics producers have been able to invest profits from mature sectors in newly emerging sectors due to the vertically integrated structure of the industry.

The third feature is that major electronic products have been manufactured by only a few companies. Popular products in consumer electronics shifted from black-and-white televisions (TVs) in the early 1960s to colour TVs in the 1970s and to video tape recorders (VTRs) in the 1980s. The majority of these products were manufactured by five or six makers – Sony, Toshiba, Hitachi, Matsushita, Mitsubishi Electric and Sanyo. This is also the case in semiconductor production. The five top producers – NEC, Toshiba, Hitachi, Fujitsu and Mitsubishi Electric – account for roughly 75 per cent of the total semiconductor output in Japan (Shimura 1992, p.49). As described later, this oligopolistic market structure has often led to excessive competition.

Internationalization

The electronics industry spearheaded multinational production in Japanese industry. The industry has had three surges of FDI: from the end of the 1960s to 1973; from the end of the 1970s to 1985; and after 1985 (Table 5.2). FDI in the first phase was directed at the East Asian

Table 5.2   Foreign direct investment by Japanese electronics producers by destination, 1970–94 (US$ million)

Year	North America	South America	Asia	Europe	Other	Total
1970	–	5	15	1	1	22
1971	6	4	19	–	1	30
1972	20	10	36	2	1	69
1973	31	35	83	4	3	156
1974	26	23	30	13	7	99
1975	43	11	36	4	2	96
1976	75	31	44	9	5	164
1977	87	29	32	5	8	161
1978	116	20	93	13	1	243
1979	88	12	55	21	4	180
1980	167	16	71	55	–	309
1981	330	39	57	46	3	475
1982	150	22	43	53	–	267
1983	368	18	45	68	3	502
1984	242	8	93	57	9	409
1985	403	7	51	48	4	513
1986	577	17	262	125	6	987
1987	1,719	42	467	179	14	2,421
1988	1,501	125	852	557	6	3,041
1989	2,734	45	934	755	12	4,480
1990	2,413	101	827	2,305	37	5,684
1991	868	46	871	501	10	2,296
1992	740	80	540	434	22	1,817
1993	1,445	11	884	418	4	2,762
1994	891	34	1,376	329	3	2,634

Sources: Ministry of Finance, *Kokusai kinyukyoku nenpo* [Annual Report of International Finance Bureau], various issues.

countries, especially the Newly Industrialized Economies (NIEs). Of 211 overseas production facilities which Japanese electronics producers set up before 1974, 140 were in Asia including 109 in NIEs (EIAJ 1993b, p.iii). The original objective of local production during this phase was to capture the local market protected by import barriers, but this was later superseded by the aim to establish export-oriented overseas capacity (Yoshihara 1978, pp.152–7).

The second phase targeted North America and Europe. Between 1980 and 1984, 64.1 per cent of FDI was directed at North America and another 14.2 per cent at Europe, while the Asia's share dropped to 15.7 per cent. Of 100 overseas manufacturing facilities set up between 1980 and 1984, 25 were in North America and 26 were in Europe (EIAJ 1993b, p.iii). The aim of the FDI in the second phase was to circumvent trade friction over Japanese exports to these areas (Urata 1993, pp.18–19).

Japanese consumer electronic products had penetrated the markets in North America and Europe in quantities sufficient to drive local producers out of the market, causing local governments to restrain Japanese imports by anti-dumping suits and import quotas. Japanese electronics firms then decided to commence local production to maintain their market position. A typical example is the beginning of local production of colour TVs in the United States. The first formal allegation by the US makers against Japanese TV exporters was the anti-dumping suit of March 1968, and the trade dispute over colour TVs led to the orderly marketing agreement (OMA) from 1977 to 1979. The response of Japanese manufacturers to these import restrictions was to begin local production of colour TVs.

Compared with these two phases, the third phase, starting in the mid-1980s, was more dynamic and comprehensive. The value of FDI increased greatly from US$1,962 million in 1980–4 to US$11,442 million in 1985–9. The share of electrical machinery in total manufacturing FDI accounted for 27.5 per cent and 36.7 per cent in 1989 and 1990 respectively. The number of production facilities increased from 100 in 1980–4 to 356 in 1985–9. Although FDI experienced a downward trend in 1991 and 1992, the resumption of yen appreciation in February 1993 revitalized FDI.

Growing FDI raised the overseas production ratio. The overall ratio for the electronics industry grew modestly from 7.4 per cent in 1985 to 10.6 per cent in 1988 to 12.6 per cent in 1993. However, the changes in major consumer electronics firms were striking. The overseas production ratio of the five major consumer electronics producers – Matsushita, Sony, Sanyo, Sharp, and Pioneer – increased from 20.1 per cent in 1985 to 34.2 per cent in 1988 to 40.9 per cent in 1992 (Teranishi and Yamasaki 1995, p.53). The volume of overseas production surpassed that of domestic production in colour TVs in 1988 and in VTRs in 1994.

A sharp appreciation of the yen after the Plaza Agreement in September 1985 encouraged electronics firms to expand foreign investment. At the same time, multinational production was undertaken as a corporate strategy. Japanese electronics producers developed an integrated production system based on an international division of labour, seeking, in their domestic production, to specialize in high value-added technology-intensive goods and to transfer manufacturing of low- and medium-value-added products to foreign countries. Items manufactured at plants in East Asia have expanded from radio cassette recorders, fans, and colour TVs to medium-technology products such as VTRs and CD players, whereas the production of technology-intensive, high value-added goods such as high-quality TVs and camcorders has been retained by domestic manufacturing plants.

International division of labour has also been pursued in overseas production bases. In order to minimize production costs, Japanese electronics producers divide production categories or entire production processes and locate each category or sub-process in specific countries or plants (Urata 1993, pp.29–30). In the past, some overseas Japanese subsidiaries manufactured a wide range of products. For example, Matsushita established the so called 'mini Matsushita' in Asian countries, which manufactured a wide range of products such as radios, fans, rice cookers, TV sets and so on. However, subsidiaries began to specialize in specific items and specific production processes. This is typically shown in Matsushita's production of audio equipment in Asia. Parts and components for audio equipment are manufactured as follows: transistors and integrated circuits, switches, and speakers in Singapore; variable resistors, capacitors, tuners, electric capacitors in Malaysia; electric capacitors in the Philippines; and speakers in Indonesia. These parts and components are assembled in plants in Taiwan, Singapore, Thailand, the Philippines, and Indonesia. The first two plants aim to export to other regions, while the others sell to local markets (Dobson 1993, p.42). In this international division of labour, each production unit has a specialized function according to its technology level, and intermediate and final products are exchanged mainly through the inter-corporate network.

In recent years, corporate alliances between Japanese and foreign electronics producers have increased mainly in the high-technology fields such as semiconductors, telecommunications and computers. The semiconductor field, in particular, has become a locus of complicated networks through corporate alliances. Although corporate alliances in the semiconductor sector were forged before the 1980s, their primary objective was a transfer of advanced US technology to latecomer Japanese makers. The flow of technology was one way, from the United States to Japan. There were almost no alliances in production, marketing and servicing, or general purpose cooperation (National Research Council 1992, p.11). After the second half of the 1980s alliances became a two way flow of technology and management resources, taking a variety of forms and pursuing a range of objectives.

Although the promotion of alliances is a general trend in the current business world, the semiconductor field has a greater need for the alliances owing to rising research and development (R & D) and production costs. The semiconductor sector has required massive R & D expenditure. For instance, the ratio of R & D to total sales is more than five times the manufacturing average in Japan.[5] Higher integration in semiconductor chips and the development of next generation devices have imposed enormous costs on firms.[6] For one company to assume these spiralling costs and risks is not a feasible strategy. Companies with the same objective share the risk through alliances. In addition, the combination of specialized technologies and core skills that each company possesses is indispensable for acquiring the initiative in developing next generation products such as flash memories, which are expected to have a market scale of 1 trillion yen in the world.

Japanese semiconductor producers have actively promoted corporate alliances. Not only have the alliances increased in number but they have also incorporated various types of alliances in the areas of R & D, manufacturing, marketing and service.[7] Recent alliances also include combined objectives. For instance, Toshiba and National Semiconductor reached an agreement in May 1992 regarding complementary metal oxide semiconductor (CMOS) standard logic integrated circuits. This alliance included joint development of new products, mutual second sourcing, and mutual supply under original equipment manufacturing (OEM) contracts. Fujitsu and Advanced Micro Devices also concluded an agreement in July 1992 to conduct joint development, manufacturing and sales of flash memories.

Furthermore, alliances have become international. Alliances with domestic firms are less attractive not only because these firms are direct competitors but also because they have similar kinds of technological and managerial skills. Japanese electronics producers looked for foreign partners, but most of them were US makers. In the 1990s, however, they formed alliances with Korean makers. Fujitsu concluded an agreement with the Hyundai group on cooperating in 4M and 16M dynamic random access memory (DRAM) production in October 1993, and NEC agreed with Samsung Electronics to share the technology for the development of 256M DRAM in March 1994.

INDUSTRY REACTION TO INCREASES IN IMPORTS OF ELECTRONIC PRODUCTS

What effects have the expansion of multinational production and corporate alliances had on firms' trade policy stance and trade structure? The effects of the internationalization of corporate activity can be seen in the reaction of electronics firms to a rise in imports of electronic products. Imports of electronic products have rapidly expanded in recent years. Total imports of electronic products grew 3.8 times from 1,035 billion yen in 1985 to 3,965 billion yen in 1995 (Table 5.3). Imports of consumer electronic products in particular are notable. Between 1985 and 1995, imports grew 14 times from 24 billion yen to 333 billion yen in value.

The rise in imports is notable in individual products such as air-conditioners, washing machines, and colour TVs (Table 5.4). The number of imported colour TVs jumped from 1.7 million in 1989 to nearly 6 million in 1994. As a consequence, the ratio of imports to total domestic sales exceeded 50 per cent in 1994.

In addition to rising imports, the consumer electronics sector is facing several other problems. Demand for major consumer electronic products is already saturated in Japan, and there are no hit products in the 1990s such as colour TVs in the 1970s and VTRs in 1980s. Moreover, diversification in the preferences of consumers in Japan and other advanced countries has made it less feasible to rely on mass production techniques which were earlier a source of the international competitiveness of Japanese electronics producers.

In spite of this critical situation, there is no move to restrain imports. Instead of demanding protectionist measures, major electronics producers have undertaken internal adjustment strategies. Toshiba with-

Table 5.3   Foreign trade of the Japanese electronics industry, 1960–95
(billion yen; per cent)

	1960	1970	1980	1985	1990	1992	1994	1995
Exports								
Consumer	57	587	2,047	3,805	2,618	2,258	1,542	1,313
electronics	(78.1)	(68.1)	(44.9)	(39.3)	(23.8)	(20.0)	(13.9)	(11.3)
Industrial	3	137	1,049	2,919	3,443	3,692	3,143	2,944
electronics	(4.1)	(15.9)	(23.0)	(30.1)	(31.3)	(32.6)	(28.3)	(25.4)
Electronic	13	138	1,462	2,971	4,933	5,361	6,419	7,340
components	(17.8)	(16.0)	(32.1)	(30.6)	(44.9)	(47.4)	(57.8)	(63.3)
Total	73	863	4,558	9,695	10,994	11,310	11,104	11,597
Imports								
Consumer	0.2	5	38	24	113	156	238	333
electronics	(2.2)	(2.6)	(5.4)	(2.3)	(5.7)	(7.7)	(8.8)	(8.4)
Industrial	6.1	121	298	398	692	633	881	1,433
electronics	(66.3)	(62.0)	(42.3)	(38.5)	(34.6)	(30.9)	(32.5)	(36.1)
Electronic	2.9	69	368	613	1,195	1,256	1,589	2,199
components	(31.5)	(35.4)	(52.3)	(59.2)	(59.7)	(61.4)	(58.7)	(55.5)
Total	9.2	195	703	1,035	2,001	2,046	2,709	3,965

Note: The figures in parentheses are percentage share in total.
Sources: Urata (1993, p.54); EIAJ, *Nihon no denshi kogyo* [The electronics industry in Japan] 1997/98, pp.11,13.

drew from the consumer audio business in April 1993, and consolidated its consumer electronic and information equipment divisions in October 1993 in order to integrate consumer electronic products into multi-media products. Hitachi decided to introduce 'second brand' consumer electronic products in 1995 with prices that were 20 to 30 per cent lower than those of the normal brand.[8] In April 1995, Hitachi also merged with Hitachi Sales Corporation, the sales company of Hitachi's consumer electronic products. This merger aimed at forming an integrated system covering all phases from product planning to development, production, sales and services, and to speed up decision making.

The increase in imports has been associated with the growth of intra-industry trade, and the industry still enjoys huge trade surpluses despite the recent surge in imports.[9] Japanese electronics firms have stopped production of uncompetitive goods and procured them from other Japanese producers and foreign producers in the NIEs under OEM agreements. This has led to increased imports of finished prod-

Table 5.4   Import volume of major electronic products, 1987–94
(1,000 units; per cent)

Product	1987	1988	1989	1990	1991	1992	1993	1994
Air-conditioners	60 (1.4)	156 (3.0)	188 (3.6)	144 (2.6)	738 (8.8)	622 (10.1)	597 (13.0)	497 (7.9)
Washing machines	13 (0.3)	55 (1.3)	67 (1.5)	56 (1.2)	131 (2.7)	145 (3.2)	170 (3.7)	230 (4.9)
Refrigerators	64 (1.6)	143 (3.3)	282 (6.2)	340 (6.9)	436 (8.4)	343 (7.9)	401 (9.2)	471 (9.4)
Fans	5,334 (46.0)	5,511 (48.9)	4,989 (53.8)	5,553 (43.1)	7,409 (42.3)	6,950 (49.1)	4,016 (54.6)	3,760 (55.7)
Microwave ovens	– –	3,047 (4.9)	2,594 (12.2)	2,750 (5.6)	2,603 (2.5)	2,550 (2.6)	2,638 (6.3)	2,929 (16.4)
Colour TVs	349 (3.2)	740 (7.2)	1,714 (14.9)	1,063 (10.1)	1,851 (16.3)	2,267 (22.2)	3,657 (33.0)	5,844 (50.4)
VTRs	128 (2.7)	367 (5.5)	473 (8.5)	264 (11.3)	317 (6.5)	487 (20.2)	680 (39.9)	1,340 (89.6)

Note: The figures in parentheses are percentage share of imports in total domestic demand calculated by imports/domestic production – exports + imports. Imports include those under OEM contracts.
Sources: JEMA, Electrical Industries in Japan, 1995, pp.34–5; EIAJ, Facts & Figures, 1995, pp.18–19.

ucts. Moreover, the increase in imports is linked to a rise in exports from Japan. The expansion of final product manufacturing in East Asia has stimulated increasing demand for Japanese electronic components used in final electronic products, especially in the Association of Southeast Asian Nations (ASEAN) countries where the components industry has not been extensively developed. Exports of electronic components increased by 147 per cent between 1985 and 1995, raising the share of electronic components in total exports of electronic products from 30.6 per cent to 63.3 per cent (Table 5.3).

Other factors link imports tightly to the multinational operations of Japanese electronics firms, so these firms have little incentive to restrain imports. First, a large proportion of imports is dominated by Japanese firms. Urata (1992, p.25) points out that in 1986, exports of Japanese affiliates in Asia to Japan were concentrated in electrical machinery, accounting for 41.7 per cent of total exports in the manufacturing sector. In addition, the share of exports to Japan by affiliates

Table 5.5   Shares of exports to Japan by overseas affiliates of Japanese electronics firms, 1980–95 (per cent)

Region	1980	1983	1986	1989	1992	1995
North America	0.4	0.1	1.2	1.5	2.6	2.4
Asia	16.2	21.0	22.2	26.9	27.2	28.7
Europe	0.8	3.4	1.5	0.8	1.2	2.0
Total	6.6	8.1	5.4	8.3	9.3	13.6

Sources: MITI, *Kaigai toshi tokei soran* [Statistical Report on Foreign Investment], No.1–No.6.

of Japanese electronics firms in Asia in total sales increased steadily from 16.2 per cent in 1980 to 28.7 per cent in 1995 (Table 5.5). These imports from overseas affiliates, or so-called 'reverse imports', have been expanding in consumer electronic products such as colour TVs, and cassette tape recorders. For example, Matsushita increased reverse imports of colour TVs from 100,000 units in 1991 to 150,000 units in 1992, while Sanyo's increase was from 360,000 units in 1993 to 620,000 units in 1994.[10]

The high level of reverse imports has much to do with the deep commitment of electronics firms to distribution channels. Electronics firms have organized *keiretsu* retail shops into their distribution outlets.[11] Electronics producers have sustained *keiretsu* retailers, which are small-sized family-owned firms, by offering financial assistance and information. *Keiretsu* retailers have enabled electronics producers to control retail prices and maintain stable market shares. Electronics distribution *keiretsu* is more open than car distribution *keiretsu* because retail shops deal in products of a number of electronics producers (Niihanda and Mishima 1991, p.98). The growth of large-scale retail stores after the late 1970s reduced the status of *keiretsu* retailers in sales of electronics products. The share of sales by *keiretsu* retailers declined significantly from 69 per cent in 1975 to 32 per cent in 1990.[12] Furthermore, a protracted recession in sales of consumer electronic products in the 1990s forced major electronics firms to revise the *keiretsu* system.[13] The maintenance of *keiretsu* retail shops now imposes a burden on major electronics firms. Hence, reverse imports have not been facilitated by the *keiretsu* distribution system alone.[14] A critical point is that the influence of electronics producers extends to large-scale retail stores. In the past, the large-scale retail stores expanded their business by challenging the retail price controls set by electronics producers. However, they have gradually fostered interdependent relationships with electronics producers. Electronics producers have equity in leading retail stores.[15] In addition, some executives of leading stores formerly worked at major electronics firms (Nikkei Ryūtsū Shimbun (ed.) 1993, pp.87–8).[16] The overall influence on distribution channels by electronics producers has facilitated reverse imports and OEM supply from overseas.

Second, the negative effects of imports have been weakened by the efforts of Japanese electronics firms to promote an international division of labour. As explained before, Japanese electronics firms transfer the production of low value-added goods to overseas plants and retain domestic production bases of high value-added products. This division of products lessens the possibility of a direct clash between imported and domestic products. Furthermore, since Japanese electronics producers retain multiple product lines, they can easily shift their businesses from declining to more profitable products. In recent years, they put more emphasis on high-value industrial electronic products represented by office automation products such as personal computers, word processors, work stations, and electronic parts and components. Not only do these products have a high possibility of future growth, but they are suitable for differentiating imported products. Japanese electronics producers have successfully adjusted their businesses from consumer electronic products to industrial electronic products and electronic components.

To summarize, rising foreign competition has not promoted a protectionist response from the Japanese electronics industry. The industry has enjoyed huge trade surpluses and the rise in imports has occurred as intra-industry trade. In addition, Japanese multinationals in the electronics industry have not only carried out intra-firm trade but have also successfully adjusted their business from declining to newly emerging sub-sectors as part of their own internal strategies. There is a limited possibility that they will suffer from rising imports. Accordingly, they can maintain a policy stance on open trade when there is a sharp rise in imports.

MARKET-OPENING ACTIVITIES

Cooperation programmes for market access expansion

The Japanese government has been keen to promote market access for foreign goods since the mid-1980s, and has implemented various policies for this objective. How did the electronics industry react to these policies? If major electronics firms had shifted their stance in favour of an open domestic market, it follows that they should have taken action to expand the access of foreign products to Japan. These firms announced international cooperation programmes to expand market access in 1989. Matsushita is an example. Matsushita named 1989 as the first year for mitigating trade friction, and President Akio Tanii ordered an examination of the trade balance of the group. There were neither statistics nor business plans relating to the imports of the Matsushita group until 1988. Matsushita drew up an action programme for international cooperation in July 1989. The programme consisted of three pillars: to double the value of imports by 1993; to freeze the increase in exports by 1993; and to increase the share of overseas production in total overseas sales from 25 per cent in 1988 to 50 per cent by 1993. In order to achieve these objectives, Matsushita established a promotion office for international cooperation in October 1989, under the direct control of the president. Matsushita strove to raise imported components and equipment to 10 per cent of total consumption as well as to import 10 per cent of the products manufactured in its overseas plants.

In December 1991, Matsushita drew up another action programme for international cooperation. In the previous programme, Matsushita had intended to import goods to the value of 420 billion yen by 1993. However, the company's imports totalled 440 billion yen in 1991, achieving the objective two years earlier than targeted. The new programme included plans to import 600 billion yen worth of imports by 1993. The programme also aimed to improve local content by promoting technology transfer through overseas production technology centres.[17]

Toshiba also drew up an action programme called the Globalization Action Project in November 1989. The programme aimed to double its 1988 import value to 200 billion yen by 1992, and to freeze the increase in exports. The value of local production would also be boosted from 300 billion yen in 1988 to 500 billion yen in 1993.[18] Hitachi followed Toshiba by drawing up an international cooperation programme in December 1989. The programme pursued the promotion of international business with balanced imports and exports by attempting to double the value of the 1988 imports by 1992 and to triple it by 1994. In 1994, the value of imports would reach 410 billion yen, improving the trade balance by 130 billion yen. Hitachi established a committee on the improvement in the import–export balance in August 1990 and the division on overseas activities promotion in December 1990, whose aim was to promote the programme.[19]

Motivations for the programmes

Why did Japanese electronics firms announce international cooperation programmes in 1989? Did these programmes stem from the shift in firms' preferences for the opening of the domestic market? International cooperation programmes were often regarded as a reluctant and formal response to MITI's guidance to import more foreign products. In fact, MITI committed the electronics industry to expand imports. In June 1989, MITI held an import promotion meeting. The Minister encouraged executives from 162 companies to boost finished product imports by 30 per cent in 1989.[20] MITI also organized special meetings with the heads of industrial associations in the electronics industry. In May 1989, the Minister met the executives of five electronic-related industrial associations, and proposed that the industry should strive to cooperate in the promotion of imports.[21] The Minister held a further meeting in July 1989 with the heads of four industrial associations in the electronics industry. He requested that they make vigorous efforts to expand imports.[22]

Although MITI's guidance certainly encouraged electronics firms to take action to expand market access for foreign products, it was not the only factor. MITI's encouragement to expand imports did not start in 1989. MITI had held import expansion meetings since 1985 requesting major companies to undertake measures to expand imports. In addition, some electronics firms formulated corporate strategies on the basis of international cooperation programmes. For example, Matsushita invested 100 billion yen in Asia between 1989 and 1991. This investment aimed at introducing the newest high-technology equipment in local plants. In order to achieve its international cooperation programme, Matsushita tried to make plants in Asia export bases for Japan.[23] This indicates that the programmes were set up in line with overall corporate strategies. It is necessary therefore to take a closer look at why corporate strategies changed and whether the changes were relevant to shifts in the stance of major electronics producers on market access issues.

In the second half of the 1980s, the Japanese electronics industry gradually reduced its dependence on exports. The ratio of exports to total production in the electronics industry decreased from 51.9 per cent in 1985 to 45.5 per cent in 1990. However, Japanese electronics producers rapidly expanded their international operations after the mid-1980s. Matsushita is typical in this respect. Matsushita was heavily dependent on exports. In 1988, its exports were valued at 1,700 billion yen, while its imports were 220 billion yen. The 1,480 billion yen trade imbalance accounted for one-sixth of Japan's total trade surplus.[24] Matsushita has steadily expanded multinational operations and pursued a globalization strategy since 1961 when it established a joint venture in Thailand. Matsushita accelerated its international operations in the late 1980s. Matsushita had 69 manufacturing subsidiaries all over the world in 1988, 20 per cent of which were built between 1987 and 1988.[25] As a result, overseas production increased rapidly from US$3.45 billion in 1987 to US$4.46 billion 1988 and US$5.43 billion in 1989, while the ratio of local production in total overseas sales climbed from 25 per cent in 1988 to 30 per cent in 1989.[26]

In addition to extending its multinational operations, Matsushita changed its internal organization to pursue a more effective globalization strategy. In April 1988, Matsushita merged with Matsushita Electric Trade, which primarily developed the overseas strategies of the Matsushita group. This merger aimed to establish an integrated system of manufacturing and marketing in overseas markets as well as to speed up decision making on globalization strategies. In addition, a regional headquarters system was introduced in the late 1980s. The headquarters in America, and Europe and Africa were established in October 1988, while the Asian headquarters was established in Singapore in April 1989. Matsushita formulated guidelines for overseas activities in 1989. These guidelines, which included a framework for promoting contributions to the local community and the recruitment of local employees to managerial positions, aimed to foster the corporate image that Matsushita was a localised company.[27]

As Japanese electronics firms have intensified their multinational operations and have been required to make more commitments to local markets, they have changed their competition patterns. A typical pattern of competition among Japanese firms was side-by-side competition. Japanese firms tended to imitate successful products or excellent production methods developed by competitors. This strategy led to the production of similar goods without distinctive sales points and resultant fierce price competition. In order to be competitive in price, Japanese firms pursued market share because mass production was the easiest way to reduce prices. Japanese electronics firms repeated this competition pattern in radio cassette recorders, colour TVs, VTRs, and other electronic products. The market structure which ensured that there were five or six producers with a similar level of corporate power, intensified competition for the top market share.

In the semiconductor sector, memory producers have had to make enough profit in four to five years to pay off their immense capital and R & D expenditure as well as creating funds to prepare for the next generation of memories.[28] Furthermore, steep learning-curve effects – production costs decline by 30 per cent for every doubling of cumulative volume – are seen in the semiconductor field.[29] As a consequence, a fundamental strategy of Japanese semiconductor producers has been directed towards increasing market share rather than maximising profitability. In order to expand market share, Japanese semiconductor producers pursued a 'forward pricing strategy' – offering products at low prices when they are introduced so as to stimulate demand, even if producers are unable to make profits at these prices. They could take this strategy because they were vertically integrated producers engaging in a wide variety of businesses. The losses in the semiconductor sector were compensated for by profits in other sectors.

Japanese electronics firms tended to regard exports and multinational production as an extension of domestic activities. Consequently, they transferred the pattern of excessive competition from the domestic to overseas markets, which caused friction with local firms and governments. For instance, the US colour TV market was severely disrupted by the aggressive advance of Japanese electronics makers in the 1970s. After the 1974–5 recession, Japanese electronics firms created an avalanche of exports of TV receivers, shown in a 153 per cent rise in exports in a single year (1976). Several US firms incapable of meeting this aggressive competition were acquired by Japanese electronics firms. Consequently, while in 1977 direct imports from Japan were 14 per cent of US colour TV consumption, the actual aggregate market share of Japanese firms, including American and third-country subsidiaries was estimated to be 44.2 per cent (Yamamura and Vandenberg 1986, pp.258–9).[30] Now, no US companies manufacture audio-visual goods such as CD players, VTRs and stereos.

In the semiconductor field, Japanese firms have concentrated their efforts on DRAM, and have made massive capital and R & D investments since the late 1970s.[31] They gradually increased their world market share in this area from 70 per cent of 64K DRAM at the end of 1981 to 90 per cent in 256K DRAM at the end of 1986. The US share for all memory products in the world fell from 75 per cent in 1980 to just over 25 per cent in 1986, while the Japanese share rose from 25 per cent to 65 per cent in the same period (Prestowitz 1988, p.45). This process of establishing market dominance was attended by fierce price competition during 1981–2 and 1984–5. During both these periods, Japanese semiconductor producers undertook a massive build-up of production capacity, with an over-supply that the world market could not absorb (Howell, Bartlett and Davis 1992, p.104).[32] Excess production capacity led to a downward price spiral.[33] Whereas the imported price of Japanese 64K DRAM fell from US$3.53 in September 1984 to US$0.82 one year later, that of Japanese 256K DRAM fell from an index of 100 to 7 in the same period (Howell *et al.* 1988, p.86). As a consequence, most US merchant producers ceased production of DRAM.[34] While 11 US merchant firms had been producing DRAM at the 16K level in 1980, by 1986, only two US firms, Texas Instruments and Micron Technology, remained in the market at the 256K level (Howell, Bartlett and Davis 1992, p.105).

Internationally oriented electronics firms like Matsushita gradually recognized that, to be true insiders in each local market, they had to refrain from the excessive pursuit of market share which was accompanied by fierce price competition and a resultant market disruption. Enhanced overseas operations have induced some Japanese electronics firms to view the world as one big market, to integrate their home market into one global entity, and to expand the global market through competition and cooperation with their rivals. Multinational operations have also raised the sensitivity of major electronics firms to foreign criticism of huge trade imbalances.[35] Not only did the electronics industry share a large portion of the trade surplus, but its surplus expanded from US$34.8 billion in 1987 to US$41.1 billion in 1988, and to US$41.5 billion in 1989, in spite of Japan's overall trade imbalances being rectified in this period (Namura 1991, p.76). The electronics firms that strengthened dependence on overseas markets increasingly appreciated the crisis over trade imbalances. For example, Matsushita's international cooperation programme sprang from a belief that conventional macro-level adjustment measures alone could not resolve trade friction, and that trade imbalance would become a critical issue if each company did not tackle it seriously.[36] Moreover, some internationally oriented firms feared that foreign criticism of the Japanese style of competition and the closed home market might lead to some form of restraint on their operations. They recognized the need for individual firms to make efforts to revise the Japanese market system by promoting access of foreign products in order that they would be accepted into the international community.

In addition to the internationalization of corporate activities, there was another stimulus to changing the preferences of Japanese electronics firms in favour of an open domestic market: the appreciation of the yen after 1985. The doubling of the yen's value between 1985 and 1988 undermined the international competitiveness of Japanese electronics products by raising their prices. In order to lessen the effects of the yen revaluation, electronics firms accelerated FDI, and increased the procurement of overseas components and materials. This deepened involvement in international production, and reinforced the interest of major electronics firms in market access for imported products.

The change in stance is shown by the statements of senior executives of leading electronics companies. For instance, Masahiko Hirata, a vice-president of Matsushita, stressed the significance of cooperation with foreign partners as follows: 'a big company like Matsushita needs to promote cooperation in international society by imposing a burden on itself. It is not sufficient to get profits through production and sales. As a company grows, it is necessary to assume a corporate responsibility in line with this growth.'[37]

This thinking reflects the stance of the Japanese electronics industry as a whole. The industry acknowledged more responsibility for promoting mutual understanding with its foreign counterparts. For instance, an EIAJ report on the Japanese semiconductor sector maintains that:

> In order to resolve trade issues, continuous communication and mutual understanding between industries are indispensable. The basis for coping with trade issues is that the industries have explicit prospects and policies, and seek to play a plus sum game with their foreign counterparts through mutual understanding. Anyway, it is almost impossible to find an effective solution if we cling only to the free competition rule and continue to maintain general principles with a myopic perspective. (EIAJ 1994b, p.110)

Some business leaders are more concerned with the criticism of the Japanese market mechanism and advocate compatibility of Japanese customs and institutions with international norms. Akio Morita,

Chairman of Sony, initiated the controversy in early 1992, suggesting a revision of Japanese management style. Morita, believing that the Japanese competition rule which stresses the expansion of market share was different from that in western nations, suggested reviewing Japanese practices such as a low proportion of value-added going to employee compensation, a low level of stock dividends, and unequal relationships with vendors (Morita 1992). He maintained that companies should adopt pricing methods which took into account appropriate margins on each product. Morita also outlined his views in the article 'Rethinking the Global Free-Market Trade', where he argued that compared with the European Community and the United States, which have transcended national boundaries and opened up their markets, Japan's efforts to open its market have been slow and piecemeal – the result of direct foreign pressure. He proposed that Japan transform its traditional systems by eliminating excessive regulation and licensing (Morita 1993).

To summarize, the Japanese electronics industry has taken action to promote market access for foreign products. This action was promoted partly by the rapid appreciation of the yen. However, enhanced multinational operations had made major electronics firms vulnerable to foreign criticism of the closed Japanese market and excessive competition. In order to ensure sound overseas operations, electronics firms announced and implemented programmes to promote market access for foreign products as well as cooperation with foreign firms.

Other action towards market opening

Japanese electronics producers had an effect on market-opening policy in the 1990s. MITI announced the Business Global Partnership (BGP) Project in November 1991. This project consisted of three pillars: the expansion of imports, the expansion of local content by Japanese affiliates, and the promotion of industrial alliances. The uniqueness of this project lay in the establishment of joint ventures and technical tie-ups in addition to conventional import promotion plans. This programme was formally set up in response to the US–Japan Structural Impediments Initiative (SII) talks, and was announced in the second report of SII in July 1992.[38] However, the content of the programme was affected by preferences of the private sector. MITI's request to rectify trade imbalances intensified in the 1990s. For example, MITI requested major firms in July 1991 to set up action programmes to expand manufactured imports by 10 per cent in 1991 and 1992.[39] Some companies resisted this request, noting that import expansion alone could not resolve trade friction, and suggesting that the solutions to trade friction need to be considered from a broader viewpoint.[40] MITI accepted this view and added the promotion of industrial alliances as a pillar of the BGP Project.

THE US–JAPAN SEMICONDUCTOR ARRANGEMENT

The US–Japan Semiconductor Arrangement is one of the most important trade accords concluded between the United States and Japan. Not only were both governments involved in arduous negotiations before its conclusion and in the process of its implementation, but the accord is regarded as a model of the results-oriented trade approach that came to be favoured by the US government. It is useful to examine how the stance of Japanese electronics firms on the market access issue in semiconductors has changed, and what effects this has had on the implementation of the accord.

Background to the arrangement

The semiconductor dispute between Japan and the United States started in the early 1980s.[41] It escalated in 1985 when the US Semiconductor Industry Association (SIA), several semiconductor producers and the US government resorted to a set of legal petitions.[42] SIA filed a Section 301 petition of the 1974 Trade Act in June 1985 against unfair Japanese trading practices such as market targeting by the Japanese government and barriers to semiconductor sales in the Japanese market.[43] Around a week after the Section 301 petition by SIA, Micron Technology charged seven Japanese chip producers with the dumping of 64K DRAM. Then, Intel, Advanced Micro Devices and National Semiconductor filed a suit in late September claiming that eight Japanese makers were dumping EPROM (erasable programmable read only memory). In December 1985, the US Department of Commerce itself initiated an anti-dumping case in 256K DRAM and 1M DRAM. Finally, the US International Trade Commission initiated a Section 337 investigation in March 1986, responding to a petition from Texas Instruments which alleged infringement of patents on semiconductors by eight Japanese chip producers and one Korean firm. In response to these complaints from the US semiconductor industry and government, Japanese officials began negotiations with their US counterparts on 28 August 1985. The two governments convened talks over the assurance of market shares by the Japanese government, the measures which the Japanese government might take concerning third-country dumping – dumping in the countries other than Japan and the United States – and the submission of proprietary manufacturing data by Japanese electronics firms to the US Department of Commerce.

The Japanese and US governments reached a five-year agreement on 31 July 1986. The accord consisted of two parts. The first part described measures to boost the sales of foreign semiconductors in the Japanese market.[44] In a confidential side letter accompanying the formal agreement, 'the Japanese said that they understood, welcomed, and would make efforts to assist the U.S. companies in reaching their goals of a 20-percent market share within five years' (Prestowitz 1988, p.65). The second part was concerned with the suspension of dumping. The US Department of Commerce would, on the basis of cost information provided by Japanese manufacturers, set fair market values (FMVs) for EPROMs and DRAMs of 256K and above manufactured by each producer. The Japanese government agreed to monitor costs and export prices, including export prices in third countries. On the condition that the accord would come into force, Japanese electronics firms signed agreements with the US Department of Commerce which suspended the dumping investigations on EPROMs and DRAMs.

In June 1991, the Japanese and US governments agreed to renew the Semiconductor Arrangement. The new agreement stipulated a more than 20 per cent share for foreign semiconductors in Japan by the end of 1992, and incorporated a common method for calculating the share.

Industry reaction to the arrangement

MITI started measures to stop selling chips below production cost just after the Semiconductor Arrangement came into force (Table 5.6). Some electronics firms were unwilling to cooperate with MITI. MITI requested a 20 per cent production cut of 256K DRAM in autumn 1986. Although major semiconductor producers such as Toshiba, Hitachi and Mitsubishi Electric accepted MITI's guidance, NEC did not comply (Uchihashi 1994, p.67). After warning of sanctions in January 1987, MITI persuaded the leading semiconductor producer

Table 5.6   MITI's commitments to the semiconductor arrangement

12/9/86	MITI requested major semiconductor makers and users in writing to eschew dumping exports of semiconductors and to promote the purchase of foreign semiconductors.
22/9/86	A semiconductor monitoring office was established in MITI.
11/86	MITI requested major semiconductor producers to ensure that export prices to third countries should coincide with FMVs to the United States.
1/1/87	The threshold value at which firms did not necessitate export licensing was lowered from 1 million yen to 50,000 yen.
16/2/87	MITI announced a 10 per cent downward forecast for the January–March quarter, and encouraged semiconductor producers to reduce their production.
4/3/87	The International Semiconductor Cooperation Centre (INSEC) was established.
20/3/87	The Minister convened an emergency meeting, and requested the presidents or vice-presidents of ten major electronics makers to continue reducing 256K DRAM production, to stop third-country dumping, and to promote the purchase of foreign chips.
23/3/87	MITI released a guideline post for the April–June quarter which represented a 20 per cent cut in production volume from the previous quarter.
24,25/3/87	MITI requested 43 semiconductor users to increase the purchase of foreign semiconductors.
26/4/87	MITI requested that the private sector observe minimum export prices on five types of semiconductors.
25/5/87	The Minister directly asked the presidents of ten major semiconductor firms to expand the purchase of foreign semiconductors and to cut production capacity so as to arrest dumping.
17/4/89	MITI held the first meeting on market access expansion of foreign semiconductors.
9/1/92	MITI expanded the target of request to purchase foreign semiconductors from 60 to 226 user companies.
25/5/92	The Minister had a meeting with the presidents of ten top semiconductor users.
19/6/92	62 semiconductor users held a breakfast meeting attended by the deputy director-general of the Machinery and Information Industries Bureau.
24/8/92	The deputy director-general of the Machinery and Information Industries Bureau organized a meeting with the executives of ten major companies.
10/9/92	The deputy director-general of the Machinery and Information Industries Bureau organized a meeting with the executives of 62 companies.

Source: Compiled from UCOM (1993) and various newspapers.

to abide by a 20 per cent production cut. NEC countered with a 10 per cent cut, but eventually accepted a 20 per cent cut in March 1987.[45] Moreover, several semiconductor producers applied for export licences above the volume prescribed. For instance, NEC applied for licences to export 20 million units in January 1987, although NEC's monthly production volume was 8.5 million units. The volume was reduced to 6 million units under MITI's guidance.[46] In spite of MITI's efforts, the US government approved a punitive sanction against Japan for alleged non-compliance. On 17 April, the Reagan administration imposed US$300 million in punitive tariffs on Japanese exports of portable computers, selected power hand tools, and some colour TV sets: the first penalties against Japan since the Second World War.

Some data collected by EIAJ indicate a lukewarm response from the electronics industry regarding market access in 1986 and 1987. The number of companies which established special internal sections for expanding market access increased by 19 in 1988, while the figure was 5 in 1986 and 11 in 1987.[47] The number of seminars sponsored by semiconductor users doubled between 1986 and 1987, and grew five-fold by 1988.[48] Furthermore, the average number of foreign semiconductor suppliers that each Japanese user dealt with increased slightly from 20.6 in 1986 to 24.9 in 1987, but jumped to 34.1 in 1988.[49] The Japanese electronics industry contended that it had made positive efforts to implement the accord since its conclusion.[50] However, judging from the above data, the industry's response to implement the accord appeared to be sluggish in 1986 and 1987.

The dumping issue was almost resolved in 1988 through monitoring by MITI, production cuts by electronics firms, and the gradual recovery in semiconductor demand. But the market access issue remained problematic. The electronics industry intensified its efforts to break the deadlock on the issue (Table 5.7). EIAJ and SIA discussed the issue of market access in California in March 1988, and agreed on five measures in this regard.[51] The agreement was crucial both because it broke the previously chilly relations between the two industries and because it presented such effective measures to expand market access as the promotion of design-in and a focus on the consumer electronics and automobile sectors.[52]

In May 1988, EIAJ organized the Users Committee of Foreign Semiconductors (UCOM) composed of some 60 members which accounted for three-quarters of Japan's total semiconductor consumption. The establishment of UCOM had significant implications.

Table 5.7   EIAJ's commitments to expanding market access for foreign semiconductors

3/1988	EIAJ and SIA discussed the issue of market access to Japan in California.
5/1988	EIAJ organized the Users Committee of Foreign Semiconductors (UCOM).
9/1988	EIAJ announced an Action Plan that aimed to improve market access opportunities for foreign semiconductor producers.
6/1989	EIAJ proposed SIA establish a task force on consumer electronics, to participate in joint development of semiconductors for high-definition TVs, and to hold a joint round table on chips for automobiles.
12/1989	EIAJ made constructive proposals to SIA to assist foreign semiconductor access to Japan.
6/1991	EIAJ and SIA established a joint steering committee in order to conduct preliminary and follow up investigations concerning EIAJ–SIA joint activities.
10/1991	UCOM distributed to SIA a list of contact persons in charge of design-in projects at 62 Japanese user companies.
6/1992	EIAJ proposed SIA submit lists of planned chip purchases by ten major Japanese users.
6/1992	UCOM established a branch in California.

Source: Compiled from various newspapers and EIAJ internal documents.

Even if company executives understood the necessity for expanding the purchase of foreign semiconductors, this aim would not be realized unless purchasing divisions changed their perceptions of foreign products and service quality. The establishment of UCOM implied that users' divisions recognized the necessity for implementing concrete actions for expanding the market access of foreign semiconductors.[53]

In June 1989, EIAJ proposed to SIA that they establish a task force on consumer electronics, participate in the joint development of semiconductors for high-definition TVs, and then hold a joint round-table on chips for automobiles.[54] EIAJ also made constructive proposals to SIA in December 1989 that Japanese electronics firms assist foreign semiconductor access to Japan, by providing information as to the products Japanese users require. Sales of foreign chips through Japanese firms' distribution channels, and collaborative development of new products and technology were also proposed. After the renewed Semiconductor Arrangement came into force on 1 August 1991, activities for expanding foreign semiconductor sales intensified.

Table 5.8   Market shares of foreign semiconductors in Japan, 1986–94
(per cent)

	1986	1987	1988	1989	1990	1991	1992	1993	1994
F1	8.7	10.2	10.6	12.9	13.2	14.4	20.2	20.7	23.7
F2	11.1	12.4	13.2	16.3	19.0	16.1	22.5	22.1	24.7

Note: All figures are those at the fourth quarter. Between 1986 and 1990, F1 is based on data collected by World Semiconductor Trade Statistics (WSTS), while F2 is based on survey data collected by MITI. After 1991, F1 and F2 mean Formula 1 and Formula 2 defined in the 1991 New Semiconductor Arrangement.
Sources: EIAJ's internal documents.

EIAJ proposed in June 1992 to SIA that it submit lists of planned chip purchases by ten major Japanese users. In the same month, UCOM established a branch in California in order to offer Japanese users' information to small and medium-sized suppliers who did not have direct access to the Japanese market as well as to introduce the technology and products of these firms to Japanese users.

The commitments by the industrial associations yielded positive efforts of individual firms and assisted in achieving a substantial improvement in the market share of foreign semiconductors.[55] Although there was only a moderate increase in the share of foreign semiconductors up to the first half of 1992, the share climbed sharply in the fourth quarter of 1992, exceeding the 20 per cent target (Table 5.8).

Stance of electronics firms on market access before 1988

What influence did the stance of electronics firms have on the implementation of the Semiconductor Arrangement? The sanctions in April 1987 were the result of the alleged non-compliance of the Japanese government and firms. SIA attributed the cause of the non-compliance to 'Japanese government and industry perceptions that limited efforts to increase market access would be sufficient to appease American concerns' (SIA 1990, p.2). Indeed, in part, MITI made the mistake of not taking US intentions seriously (Prestowitz 1988, p.67). Yet, MITI undertook measures immediately after the accord came into force. A more crucial cause of non-compliance lay in the response of the private sector in 1986 and 1987.

The unwillingness of Japanese electronics firms to implement the arrangement in 1986 and 1987 stemmed partly from their perception of market structures in the Japanese semiconductor sector. Reflecting vertically integrated corporate structures, major chip producers are major users in Japan. Eight out of the ten largest users are among the ten top producers, and only two users do not produce semiconductors. Accordingly, room for foreign chip producers to penetrate the Japanese market was limited. In addition, the Japanese semiconductor market depends heavily on consumer electronics demand. Consumer electric applications accounted for 43 per cent of total semiconductor demand in Japan in 1986, compared with 7 per cent in the United States. In contrast, semiconductor use in the government and military sectors accounted for 21 per cent of total use in the United States, while there was no such comparable end use in Japan (EIAJ 1988, p.24). Most US suppliers had little manufacturing expertise in and production varieties for consumer electric applications.[56] These features of the Japanese semiconductor market made it almost impossible to raise the market share of foreign devices in a short time.[57]

As far as the internal organization of electronics firms is concerned, the purchase of foreign semiconductors is handled by the procurement divisions rather than the semiconductor divisions. The independence of each division is stronger than is usually recognized in Japanese electronics firms which manufacture a wide variety of products. The procurement divisions regarded themselves as victims of the semiconductor divisions. This was because they were forced to take action for expanding access of foreign devices as a result of the arrangement which was triggered by dumping problems caused by the semiconductor divisions. They were therefore not inclined to be fully cooperative in purchasing foreign semiconductors.[58] The relationships between assembly makers and parts suppliers in the electronics industry have two differences compared to the automobile industry. First, electronics producers, which manufacture a large portion of parts in-house, are less dependent on parts suppliers than auto producers (Takeuchi 1994, p.88).[59] Second, unlike auto producers, electronics producers procure parts belonging to 'marketed goods' (*shihanhin*), such as semiconductors, condensers, and resistors.[60] A survey shows that in the TV production at an electronics company, 20 per cent of the parts belong to this category (Wu 1991, p.70). However, there is a close relationship between parts suppliers and assembly makers in the electronics industry. Electronics makers encourage suppliers to organize supplier associations.[61] The makers negotiate with parts suppliers over various trade conditions through the supplier associations (Chen 1994, p.83). Moreover, the electronics makers and subcontracting parts suppliers jointly undertake activities for quality improvement and cost reduction.[62] Accordingly, electronics producers have traded with selected parts makers for a relatively long period (Hiramoto 1994, p.305). The procurement divisions that cultivated tight linkages with domestic firms were one of the most domestically oriented divisions.[63] It took considerable time to change their procurement patterns.

The unwillingness of Japanese electronics firms to implement the arrangement also stemmed from a political factor. Japanese electronics firms were dissatisfied with the process as well as with the result of the negotiations over the accord. MITI officials sought to resolve the dumping issues which were of concern to the semiconductor producers together with the Section 301 file. MITI hoped to limit the electronics industry's influence in the negotiations.[64] The negotiations were carried out secretly, and MITI officials did not consult sufficiently with electronics companies during the negotiations.[65] For instance, a general framework for agreement was reached in talks between Michio Watanabe, Minister of MITI, and US Trade Representative Clayton Yeutter on 29 May 1986.[66] Before the talks, MITI had no prior consultations with the electronics industry.[67] MITI officials expected electronics firms to accept the result of the negotiations. In fact, however, the firms were dissatisfied with the agreement reached at the talks.[68]

After the Watanabe–Yeutter talks, MITI sought to persuade the US government to withdraw the anti-dumping petitions. However, the US government requested both that the Japanese electronics firms submit proprietary manufacturing data to prove that they were not exporting at cheap prices and that the Japanese government monitor export prices to third countries. Furthermore, the US government demanded government insurance for market access and eventually the side letter was submitted.[69] The substantial agreement on 30 June 1986 included requests which were seemingly unacceptable to the Japanese electronics industry such as third-country monitoring and provision of proprietary data to the US government. After the agreement was reached, MITI spent two months trying to persuade the electronics firms to accept the agreement.[70] Japanese electronics firms reportedly preferred to accept anti-dumping duties rather than agree to the provisions required in the agreement.[71]

As Japanese electronics firms were insufficiently consulted during negotiations, and were also dissatisfied with the provisions of the accord, they had little incentive to cooperate in implementation of the arrangement (Satō 1991, p.128; Krauss 1993, p.287). Prestowitz (1988, p.66) says that although MITI had promised in November 1986 that the US market share would rise to 10 per cent by March 1987, it had difficulty in obtaining cooperation from electronics firms.

The dissatisfaction of the electronics firms with the arrangement escalated when the Reagan administration announced retaliation against alleged Japanese non-compliance. The Japanese electronics industry and firms criticised the sanction.[72] On the dumping issue, the Japanese electronics industry disagreed with the US interpretation of the cost-based fair value for third-country exports as being equal to the FMVs set by the US Department of Commerce (EIAJ 1987, p.16). In addition, the side letter made the situation more complicated.[73] The managers of Japanese electronics firms did not understand why the US government and semiconductor industry took such an extreme position. The top executives of major firms were allegedly shown the side letter, but they considered it as merely a personal memorandum from a MITI official.[74]

The views of the Japanese electronics industry did not coincide with US perceptions of the arrangement. The US government and semi-conductor industry believed that there had been little or no improvement in market access for four years.[75] In addition, in late January 1987, the US government gave MITI 30 days to stop third-country dumping and 60 days to improve market access, otherwise the United States would have to retaliate.[76] As far as the application of FMVs to third-country exports was concerned, the US government asserted that not only would FMVs become a yardstick for third-country exports, but it would be sufficient to substantiate dumping because semiconductors were exported at the half price of FMVs.[77] The US government also believed that the side letter was the core of the arrangement because it was proof of the intention to implement the arrangement.[78] Thus, the Japanese electronics industry underestimated the strength of US dissatisfaction. What is important here is that Japanese electronics firms had little incentive to implement the accord during 1987, owing to their dissatisfaction with US sanctions and the side letter to the Semiconductor Arrangement.

Stance of electronics firms on market access after 1988

Japanese electronics firms undertook cooperative actions to implement the accord after 1988. Several interpretations to account for this change have been advanced. The first interpretation stresses the success of the Semiconductor Arrangement. The positive actions of electronics firms on market access expansion were related to the dumping issues. Major Japanese electronics firms benefited from the arrangement because they avoided the image problems as well as dumping duties as a result of the suspension of dumping suits under the arrangement. These benefits made up for the disadvantages of concessions on market access.[79] The electronics firms also gained huge profits from the semiconductor business as a result of the arrangement. As explained above, MITI encouraged semiconductor producers to cut production capacity in order to observe the arrangement. The production cut as well as price monitoring helped to raise chip prices.[80] The major electronics firms refrained from criticizing the arrangement and became more cooperative in market access. Others maintain that continuous US pressure triggered cooperative actions from the Japanese electronics industry in 1989 and 1990 (Tyson 1992; Tyson and Yoffie 1993). Tyson (1992, p.136) asserts that SIA's commitment to list semiconductors as a primary practice under Super 301 of the 1988 Omnibus Trade Act led to a sharp increase in the market share of foreign semiconductors.

The second interpretation is that MITI's guidance led electronics firms to expand the market access of foreign suppliers. As explained above, MITI worked assiduously to expand the access of foreign semiconductors. In addition to official measures, there were a number of episodes in which MITI influenced Japanese electronics firms' activities to promote market access. Although UCOM was established as an affiliated organization of EIAJ, the director of the Industrial Electronics Division of MITI persuaded major semiconductor users to join the organization. After he gained agreement from 56 firms, EIAJ assumed the Secretariat of UCOM.[81] When EIAJ suggested constructive proposals to SIA in December 1989, it sought to publish the content of the proposals in a US newspaper. This plan was aborted because MITI recommended against publishing the semiconductor access issue in the United States.[82] Furthermore, Hitachi abandoned the advertisement of its development of 4M DRAM at MITI's recommendation in summer 1989.[83] This was in spite of the fact that Hitachi had already printed advertising posters. Lagged behind Toshiba in the development of 1M DRAM, advertising was important for Hitachi. MITI hoped to avoid stimulating the US semiconductor industry which was behind its Japanese counterpart in DRAM development.

These factors helped to explain the actions of Japanese electronics

Table 5.9   Shares of foreign semiconductors in major electronics firms,
1986–91 (per cent)

Company	1986	1988	1989	1990	1991
NEC	20.5	20.8	21	22	24
Toshiba	12	16.3	18.5	20	20.8
Hitachi	8	15	17	20	–
Fujitsu	8	15	18	20	–
Mitsubishi Elect.	20	20	20	21	22
Oki Electric	21	22.5	23	23	–
Matsushita	–	9.5	13	–	20
Sony	4.2	7–8	13–14	–	20

Sources: *Nikkei Bijinesu* (26 March 1990, p.14); *Nihon Keizai Shimbun*
(26 March 1989; 12 April 1990).

firms which were the leading semiconductor producers. Although the
overall share of foreign semiconductors reached 20 per cent in the
fourth quarter of 1992, the leading semiconductor producers attained
the goal earlier (Table 5.9). While NEC and Mitsubishi Electric
attained 20 per cent by 1988, Hitachi, Toshiba and Fujitsu reached it
in 1990.

The Semiconductor Arrangement was a critical factor in inducing
the major semiconductor producers to commit themselves seriously
to expanding market access. General managers of major electronics
firms admitted that the arrangement functioned as a catalyst in
encouraging them to undertake market-opening activities.[84] However,
any interpretation of developments that focuses exclusively on the
effects of the accord alone seems to be naive. The semiconductor
sector alone did not expand market access in Japan in the late 1980s.
A sharp expansion in imports was seen in various electrical and electronics products. US producers alone did not increase semiconductor
sales in Japan. In the 1990s, exports of Korean semiconductors grew
more rapidly than those of the United States, while the US share
of total imports of integrated circuits fell from 70 per cent in 1990 to
50 per cent in 1995 (Table 5.10).

The assessment on the role of SIA's pressure in expanding market
access also needs qualification. SIA wielded political pressure effectively, but its members, big semiconductor producers in particular,
preferred cooperative relations with Japanese semiconductor users
to political pressure.[85] The Japanese users have acknowledged this
stance. When SIA requested the US Trade Representative to list semi-

Table 5.10   Imports of integrated circuits, 1990–95 (billion yen; per cent)

	1990	1991	1992	1993	1994	1995*
United States	265,630	280,084	250,137	286,263	331,338	196,362
	(70.8)	(68.8)	(64.5)	(60.9)	(53.5)	(50.2)
Europe	36,788	31,717	26,995	26,807	27,014	14,029
	(9.8)	(7.8)	(7.0)	(5.7)	(4.4)	(3.6)
South Korea	32,658	40,594	43,435	80,678	155,901	108,800
	(8.7)	(10.0)	(11.2)	(17.2)	(25.2)	(27.8)
Taiwan	15,124	19,642	14,836	19,084	28,051	17,966
	(4.0)	(4.8)	(3.8)	(4.1)	(4.5)	(4.6)
Others	25,224	36,167	52,316	56,894	76,961	53,692
	(6.7)	(8.6)	(13.5)	(12.1)	(12.4)	(13.7)
Total	375,424	407,204	387,719	469,726	619,265	390,849

Note: The figures in parentheses are the percentage share in the total imports. *from January to June.
Source: EIAJ, Internal document.

conductors as a primary practice under Super 301, UCOM, which continued cooperative programmes with SIA for expanding the sales of US semiconductors in Japan, asked SIA its reasons for the request. The answer from SIA was that there was little possibility that the US government would list semiconductors, but it was desirable that semiconductors should remain on the agenda.[86] In addition, although governmental negotiations over semiconductors have always been intense, business-level meetings have been constructive and cooperative.[87]

The semiconductor sector was originally fostered under MITI's encouragement and protection. MITI protected the domestic semiconductor market from foreign firms by initially rejecting applications for wholly owned or majority owned subsidiaries to establish themselves in Japan, and by controlling the approval of all patent, technical assistance and licensing agreements (Tyson 1992, p.93). MITI actively encouraged Japanese electronics firms to develop the semiconductor sector through various public projects.[88] As a consequence, the semiconductor divisions of Japanese electronics firms maintained closer relations with MITI than other divisions, such as consumer electronics, using formal and informal communication channels. Business leaders in the semiconductor sector and MITI officials exchanged information, some of which touched on sensitive issues.[89]

Business leaders willingly divulged proprietary corporate information to MITI officials because they believed that it would not be leaked (Okimoto 1984, p.101). This did not mean that the semiconductor producers always accepted MITI's guidance. Electronics firms criticised MITI's concessions in the negotiation of the Semiconductor Arrangement, and NEC rejected MITI's recommendation to cut production capacity until relations with the United States entered a critical phase.

To understand how the industry changed its stance on market access, attention needs to be paid to the actions of consumer electronics producers represented by Matsushita and Sony. They are not leading semiconductor producers, but they are the leading semiconductor users.[90] Compared with other electronics giants, they had difficulty in expanding the purchase of foreign semiconductors because of their high demand for devices used for consumer electronic products.[91] Most US suppliers had little experience in manufacturing chips for consumer electric applications and their production varieties were limited. The proportion of foreign semiconductors Matsushita and Sony used was below 10 per cent in 1988 when that of other major electronics firms was 15 per cent or more (Table 5.9). However, they made serious efforts to boost their purchase of foreign devices. Matsushita organised joint exhibitions for foreign suppliers after 1989, and sent missions for semiconductor procurement. The leading consumer electronics maker also quadrupled the number of design-ins from 40 to 200 between 1986 and 1990.[92] Matsushita steadily elevated the share of foreign semiconductors from 9.5 per cent in 1988 to 13.0 per cent in 1989 to 20 per cent in July 1991. The foreign share of total chip purchases in Sony also increased sharply from 4.2 per cent in 1986 to 13–14 per cent in 1989 to 20 per cent in April 1991, and the value of foreign semiconductors purchased grew tenfold between 1986 and 1990.[93]

The internationalization of corporate activity provides an explanation for the stance taken by the major electronics firms, especially Sony and Matsushita. The trend was towards multinational production in the semiconductor sector in the late 1980s. Major electronics firms opened DRAM fabrication plants in the United States between 1989 and 1991.[94] The major electronics firms have promoted further internationalization, and they became more cooperative in promoting the access of foreign semiconductors to the Japanese market. Rising internationalization increased the vulnerability of Japanese electronics firms towards reactions from foreign governments and firms. The semiconductor sector was all the more sensitive to foreign reactions because it had experienced retaliation from the US government in April 1987. Although they criticised the retaliation vocally, and semiconductors were not included in the sanctions list, the US response increased the vulnerability of Japanese electronics firms.[95]

Matsushita and Sony were the two major electronics firms that first began multinational productions, and developed them to maturity. Sony established a TV manufacturing plant in the United Kingdom in May 1968, and in the United States in August 1972. Matsushita was behind Sony in moving to developed countries, but it established a TV plant in Thailand in 1961. The two companies steadily expanded multinational production. In 1992, the ratio of foreign employees was 55 per cent in Sony and 75 per cent in Matsushita. The overseas production ratio in 1993 was 36 per cent in Sony and 39 per cent in Matsushita.[96] These two companies also experienced trade friction in the 1970s when the US government introduced the orderly marketing agreement (OMA) in 1977 over Japanese exports of colour TVs. They were relatively more sensitive to foreign reactions than other electronics companies. The positive actions of Matsushita and Sony can be explained in this context.[97] The fact that Matsushita and Sony, which had been deeply involved in multinational operations, committed themselves to purchasing foreign semiconductors seriously is consonant with the automobile case where Nissan, the most active in multinational operations, took the lead in announcing an international cooperation programme in 1989.

Technical features of semiconductors are also relevant to the expansion of the market access of foreign suppliers. Electronics firms manufacture core semiconductors for applied products in-house because these devices determine the features and competitiveness of applied products. At the same time, they purchase supplementary semiconductors from other semiconductor makers. Most semiconductors originally belonged to the 'marketed goods' category, which other large semiconductor producers sold directly to the market. The supply of semiconductors was not undertaken under subcontracting *keiretsu* relationships. The relationship between electronics makers and semiconductor suppliers has become closer as design-in has become popular in semiconductor development. It is less intimate than conventional subcontracting *keiretsu* relations, however. In addition, foreign semiconductor producers have enhanced their advantage, as the Japanese electronics industry has experienced changes in market structure. The spread of CD players and high-definition TVs raised the demand for digital chips in which US suppliers have an advantage. US semiconductor producers excel in application specific integrated circuits (ASICs) or custom chips represented by gate array and standard cell, which require small-scale, tailored production to meet specific user requirements rather than mass production. Furthermore, the rising importance of differentiation in product function, which is a key measure to enhance the competitiveness of final products, increased the demand for foreign devices. Since Japanese makers tend to manufacture similar types of products, differentiation is all the more crucial for them. The nature and degree of differentiation depends on the function and quality of chips used in products. Japanese consumer electronics makers look for a wide variety of chips for this purpose, and require suppliers to produce chips only for specific uses. Foreign suppliers are more suitable for differentiation than Japanese suppliers in semiconductor supply because they are not competitors in the consumer electronics sector.[98]

The evolution of electronics firms' position on market opening is revealed in the statements of company executives. Akio Tanii, President of Matsushita, explained the decision to pursue a 20 per cent target as follows: 'it is useless to quibble about the 20 per cent target. We should behave so that Japan will not become an orphan in the world.'[99] Sony also acknowledged responsibility for expanding the purchase of foreign semiconductors. Masayoshi Miyazaki, a general manager of Sony, points out:

> The Semiconductor Arrangement was concluded following the trigger of dumping by major semiconductor producers in the US market. Therefore, it might be possible to argue that Japanese firms other than major producers named in the dumping cases were, so to speak, victims with respect to market access. However, as an enterprise in a country with huge trade surpluses, we must make efforts to reduce them through the purchase of foreign goods.[100]

Market access to the Japanese semiconductor market has also been promoted by corporate alliances, especially in the 1990s. It is often argued that Japanese semiconductor firms formed alliances with US producers in order to alleviate the semiconductor friction (Kuwata 1990, p.91). Indeed, this motivation can explain the formation of alliances between Japanese users and foreign suppliers in the marketing and service area. The fact that in 1992, Japanese electronics firms forged alliances with National Semiconductor, Advanced Micro

Devices, and Micron Technology – the hardliners of SIA – is explicable in this context as well.

This factor does not explain the whole motivation of Japanese electronics firms in forging international alliances, however. Alliances have often been agreed after deliberate consideration as a major corporate strategy. For instance, the alliance between Toshiba and Motorola was the result of cautious and deliberate calculation by Motorola, which had previously had two joint ventures with Japanese companies. Negotiations took more than a year and continued against a background of a severe industry slump and during the negotiations over the Semiconductor Arrangement (National Research Council 1992, p.94). In addition, Japanese electronics firms forged alliances with Korean firms. If alliances were directed to calm down the trade dispute alone, Japanese electronics firms would not have forged alliances with Korean firms with which they did not have severe trade friction. More significantly, Japanese electronics makers have deepened their commitment to the alliances. In the late 1980s, alliances regarding joint R & D and joint manufacturing were rare. However, these have substantially increased in the 1990s (Table 5.11). Individual firms have also developed their relations typically shown in the alliance between Hitachi and Texas Instruments.[101] If Japanese electronics firms forged alliances with US firms with an eye to mitigating the semiconductor friction alone, they did not have to develop the alliances. In reality, most alliances stem from the strategic perception that Japanese firms derive benefits from them (Enomoto 1991, p.60).

Table 5.11   Number of alliances between Japanese and foreign semiconductor firms, 1985–94

Year	Sales cooperation	Exchange information	Joint R & D	Production cooperation	Joint venture	Total
1985	–	1	–	–	1	2
1986	–	–	1	1	–	2
1987	–	1	–	–	–	1
1988	1	–	2	–	1	4
1989	1	–	–	2	–	3
1990	1	2	1	4	2	10
1991	–	–	8	1	–	9
1992	3	1	12	4	–	20
1993	4	1	11	14	2	32
1994	–	6	10	10	1	27

Source: EIAJ (1995, p.2.8).

The semiconductor dispute functioned only as one factor conducive to alliance formation.

Corporate alliances have played a critical role in improving the access of foreign semiconductors to the Japanese market in various ways. First, various forms of alliances have directly contributed to improving market access. Marketing and sales alliances with an eye to expanding the sales of foreign semiconductors in Japan naturally led to an increase in semiconductor sales.[102] Manufacturing alliances such as OEM and second sourcing agreements also facilitated market access. These alliances encouraged a division of labour in product categories, and ensured a certain volume of foreign semiconductors.[103]

Second, the alliances in joint development and joint manufacturing have facilitated design-in. Design-in has functioned as a key factor facilitating market access of foreign suppliers. The design-in of application specific integrated circuits (ASICs) is particularly important for US suppliers who hope to enter Japan's huge consumer electronics market (Tyson and Yoffie 1993, p.54). As the number of design-ins has increased, market access for foreign devices has improved.[104] Alliances in joint manufacturing and joint development enable partners to exchange information as to production methods and commitment to quality, which constitute the basis in undertaking design-in. For instance, Motorola learned 'soft technology' such as the importance of training operatives on equipment to be used through joint manufacturing with Toshiba.[105]

Third, corporate alliances have contributed to changing the stance of major electronics firms on market access. This is shown typically in Toshiba's case. Toshiba has spearheaded the industry thrust for corporate alliances. Toshiba has had substantial experience in alliances seen in its 80-year-alliance with General Electric and it has developed 24 partnerships and joint ventures in numerous fields.[106] Toshiba has learned the political as well as the economic merit of alliances. Toshiba Machine, a subsidiary of Toshiba, provoked a Coordinating Committee on Multilateral Export Controls (COCOM) breach incident in 1987.[107] Robert Galvin, Chairman of Motorola, did not criticise Toshiba for this incident, even though he had been known as a hard-liner towards Japan. On the contrary, he made efforts to explain Toshiba's stance to the members of the US Congress, when Congress indulged in 'Toshiba bashing'.[108] It was deemed that the alliance with Toshiba in the semiconductor field motivated him to take those positions. Toshiba appreciated the political importance of corporate alliances through this incident.[109]

As a result of experiences, Toshiba has become more positive about expanding market access through alliances. Not only did Motorola resume the DRAM business but it also increased sales in Japan due to the alliance with Toshiba. Toshiba and Motorola established a sales company, Nippon Motorola Microelectronics in October 1989 in order to sell Motorola's products to Toshiba's group members.[110] Toshiba also made serious efforts to sell General Electric's home electrical appliances after the two companies concluded alliances in the home electrical appliance business in April 1991.[111]

CONCLUSION

The electronics case appears to support the argument that firms with extensive multinational operations and corporate alliances have preferences in favour of an open home market.

In the electronics industry, rising imports in electronic products have not led to a demand for import restrictions. In addition to the huge trade surplus in the electronics industry, a rise in intra-industry trade has reduced the industry's incentive to restrain the increase in imports. Furthermore, imports were largely carried out by Japanese multinational electronics firms as reverse imports. Reverse imports took place on the basis of the division of manufacturing products, that is, high value-added electronic products in Japan and standardized consumer electronic products in overseas plants. Major electronics firms were restructuring away from an import-competing consumer electronics sector to industrial electronics and electronic components sectors. There was little possibility that imports would jeopardize the interests of multinational electronics firms. The Japanese electronics firms, which have been intensively engaged in intra-firm trade and have successfully adjusted their business, could maintain an open trade stance.

Enhanced international activities also affected electronics firms' stance on market access activities. In 1989, major electronics firms drew up international cooperation programmes designed to expand market access of foreign products to Japan. These programmes were designed to mitigate the effects of the yen appreciation after 1985 by using cheaper foreign products. At the same time, they stemmed from changes in corporate strategies and trade policy stance. In the past, the five or six producers had indulged in intense competition to boost market share, sometimes forcing local producers out of the market. They paid little attention to the criticism by foreign governments and firms of the closed Japanese market. However, as they strengthened multinational operations, they began to revise competition strategies, to pay more attention to cooperation with their competitors and to the harmonization of Japanese institutions and customs with international norms. This change in stance encouraged major electronics firms to draw up international cooperation programmes.

The US–Japan Semiconductor Arrangement illustrated the effects of the change in firms' stance on the market access issue. The arrangement failed to produce substantial outcomes during its first two years. This was a result of the lukewarm response from the private sector. Some electronics firms did not accept MITI's guidance on production cuts. The commitment of the industry to market access was also slow. This inert response sprang from the perception that a swift increase of foreign semiconductors would be difficult in the Japanese semiconductor market because of high demand for devices used for consumer electronic products for which US suppliers had little manufacturing expertise and few production varieties. An additional political factor was that the industry had not been clearly involved in the negotiations by MITI, and the final accord included clauses which it considered unreasonable.

The electronics industry became more cooperative in promoting market access in 1988. While EIAJ launched various programmes to aim at removing impediments to access of foreign semiconductors, individual firms undertook activities such as a dispatch of procurement missions, seminars and exhibitions of foreign devices. This change has been interpreted as resulting from a variety of factors such as benefits from the Semiconductor Arrangement, effects of SIA's pressure, and MITI's persistence. However, the changed approach of major electronics firms on market access for foreign products was also a critical factor, especially that of consumer electronics producers. These firms were not leading semiconductor producers, which had caused the dumping problems in the US market and had gained huge profits under the arrangement. Consumer electronics producers also had difficulty in expanding their use of foreign semiconductors owing to their high demand for consumer product devices. However, they made serious efforts to elevate the share of foreign semiconductors used in Japan. As they expanded their multinational operations, they became more and more sensitive to foreign criticism of Japanese corporate behaviour and the closed nature of the Japanese market. Their motivation was to discourage the US government from taking retaliatory action, and to promote cooperation with foreign firms.

Corporate alliances have played a crucial role in improving market access. Some of the alliances incorporated direct measures to promote market access, providing an environment where mutual understanding and communication would develop more deeply. The parties to alliances deepened their understanding of market conditions, production methods, and the kinds of semiconductors partners need. Corporate alliances led to a changed stance of some Japanese electronics firms on market access. They promoted market access in order to maintain stable relationships with alliance partners. The change in private firms' strategies was, thus, a vital factor ensuring success in expanding market access to the Japanese semiconductor market.

Thus, the electronics industry showed similar characteristics to the automobile industry in the relations between the internationalization of corporate activities and firms' trade policy preferences. In both industries, greater international operations made Japanese firms more sensitive to foreign criticism of the closed Japanese market. These firms changed their position on free trade and market access and strove to facilitate the access of foreign products to the Japanese market.

6 Trade Policy Preferences in the Japanese Textile Industry

The automobile and electronics industries have advanced international operations in the form of multinational production and corporate alliances, and these moves have become a catalyst of changes in corporate preferences for open trade. This chapter approaches the central interest of this study, the relationship between the internationalization of corporate activities and its influence on pro-liberal corporate preferences from a different viewpoint; that is, how internationally oriented firms react to protectionist tendencies in an import competing industry.

The Japanese textile industry, which had been the leading industry in terms of production output and exports until the 1950s, gradually lost international competitiveness in the labour-intensive sectors in the 1970s and 1980s. The industry suffered first from a dramatic decline in international market share and then from a rise in imports from Asian neighbours.[1] In order to circumvent a sharp rise in imports, some textile producer associations resorted to anti-dumping and countervailing suits, while major textile industrial associations called on the government to invoke the Multi-Fibre Arrangement (MFA), the protectionist agreement in international textile trade.

There are many different kinds of firms in the textile industry, reflecting a vertically layered structure. While the weaving, knitting, dyeing and garment manufacturing sectors consist of a number of small and medium-sized firms, the fibre making and spinning sectors are dominated by big companies owing to their capital-intensive character.[2] The degree of internationalization is also diverse. The small and medium-sized firms in the weaving and knitting sectors have developed few international operations. In contrast, spinning and synthetic fibre companies started foreign direct investment (FDI) in the late 1960s and early 1970s, while the apparel makers have actively expanded international operations since the mid-1980s. The aim here is to confirm whether the internationalization of corporate activity has functioned as a critical factor in determining trade policy attitudes, and in particular whether it has mitigated the demand for import restrictions in the industry.

The next section looks at the features of the textile industry as well as examining the internationalization of the industry. The second section outlines the rise in textile imports and government policies in response to this trend. The third section describes two reactions by textile producers to rising imports: anti-dumping and countervailing suits, and the demand for introducing the MFA. The fourth section examines the stance of various industrial associations towards import restrictions. Then, it highlights the policy stance of large textile producers and examines why they took the stance that they did.

INDUSTRIAL CHARACTERISTICS AND INTERNATIONALIZATION

Industrial characteristics

Management resources, a company's perspective on markets, and decisions by executives are among the factors which influence the formation of corporate preferences. The characteristics of industries to which firms belong also influence the formation of corporate preferences. The Japanese textile industry has several particular industrial characteristics. First, the textile industry is multi-layered consisting of fibre production, primary processing, and secondary processing.[3] Fibre production involves the manufacturing of two kinds of fibres – staple and filament – from raw fibre materials. The main synthetic fibres today are nylon, polyester and acrylic. The primary processing operations include spinning, twisting, weaving, knitting, dyeing and finishing. Intermediate products produced in primary processing are transformed into final goods in secondary processing operations, including such activities as garment manufacturing and the production of soft furnishing and other textile goods (Yoshihara 1978, p.94). These three sets of manufacturing operations are normally called upstream, midstream and downstream stages.[4]

Market competition in the textile industry is intensive from the upstream to midstream and then to the downstream stages (Yoshihara 1978, p.94). The fibre production stage is oligopolistic because large capital investments are necessary to attain the optimum scale of production, and the level of technology and expenditure for research and development (R & D) is high. The spinning sector is less oligopolistic than fibre making, but exhibits a relatively high degree of company concentration. Market structure in the midstream stage – weaving, dyeing and finishing, and knitting – is far more competitive than that in the spinning sector. Lastly, there are numerous garment manufacturers in the downstream stage, which is more competitive. Thus, the industrial structure of the textile industry is exactly the opposite of the automobile and electronics industries, which become oligopolistic as manufacturing proceeds downstream and approaches the final product stage (Hirai 1991, p.52).

The multi-layered relationship between firms in the textile industry leads to a dualistic structure. The industry consists of a dozen big companies that specialize in synthetic fibre making and spinning, and a large number of small and medium-sized firms that engage in weaving, knitting, dyeing, and garment manufacturing. The majority of small and medium-sized firms subcontract with upstream firms or local trading companies that supply yarn, sell products and often offer financial assistance.

The second feature of the textile industry lies in its role in the national and local economies. The textile industry was the leading industry from the Meiji era to the 1950s in Japan.[5] Although its status has declined since the 1960s in terms of production and exports, the industry still accounts for a considerable share in all manufacturing establishments and employment. In 1993, for example, the industry employed 1.15 million people in 117,327 establishments in the manufacturing section, accounting for 10 per cent of the total Japanese manufacturing labour force, and 16.9 per cent of total manufacturing establishments.[6] In addition, textile manufacturing companies are concentrated in specific textile districts (*sanchi*). There are 127 textile *sanchi* including 36 handling silk and rayon fibre weaving and 30 handling cotton and staple fibre weaving (Hirai 1991, pp.56–7). In these districts, the industry creates employment and sustains the local economy. In 1992, for instance, the share of textiles in the total manufacturing labour force was more than 20 per cent in 12 prefectures.[7]

Industrial associations

Policy stances are often formed on a sectoral basis, and are expressed by industrial associations in each sector. Because of its vertical multi-layered structure, the textile industry has numerous industrial associations (Table 6.1).[8] In the upstream sector, the Japan Chemical Fibres

Table 6.1   Major industrial associations in the textile industry

Association	Stage	Sector	Firm size
JCFA	upstream	fibre making	big
JSA	upstream	spinning	big
JCSFWA	midstream	weaving	small
JSRFWA	midstream	weaving	small
JKIA	midstream	knitting	small
JTMA	midstream	towel making	small
JAIC	downstream	apparel	mixed
JTIA		importing	mixed

Source: Compiled from industry sources.

Association (JCFA) and the Japan Spinners' Association (JSA) are the two major associations. JCFA, established in August 1948, comprises 60 large companies that engage in man-made fibre production, yarn spinning, raw material manufacturing and allied processes. The association is dominated by the so-called seven major synthetic fibre companies.[9] As major cotton spinners have expanded their business into man-made fibre production and processing, they have become members of JCFA. Toyobo and Kanebo, which began operations in the spinning sector, are now included in major synthetic fibre companies. JSA, originally founded as the Spinners' Federation in 1882, is the association of large natural and man-made fibre spinning companies. JSA consisted of 41 members in 1995 including nine major spinning companies, but small and medium-sized spinners are not members.[10] These two associations, reflecting the corporate power of the members, are the most influential in the textile industry.

The weaving sector has two major associations. One is the Japan Cotton and Staple Fibre Weavers' Association (JCSFWA), which represents spun-yarn weavers (cotton and synthetic spun fabrics). JCSFWA consists of 56 affiliated associations at the district level, mainly located on the Pacific coast of Japan. The other is the Japan Silk and Rayon Fibre Weavers' Association (JSRFWA), which represents filament fabric weavers (silk, artificial silk, and synthetic filament fabrics). JSRFWA comprises 27 affiliated associations on the district level, mainly concentrating on the Sea of Japan coast. Both associations consist of small companies, and more than 99 per cent of the members belong to small and medium-sized firms.[11] The Japan Knitting Industry Association (JKIA) and the Japan Towel Manufacturers' Association (JTMA) are the two other major associations in the midstream sector. JKIA was formed in 1974 in the knitting sector which covers some 14,500 firms. Some 92 per cent of these firms are small firms with less than 30 employees. JTMA, founded in 1962, incorporates some 700 members which are concentrated in the Osaka and Ehime prefectures. More than 95 per cent of its members are small and medium-scale firms which operate less than 50 looms.

In the apparel sector, six major apparel associations formed the Japan Apparel Industry Council (JAIC) in 1982. JAIC consists of some 220 members, most of which are apparel wholesalers. In the textile import business, the Japan Textiles Importers' Association (JTIA) was founded in 1972 as a combination of the Japan Importers' Association of Textile Products and the Japan Importers' Association of Wool Products. The association comprises some 170 members including the major general trading companies and textile-specific trading companies.

Lastly, textile circles have a peak federation, the Japan Textile Industry Federation (JTIF). The Federation was established in January 1970 during the US–Japan textile negotiations as a counter-weight to the American textile coalition led by the American Textile Manufacturers Institute (Friman 1990, p.74). JTIF incorporates 20 prefectural subdivisions as well as 35 associations ranging from the upstream to downstream stages of the industry.

Internationalization before 1985

In examining how firms' stance on trade policy has evolved as textile firms have promoted international operations, one needs to spell out how the Japanese textile industry has become more deeply involved in multinational operations. The textile industry was the first Japanese manufacturing industry to make inroads into overseas markets and then into overseas production. Big spinning producers initiated multinational operations by investing in Latin America in the 1950s, followed by major synthetic fibre producers which had actively trans-ferred production bases to Taiwan and Hong Kong in the late 1960s and to South Korea, Singapore and Thailand in the 1970s. Annual outward investment in textiles was US$163 million in 1972 and US$326 million in 1973, which accounted for 31 per cent and 22 per cent of the total Japanese manufacturing investment, respectively (Table 6.2). The two synthetic-fibre makers, Toray Industries and Teijin, were the most active in multinational operations. By the end of 1973, Teijin was involved in 18 overseas manufacturing operations

Table 6.2   Foreign direct investment by Japanese textile producers by destination, 1965–94 (US$ million)

Year	North America	South America	Asia	Europe	Other	Total
1965	–	2	3	–	1	6
1966	3	3	2	–	3	11
1967	–	5	11	–	1	17
1968	–	2	13	–	–	15
1969	–	5	25	–	4	34
1970	3	6	37	–	3	49
1971	1	11	53	–	–	65
1972	3	23	132	–	5	163
1973	28	93	191	4	10	326
1974	10	36	118	8	3	175
1975	4	17	71	4	2	98
1976	29	27	47	6	3	112
1977	27	34	83	13	1	158
1978	37	27	35	73	–	172
1979	22	15	34	17	1	89
1980	14	12	50	12	3	91
1981	26	10	43	13	–	91
1982	10	12	40	5	–	67
1983	11	17	132	14	–	174
1984	15	16	39	15	–	85
1985	1	11	8	8	–	28
1986	22	2	21	17	1	63
1987	132	9	28	35	3	206
1988	96	11	149	59	2	317
1989	158	1	189	185	–	533
1990	107	12	298	376	2	796
1991	233	9	217	156	–	616
1992	66	23	227	108	4	428
1993	37	–	300	161	–	498
1994	49	13	496	80	4	641

Sources: Ministry of Finance, *Kokusai kinyukyoku nenpo* [Annual Report of International Finance Bureau], various issues.

in nine countries, whereas Toray was engaged in 35 offshore manufacturing operations in 15 countries (Tsurumi 1976, p.89). Even in 1974, the capacity of the overseas affiliates for these companies was 30 per cent of domestic capacity (Yoshihara 1978, p.106). Most overseas operations took the form of joint ventures with local companies and Japanese trading companies in order to diversify capital and market risk.

Motivations for FDI during this stage had domestic and international origins. Owing to a labour shortage and a resultant rise in wages, textile producers suffered from an increase in production costs. They sought to restore international competitiveness by making inroads into countries with cheap labour costs. As an external factor, the newly industrialized economies (NIEs) and the Association of Southeast Asian Nations (ASEAN) countries adopted policies to attract foreign capital in the mid-1960s. For instance, South Korea enacted the Foreign Capital Promotion Law in 1966, while Singapore introduced the Economic Expansion Encouragement Law in 1967 (Horaguchi 1992, p.172). This is one reason why some 70 per cent of investment was directed towards Asia in the late 1960s and early 1970s. In addition, export restraints by the US government, which started in the late 1950s and led to the US–Japan Textile Arrangement in 1971, encouraged Japanese textile manufacturers to promote offshore production. The tariff exemption system under the Generalized Scheme of Preferences introduced by European countries in 1971 also provided developing countries other than Japan with an advantage in achieving access to the markets of industrialized countries (Yamazawa 1980, p.451; Toyne *et al.* 1984, p.155). However, overseas investment in textiles experienced a downward trend until the mid-1980s owing to a protracted recession in the industry caused by the two oil shocks.

Internationalization after 1985

The textile industry, like other manufacturing industries, enjoyed a surge in its international operations after the mid-1980s. The main actors in this phase were the apparel, not the textile companies. The international operations of Japanese apparel makers at first took the form of technology alliances and outward processing agreements. Outward processing agreements under which local subcontractors manufactured standard clothing according to the specifications of Japanese firms in design pattern and quality were especially prominent. The number of export approvals for outward processing in China, South Korea, Taiwan and Hong Kong increased sharply from 709 in 1985 to 9,605 in 1991 (Table 6.3). One study estimates that some 80 per cent of imports in clothing from the NIEs between 1983 and 1987 were imports associated with outward processing agreement (Mukaiyama 1989, p.27).

FDI, especially in the form of joint ventures, has expanded rapidly

Table 6.3   Number of export approvals for outward processing in textiles, 1985–92

	1985	1986	1987	1988	1989	1990	1991	1992*
China	472	489	728	1,241	2,012	3,814	8,636	7,436
South Korea	201	219	246	350	401	426	483	326
Taiwan	26	25	31	38	35	45	73	44
Hong Kong	10	13	34	44	58	144	413	253
Others	–	–	–	–	–	324	747	460
Total	709	746	1,039	1,673	2,506	4,753	10,352	8,519

Note: Data on others before 1989 are unavailable. * From January to June.
Source: MITI (1994c, p.203).

Table 6.4   Number of joint ventures in textiles

	Fibre, Spinning		Weaving, Dyeing		Apparel		Total	
	1987*	1988–92	1987*	1988–92	1987*	1988–92	1987*	1988–92
China	2	4	1	7	13	108	16	119
NIES	8	1	16	5	21	17	45	23
ASEAN	35	5	47	11	14	43	96	59
US, EC	7	3	6	7	9	12	22	22
Latin America	18	1	13	1	6	1	37	3
Total	70	14	83	31	63	181	216	226

Note: *Up to 1987.
Source: MITI (1994c, p.176).

since 1987. It is difficult to obtain official data on FDI in the apparel sector proper because data on FDI issued by the Ministry of Finance (MOF) treat the textile industry as one industrial category. But other survey data indicate a remarkable rise in FDI by apparel makers since the late 1980s. Table 6.4 illustrates the number of joint ventures in textiles reported by MITI. The apparel sector accounted for 29.2 per cent, 63 out of 216 before 1987. After 1988, 80.1 per cent, 181 of the total 226 joint ventures were related to the apparel sector. The advance into China by Japanese apparel makers in the 1990s is particularly noteworthy. According to a survey by the Japan Export Clothing Manufacturers Association, 476 apparel-related plants were established between 1981 and the first half of 1994. They were set up mainly in the 1990s: 19.3 per cent in 1992, 22.5 per cent in 1993, and 14.9 per cent in the first half of 1994.[12] The main objective of apparel makers in making inroads into China was to cope with the labour shortage in

Table 6.5   Shares of exports to Japan by overseas affiliates of Japanese textile firms, 1992

	0	1–25%	25–50%	50–75%	75–100%	100%	Total
Spinning	17	5	3	–	1	1	27
Dyeing	8	2	2	1	–	–	13
Clothing apparel	3	1	2	6	7	23	42
Knit apparel	2	2	1	6	1	16	28

Note: The figures are the number of affiliates which export each product to Japan by each percentage.
Source: MITI (1994c, p.211).

Japan, and to utilize cheap labour. After the Japanese economy plunged into a protracted business slump in the 1990s, apparel makers responded to consumer preferences for low-priced clothing by accelerating the transfer of production bases for standardized garments to low labour-cost countries.

Active international operations by Japanese apparel makers led to an increase in imports of finished products into the Japanese market. Originally, Japanese apparel makers decided to advance into East Asian countries with an eye to bringing the products manufactured there back to Japan. Not only was the demand in local markets weak but exports to major developed countries were also blocked by quotas. A survey by MITI shows a high propensity for Japanese apparel makers to import their offshore output to Japan. In 1992, 23 out of 42 affiliates in clothing apparel and 16 out of 28 affiliates in knit apparel exported 100 per cent of their garments produced overseas to Japan (Table 6.5).

RISING IMPORTS IN TEXTILES AND GOVERNMENT POLICIES

As with other labour-intensive industries, the Japanese textile industry, particularly its labour-intensive sectors, has steadily lost competitiveness internationally, and suffered from a rise in imports from developing countries (Park and Anderson 1992). While the proportion of textiles in all manufacturing output halved between 1970 and 1992 from 8.9 per cent to 4.2 per cent, the proportion of textiles in total exports decreased from 12.5 per cent to 2.5 per cent in the same period.[13] The importance of the Japanese textile industry in international trade declined sharply as well. The ratio of Japanese exports of textiles and clothing in international trade decreased from 15 per cent in 1955 to 8 per cent in 1975 and then to 3 per cent in 1988 (Park and Anderson 1992, p.23).

The scarcity of domestic labour – particularly young factory workers – and a rise in wages deprived the Japanese textile industry of its international competitive edge. This led to falling competitiveness in low-quality standardized textile products. Furthermore, owing to several yen appreciations after the early 1970s, imported products gained price competitiveness in the Japanese market. Internationally, East Asian countries emerged as powerful production centres for textile goods. These economies positioned their textile industries as significant export industries, and promoted them with active investment. Not only have they rapidly augmented production capacity but they have also caught up with Japan in terms of technology and productivity by introducing the newest technology and machinery (Uryū 1990, p.5). Furthermore, because of tighter import restrictions of the MFA, developing countries shifted their exports from other industrialized countries to Japan (Cline 1987, pp.136–7). In the 1990s, consumer preferences for inexpensive clothing and emergence of discount retailings, such as roadside shops, have accelerated import penetration in the Japanese market.

Textile imports have grown sharply, especially since the 1980s. The share of imports in total domestic demand increased from 16.3 per cent in 1980 to 27.8 per cent in 1986, and to 50.8 per cent in 1993 (Table 6.6). Japan became a net importer of textiles in 1987. In 1993, the share of imported products in total domestic consumption was 42.6 per cent of cotton yarn, 49.2 per cent of cotton fabric and 69.6 per cent of knitted outerwear. Although import penetration is seen in every segment, the rise in the clothing sector is particularly striking. The import value of finished textile products grew significantly from US\$3.54 billion in 1985 to US\$14.2 billion in 1993, making for a cumulative growth of 400 per cent within this period. In 1993, the clothing sector accounted for 76 per cent of total textile imports.[14]

The sharp rise in imports had serious effects on the textile industry. The number of establishments decreased from 146,286 in 1970 to 104,493 in 1995, and some 41,800 establishments withdrew from production. Employment also fell from 1.75 million in 1970 to 0.99 million in 1995 (Table 6.7). In spite of decreases in the number of establishments and employment, the industry continued to expand the value of shipments and value added until 1990. However, these items also began a downward trend in 1991.

Table 6.6   Import shares in textile products, 1986–93 (per cent)

Product	1986	1987	1988	1989	1990	1991	1992	1993
Yarn								
Cotton	26.1	28.9	30.3	31.5	31.1	37.1	36.5	42.6
Silk	34.0	34.3	39.2	41.7	37.6	47.5	41.6	50.4
Wool	4.0	5.4	8.1	5.8	6.6	11.8	9.3	6.1
Synthetic	3.5	5.0	6.1	6.6	7.7	8.0	8.4	7.8
Fabric								
Cotton	24.9	28.8	31.3	34.2	31.4	36.6	39.0	49.2
Silk	18.7	19.3	20.0	21.5	22.7	22.9	23.4	26.8
Wool	4.7	5.9	8.1	9.1	7.9	6.4	6.7	6.6
Synthetic	15.3	8.0	4.7	11.7	7.8	9.1	11.6	7.8
Finished textiles								
Woven outerwear	28.6	33.2	40.8	46.9	47.3	51.2	59.1	64.8
Woven underwear	31.5	36.3	42.0	51.0	51.1	49.5	58.8	63.4
Knitted outerwear	34.8	46.3	53.6	55.2	53.7	57.7	64.3	69.6
Knitted sweater	49.0	54.8	65.9	69.4	66.9	72.4	77.4	81.3
Knitted underwear	25.5	36.3	46.6	50.1	47.5	50.8	55.7	55.4
All textiles	27.8	32.8	36.7	38.7	37.4	41.4	45.0	50.8

Note: The figures are the proportion of imports in total domestic demand.
Source: MITI (1995, p.246).

Table 6.7   Establishments, employees, value of shipments, and value-added in the textile industry, 1970–95

	1970	1975	1980	1985	1990	1993	1995
Establishments	146,286	157,381	147,467	142,167	130,063	117,327	104,493
	(22.4)	(21.4)	(20.1)	(19.0)	(17.8)	(16.9)	(16.0)
Employees	1,750	1,589	1,391	1,334	1,271	1,149	994
('000)	(15.0)	(14.1)	(12.7)	(11.6)	(10.8)	(10.0)	(9.1)
Value of shipments	6,127	9,404	12,878	13,340	13,953	12,462	10,701
(billion yen)	(8.9)	(7.4)	(5.7)	(5.0)	(4.3)	(4.0)	(3.5)
Value-added	2,329	3,335	4,663	5,333	6,080	5,549	4,871
(billion yen)	(9.5)	(7.9)	(6.5)	(5.8)	(5.0)	(4.7)	(4.1)

Note: The figures are for all textiles, clothing and man-made fibres. The figures in parentheses represent the percentage share in the total manufacturing industry in Japan.
Sources: MITI, *Kogyo tokeihyo: Sangyohen* [Census of Manufactures: Report by Industry], various years.

The Japanese government has treated textile problems – including rising imports – as an industrial problem rather than a trade issue, encouraging the restructuring and rationalization of the industry instead of resorting to import restriction measures. Structural adjustment in textiles has been implemented by adopting a succession of temporary laws, which aimed to provide incentives to reduce excess labour and capital equipment, to modernize small plants, and to move into higher-value products.[15] The 1956 Law on Temporary Measures for Textile Industry Equipment (Old Textile Law, 1956–63) introduced a programme to regulate spinning and weaving capacity through purchases of surplus equipment and established a registration system for spindles and looms under which the use of non-registered equipment was prohibited. The 1964 Law on Temporary Measures for Textile Industry Equipment and Related Equipment (New Textile Law, 1964–66) adopted a scrap-and-build programme in which two machines were scrapped in exchange for the installation of one new machine. The government has continued policies to purchase and scrap excess capacity by adopting additional laws.[16]

Under these industry-specific measures and general programmes for small and medium-sized firms, the government provided 52.5 billion yen in subsidies between 1956 and 1974, of which 3.6 billion yen was used for the direct purchase of excess equipment and the rest was awarded in return for losses under the voluntary restraint on textile exports to the United States (Yamazawa 1980, p.454). The government offered 329.9 billion yen in low-interest, long-term loans to promote the disposal of excess machinery, the modernization of productive capacity, and the grouping of units of production.[17] As a consequence of these measures, 205,000 looms for cotton and staple fibres, 121,000 looms for silk and rayon, and 5 million spindles were scrapped between 1956 and 1981 (Yamazawa 1988, p.400).

The Japanese government, by adopting the successive adjustment laws, has avoided protecting the textile industry from outside competition through the use of trade restrictions. Although Japan has been one of the developed country participants in the MFA, it has not imposed MFA restrictions on imports (Whalley 1992, p.77). Exceptional import restrictions are the bilateral restraint agreements on raw silk and silk fabrics from China and South Korea, and voluntary export restraints (VERs) which were agreed as a result of anti-dumping actions in December 1982 and October 1988.[18]

RESPONSE OF TEXTILE PRODUCERS TO RISING IMPORTS

Textile producer associations have taken several measures to curb steep rises in imports. One measure is the convening of periodic consultations with foreign exporters. JSA has organized meetings with its Korean and Pakistani counterparts, and JCSFWA has had consultations with its Chinese counterparts every year since 1977. However, this appeal to foreign suppliers at the private level has not worked well in maintaining orderly exports. In more direct responses, some of the textile producer associations have resorted to adopting anti-dumping and countervailing suits. Major textile producer associations have also demanded that the Japanese government put the MFA into action.

Anti-dumping and countervailing suits

The primary strategy of textile producers to curb steep import rises has been directed towards persuading the government to invoke the MFA. But they have recognised that this initiative depends on government not industry action, and that it takes time. Alternatively, several textile producer associations have resorted to anti-dumping and countervailing charges for restraining imports.[19] There have been seven anti-dumping and countervailing cases filed by Japanese industry until now, four of which were lodged by textile producers (Table 6.8).[20]

The first anti-dumping and countervailing files in Japan were petitioned in 1982. In early December of 1982, JSA notified MITI of its intention to petition MOF to institute an anti-dumping suit against South Korea and a countervailing duty suit against Pakistan. Although MITI refused to engage in bilateral discussions to restrain imports

Table 6.8 Anti-dumping and countervailing suits in Japan

Date	Actor	Country	Targeted item	Result
Anti-dumping suits				
27 Dec. 1982	JSA	South Korea	Cotton yarn	VER, withdrawal
6 Mar. 1984	JFA	Norway, France	Ferrosilicon	Withdrawal
21 Oct. 1988	JKIA	South Korea	Knit sweater	VER, withdrawal
8 Oct. 1991	JFA	China, Norway, South Africa	Ferrosilicon manganese	Dumping duties on Chinese imports
20 Dec. 1993	JSA	Pakistan	Cotton yarn	Dumping duties
Countervailing suits				
27 Dec. 1982	JSA	Pakistan	Cotton yarn	Withdrawal
6 Mar. 1984	JFA	Brazil	Ferrosilicon	Withdrawal

Note: JFA denotes the Japan Ferroalloy Association.
Source: *Kasen Geppo* (March 1994, p.12).

with either South Korea or Pakistan, the association filed the suits with MOF on 27 December.[21] The association asserted that massive imports of cheap cotton yarn from the two countries had caused serious damage to domestic cotton spinners.[22] The imports of cotton yarn from the two countries during January to October 1982 totalled 486,786 bales, 70 per cent more than over the same period in the previous year, and some 30 per cent of Japan's total production during the same period.[23] In March 1983, Korean spinners announced that they would accept VERs on cotton yarn exports to Japan set at an annual maximum of 270,000 bales for three years. The government decided in February 1983 to investigate charges that cotton yarn exports from Pakistan had been subsidised by the government. In August 1983, the Pakistani government agreed to withdraw export subsidies. In light of the responses from both countries, JSA dropped the case against South Korea in April 1983 and the case against Pakistan in February 1984 after the completion of Pakistani loans to cotton producers in January (Friman 1990, p.135).

The second anti-dumping file in the textile industry was petitioned against Korean knitted sweaters in 1988. JKIA announced on 30 May 1988 that it would lodge a complaint with MOF against Korean knitted sweaters. Imports of Korean sweaters increased 41.8 per cent in 1986, 25.9 per cent in 1987 and 77.2 per cent during January to July 1988.[24] However, MITI was anxious about a deterioration in relations with South Korea, and persuaded the association to postpone the filing. On 24 June, the Korean government announced that it would adopt a monitoring measure for price and volume of exports in July.[25] The measure had almost no effect. The export volume of Korean knitted sweaters in July was 14 million units, 29 per cent up from the previous year and 0.68 million units up from the previous month.[26] Eventually, the association filed an anti-dumping suit with MOF on October 21 1988, arguing that the export prices of Korean knitted sweaters were 30 per cent lower than normal market prices.

The major textile industrial associations supported the anti-dumping action. JTIF was a substantial co-organizer of the file. The dumping suit imposed huge costs and consumed an enormous amount of time because it required the investigation of Japanese products, Korean imported products and products sold in the Korean market. JTIF supported JKIA by collecting data and providing financial and personnel assistance.[27] JTIF also sent a mission to South Korea to investigate the implementation of the monitoring measures in August 1988.[28] It was reported that the suit by JKIA went ahead because of informal negotiations with the LDP, MOF and MITI by Kagayaki Miyazaki, Chairman of JTIF.[29] JCFA also supported the JKIA's suit. Susumu Okamoto, Chairman of JCFA, said that the dumping suit by JKIA was a natural reaction, and he expected that MOF and relevant ministries would respond to the anti-dumping action properly and promptly.[30] JCFA assisted JKIA by offering financial and personnel support. The Japan Federation of Textile Workers' Unions (*Zensen Domei*), and its supporting party, the Democratic Socialist Party also openly supported the suit.

MITI was reluctant to commence the investigation of dumping because it favoured a negotiated settlement.[31] The LDP Special Committee on Textile Measures received an explanation from MITI about the dumping, and Kabun Muto, Chairman of the Committee, visited South Korea in late December to coordinate relations between the governments and industries of both countries.[32] After five days of negotiations between the Japanese and Korean industries, South Korea announced VERs on 2 February 1989, which limited the annual growth rate to less than 1 per cent for the next three years under a price monitoring system. JKIA withdrew the petition in March 1989.

The third anti-dumping suit by the textile industry was lodged in December 1993. In January 1992, JSA commenced a dumping investigation against cotton yarn imports from Pakistan. At that time, however, JSA abandoned the petition because the Pakistani government introduced a minimum export price system on cotton yarn exports.[33] In mid-1993, low-priced exports of 20-count cotton yarn from Pakistan became a serious issue again. On 20 December 1993, JSA filed an anti-dumping suit against Pakistani 20-count cotton yarn. According to JSA, imports of cotton yarn from Pakistan accounted for some 80 per cent of sales in the Japanese market, and the price of 20-count cotton yarn imported from Pakistan was 20 per cent lower than domestic prices in Pakistan.[34] MOF and MITI decided in February 1994 to commence a dumping investigation. After two extensions of the investigation, MOF and MITI decided in August 1995 to impose dumping margins ranging from 2.1 per cent to 9.9 per cent.[35] This was the second case in which dumping duties were imposed in Japan.[36]

Demand for the introduction of the MFA

Textiles and apparel have been 'the most systematically and comprehensively protected sectors in the world' (Cline 1987, p.145). The

United States and other developed countries sought to restrain imports from Japan and other East Asian countries through VERs between Japan and the United States in 1956, the Short Term Arrangement in 1961, and the Long Term Arrangement (LTA) in 1962.[37] After the LTA was renewed in 1967 and 1970 through 1973, the MFA was concluded in January 1974.[38] The MFA, which covered woollen goods and man-made fibres in addition to cotton products under the previous accords, stipulates two import quota measures. The signatory countries are qualified to take unilateral restraints when serious damage or actual threat is provoked by imports (Article 3), or to conclude bilateral agreements with exporting countries when there are real risks of market disruption (Article 4). The MFA aims to safeguard the textile industries of developed countries against a rise in imports from developing countries as an exception to the General Agreement on Tariffs and Trade (GATT) 19.

Although the MFA had regulated the international textile trade for twenty years, liberalization of the textile trade became an issue in the GATT Uruguay Round negotiations. In the new arrangement ratified in April 1994, it was agreed that the MFA would be phased out by integrating it into the general GATT rules in three stages over a ten-year period. The new arrangement divides the transition period into three stages – the first stage for three years, the second for four years, and the third for three years – and at the beginning of each stage 16 per cent, 17 per cent, and 18 per cent of the total textile trade will be changed into the general rules. During the transition phase, any country is entitled to introduce a transitional safeguard (TSG).[39]

Japan is one of the exceptional countries which have not set quotas on textile imports based on the MFA. The introduction of the MFA (later TSG) has been persistently called for by textile circles. JCSFWA has requested the government to introduce the MFA against imports of cotton fabric from China almost every year since 1975.[40] JSA has also called on the government to introduce the MFA since the mid-1970s. JTIF set up a committee on import issues in May 1973, and persistently advocated the application of MFA provisions in import restrictions (Yamazawa 1988, p.415).

Textile producer associations intensified their demand for restricting imports under the provisions of the MFA after they experienced a sharp rise in imports in 1984, and Japan posted its first deficit in the textile trade in 1987.[41] In March 1985, JTIF decided to persuade relevant government agencies to apply the MFA quota restrictions to imported products.[42] JSA, JKIA, and JCSFWA also intensified pressure on the government to introduce the MFA. In November 1986, the Chairman of JSA stated that it would ask relevant ministries to apply the MFA for maintaining orderly imports of cotton yarn. In April and June 1987, JKIA called on MITI to safeguard its interests by introducing the MFA against textile imports. On 21 January 1988, JTIF passed a resolution to use anti-dumping suits against unfair imports and to demand that the government impose restrictions on textile imports under the MFA quota.[43] In May 1988, JCFA expressed its intention to ask the government to put the MFA into action.[44]

These producer associations lobbied the LDP as well. Textile producers have long maintained strong ties with the LDP because owners of small-sized textile factories in *sanchi* often simultaneously engage in agriculture, which constitutes LDP's traditional constituency (Ike 1980, p.538). The LDP organized the Special Committee on Textile Measures at the foundation of the party. The Committee, which mainly comprises Diet members from the prefectures of *sanchi*, played a critical role in relief funding (Ōtake 1979, p.136). The Committee has also showed an interest in textile trade issues. On 30 August 1979, the Committee passed a resolution demanding effective measures to cope with a surge of textile imports and to call for the abolition of the Generalized Scheme of Preferences. On 4 June 1985, the Committee passed a resolution requiring the government to invoke the MFA. The resolution was a result of the earnest lobbying activities by executives from textile circles to the LDP.[45]

In spite of persistent demands from textile circles, MITI has maintained a cautious stance in applying the MFA quota restraints to textile imports. It is said that the Consumer Goods Industries Bureau, which has jurisdiction over the textile industry, has become more sympathetic to textile circles. The bureau, one of the sector-specific vertical bureaus, understands the plight of the industry.[46] However, horizontal bureaus such as the International Trade Policy Bureau and the International Trade Administration Bureau, which consider the issue of the introduction of the MFA from a broader perspective, have remained sceptical about its introduction. They fear that adoption of a protectionist measure like the MFA would provoke international criticism that Japan's action runs counter to its commitment to import more and reduce its huge trade surplus. They are also concerned that the introduction of the MFA would threaten the relationship with Japan's textile trade partners, especially China and South Korea.[47] Furthermore, MITI has preferred selective support based on industrial adjustment policies to uniform protection by import restrictions which cover all firms, including inefficient ones. The Japanese government has regarded the MFA as a last resort after various industrial policies have failed to yield expected results.

Although the pace was slow, textile circles gradually extracted concessions on import restrictions from the government after the late 1980s. The change in the government's stance reflects the content of the textile industry reports.[48] The 1988 report was cautious about the possibility that import restrictions would be imposed under MFA provisions, regarding MFA restrictions as the final resort for specific products during a limited period. However, it recommended that 'appropriate measures such as anti-dumping and countervailing duties based on the GATT rules should be introduced, when a sharp increase in imports was caused by unfair trade practices'.[49] In addition, the report suggested that the investigation subcommittee under the Textile Industry Council conduct periodic investigations on import surges and make recommendations on necessary measures.

The revised textile report released in December 1993 included more flexible provisions for introducing the MFA. This report explicitly spelt out that the MFA was an internationally accepted rule and that its introduction was an international right. The report then stated that it would be desirable to adopt measures to mitigate the adverse effects of a rapid increase in imports on planned structural improvement, business conversion and industrial adjustment. More importantly, the report proposed that the government should consider detailed conditions for putting the MFA into action at a subcommittee on trade issues under the Textile Industry Council.

The Textile Industry Council had set up a subcommittee on trade issues in July 1993 in order to discuss trade issues in textiles. According to one of the recommendations of the textile report in December 1993, the subcommittee started to conduct surveys on the implementation of the MFA in other countries and to discuss detailed conditions for the introduction of the MFA in Japan. In the process of deliberation, the subcommittee organized hearings with nine relevant industrial associations.[50] The subcommittee submitted a recommendation in May 1994, outlining the conditions that would be prudent for introducing the MFA. They included political conditions such as the effects on foreign countries and consumers. They also covered the following aspects of market conditions: shares of imported products; ratio of import growth; and changes in the volume of production as well as in the number of manufacturing establishments. The recommendation also suggested that the period of introduction should be within three years under the strict selection of targeted products, and quotas should be increased at least 6 per cent over the preceding year. Although strict conditions were attached, the decision to introduce the MFA was broadly accepted as essential by textile circles.[51] Based on this recommendation, MITI published guidelines for the procedure of textile safeguards in December 1994.[52]

The change of the government's stance in favour of import restrictions was a result of the persistent commitments by textile circles through members of the Textile Committee of the Industrial Structure Council and the Textile Industry Council, and also a result of direct demands on the government. Both councils include quite a few representatives from textile industrial associations. For example, when the 1988 report was drawn up, 20 out of 44 members of the Textile Industry Council and 5 out of 13 members of the Textile Committee of the Industrial Structure Council were representatives from industrial associations which belonged to JTIF. In the 1994 report case, 15 out of 42 members of the Textile Industry Council and 3 out of 11 members of the Textile Committee of the Industrial Structure Council were from industrial associations which joined JTIF.

The change in the 1988 report reflected the opinions of these members. For example, Susumu Okamoto, Chairman of JCFA and a member of the Textile Industry Council, explicitly spelt out in May 1988 that he strove to reflect opinions of the industry on the report. Saburo Takizawa, Chairman of JSA and another member of the Textile Industry Council, expressed his dissatisfaction with import policies in the report, demanding stricter measures.[53]

The actions by textile circles in the deliberation of the 1993 report were more salient. Textile circles hoped that two points would be written in the report. One was that the MFA was an internationally accepted rule and it would be put in practice when the conditions were met. The other was that a committee to discuss the conditions and a system for introducing the MFA would be established. In April 1993, the Trade Policy Division of the Consumer Goods Industries Bureau drew up a preliminary draft of the interim report. This draft was sceptical about the introduction of the MFA, pointing out that its introduction would produce 'unfavourable side effects' such as damage to the interests of domestic consumers and users, and the survival of inefficient manufacturers in the industry, and regarded the introduction of the MFA as a measure that the government had to take in spite of these unfavourable side effects.[54] The draft did not suggest establishing an organization to discuss the issue of the MFA, either. The draft adopted the basic stance of the previous report without any significant change.[55]

When the draft was published, major producer associations were disappointed with it, and lobbied the government to revise it. JCFA submitted a paper on 11 May, which called on the government to recommend in the interim report that the MFA should be introduced when import surges caused market disruption, and that an organization to discuss concrete conditions for introducing the MFA should be established.[56] JTIF confirmed on 21 May that unless the demands from the industry were accepted, deliberation on the report should be held over to the final report, and not released as part of the interim report. The federation also demanded that a committee to discuss trade issues should include members who are familiar with the severe circumstances of the industry.[57]

The interim report announced on 8 June 1993 deleted the phrase 'unfavourable side effects' as too negative to the introduction of the MFA. The report also suggested establishing a special subcommittee to discuss the conditions for introducing the MFA. The industry also succeeded in sending a representative to this six-member subcommittee.

TRADE POLICY PREFERENCES OF INDUSTRIAL ASSOCIATIONS AND FIRMS

Textile circles have filed three anti-dumping suits and one countervailing suit and have gradually extracted concessions from the government over the introduction of the MFA. To test the argument that as firms have intensified their multinational operations, they have opposed the introduction of protectionist measures, we need to examine the preferences and actions of internationally oriented textile producers towards these moves within textile circles.

Trade policy preferences of industrial associations

Not only are the stances of the numerous industrial associations in the textile industry towards import restrictions diverse, but some industrial associations have displayed inconsistent views as users of intermediate products and as producers of competing products of imported goods. Manufacturing associations such as JCSFWA, JKIA and JSRFWA explicitly support the introduction of the MFA. These associations are composed of small and medium-sized firms whose international operations are minimal. They support the introduction of the MFA on the products they manufacture, but they do not oppose the introduction of the MFA on imports of yarns, although they are users of yarns.

Towel manufacturers are in a unique position. Since they were suffering from rising imports of towel products, they demanded the introduction of the MFA on towel imports. At the same time, as users, they were heavily dependent on imported cotton yarns. Eighty per cent of their input came from overseas, with 15 per cent directly supplied to weaving houses and only 5 per cent supplied to the market by domestic yarn spinners. Only one domestic company produced 20-count cotton yarn against which JSA filed an anti-dumping suit in December 1993.[58] Therefore, JTMA was cautious about imposing import restrictions on cotton yarns. When JSA filed the anti-dumping suit in December 1993, JTMA opposed this action. One week after the suit, JTMA sent a letter to JSA in which it called for the establishment of a stable supply system for cotton yarn.[59] JTMA also asked the textile federation to persuade the spinning association to withdraw the suit, hinting at the possibility that it might secede from the federation.[60]

JAIC also adopts an ambiguous stance on import restrictions. Apparel makers, which have developed their business with few regulations and little support from the government, prefer to operate without regulation of their activities including international trade (JAIC 1993, p.4). A more substantial reason why apparel makers are reluctant to introduce import restrictive measures lies in their international operations. The bulk of imported clothing is products manufactured by joint venture plants or local manufacturers under outward processing agreements with Japanese apparel makers. The introduction of import restraint measures in the Japanese market will impede their own exports and disrupt their overseas business. This is the reason why there is little or no move to restrain imports in the clothing sector, although the rise in imports in this sector is the most conspicuous. Thus, the position of apparel makers is similar to that of electronics firms which had little incentive to restrain rising imports of consumer electronic products. At the same time, apparel makers are users of domestic fabrics, and have cultivated linkages with the upstream and midstream manufacturers. They are concerned that the spinning and weaving sectors may lose planning and development capabilities due to rising imports. Accordingly, JAIC appreciates the need for import restrictions on cotton yarns and fabrics as a measure to sustain structural adjustment.

JTIA has been the most explicit opponent of import restrictions, and has occasionally taken action to oppose moves that would restrain imports. When the LDP's Special Committee on Textile Measures passed its resolution in June 1985, JTIA sent a letter to 42 members of the Committee asking them to oppose the introduction of the MFA.[61] JTIA's opposing stance on import restrictions was also shown when JKIA filed an anti-dumping suit against Korean knitted sweaters in October 1988. JKIA and the Knit Products Committee of JTIA organized meetings where they discussed measures to restore ordered imports of knit products. However, JKIA decided on the suit without prior consultation in the middle of ongoing negotiations.[62] Some members of the Committee hinted at the possibility that JTIA would secede from JTIF.[63] Furthermore, when the subcommittee under the Textile Industry Council held hearings with major textile associations on the introduction of the MFA, JTIA was opposed to the introduction of the MFA. JTIF, which hoped to demand the introduction of the MFA as the collective will of the industry, asked JTIA to refrain from objecting to the introduction of the MFA.[64] However, JTIA submitted a hearing paper opposing its introduction raising such problems as: the importance of free-trade principles; preservation of consumers' interests; anxiety that import restraints might spread to other items and countries; and the role of Japan in contributing to economic development in Asia (JTIA 1993, p.7).

Trade policy preferences of large textile producers

What stance, then, did JCFA and JSA, which are the associations of large textile firms, take on import restrictions? As already mentioned, JSA itself filed anti-dumping and countervailing suits in 1983 and an anti-dumping suit in 1993. Although JCFA did not lodged a suit, neither did it object to anti-dumping suits. JCFA assisted JKIA with finance and personnel when JKIA filed an anti-dumping suit in 1988. In September 1988, JCFA conducted a dumping investigation of Korean acrylic filament by organizing a special working group to investigate import routes.[65]

JCFA and JSA adopted a position of supporting the introduction of the MFA. JCFA has publicly advocated the introduction of the MFA since 1979, and has spelled out its stance on this issue on various occasions.[66] In March 1988, for instance, Ryohei Suzuki, vice-chairman of JCFA, stressed the necessity of macro-level measures like the introduction of the MFA in order to minimize economic and social costs attended by international structural adjustment in the textile industry.[67] Susumu Okamoto, Chairman of JCFA, also stated in May 1988 that Japan must limit its textile imports if the domestic industry were to survive.[68] JSA has demanded since the mid-1970s that the government put the MFA into practice.

For what reasons, then, have JCFA and JSA demanded the introduction of the MFA? As noted before, the subcommittee under the Textile Industry Council held hearings with nine industrial associations in order to assess their opinions about the introduction of the MFA. According to JCFA's hearing paper, the introduction of the MFA would have five benefits (JCFA 1993, pp.10–12):

(1) maintenance and strength of production technology and a capability to develop products.
(2) a swift and appropriate response to distorted supply pressure.
(3) a breathing space for strengthening linkages with the midstream sector.
(4) a lead time for structural adjustment.
(5) a breathing space for gaining outcomes from prior investment.

JSA maintained that the MFA would provide the preconditions for promoting the transfer to other lines of business by adjusting its speed of the transfer and minimizing friction accompanying it, and for ensuring the effects of investments for upgrading business. The association also asserted that the introduction of the MFA would not yield negative effects on the development of the textile industry for their Asian neighbours and users because it would admit a certain increase in imports. Nor would this impact on consumers because the level of imports of cotton yarns and fabrics had already been high (JSA 1993, pp.14–22).

It is difficult to know the stance of individual firms on import restrictions because it is very rare for them to reveal their views on specific policies. However, several textile producers showed support for the introduction of the MFA. For example, a general manager of Toray asserted that Toray had openly provided support for the introduction of the MFA.[69] Teijin and Kanebo also maintained that their views towards the MFA were in line with those of their industrial association.[70] Uriu (1996, p.85) asserts that the diverse stances on trade policy between large and small firms in the textile industry explain

Table 6.9   Policy stance of major industrial associations on import restrictions

Association	Sector	Firm size	International linkages	Stance on import restrictions
JCFA	fibre making	big	FDI	support
JSA	spinning	big	FDI	support
JCSFWA	weaving	small	minimal	support
JSRFWA	weaving	small	minimal	support
JKIA	knitting	small	minimal	support
JTMA	towel making	small	yarn importers	ambiguous
JAIC	apparel	mixed	FDI	ambiguous
JTIA	importing	mixed	importers	oppose

why the industry could not obtain protection. However, the analysis here demonstrates that even the large producers became supportive of protectionist measures.

To summarize, domestically oriented industrial associations composed of small and medium-sized firms have aggressively maintained the demand for import restrictions. In contrast, the associations which have some form of international linkages, such as imports of intermediate inputs, overseas production, or imports of products, give reluctant support to or oppose imports restrictions (Table 6.9). Given the fact that these associations include those composed of small and medium-sized firms, international linkages are a critical factor in formulating policy preferences of firms and sectors. What is of interest is that JCFA and JSA supported moves to implement protectionist measures, although they comprise large companies that have international operations. While JSA initiated the anti-dumping suits, JCFA positively supported the anti-dumping files by other industrial associations. Both associations have supported the move to invoke the MFA. We have to consider why large textile producers and their industrial associations have adopted a policy stance supportive of protectionist measures.

POLICY PREFERENCES OF LARGE TEXTILE PRODUCERS

Internationalization of corporate activities and policy preferences

The preference of large textile producers for protectionist measures had various origins. First of all, it is necessary to examine their preferences in terms of international activities. Recall that the textile industry was the first among the Japanese manufacturing sectors to transfer production bases overseas, and its leading companies are regarded as being involved in a vast array of international operations through direct investment and international subcontracting (Dicken 1992, p.258). However, the overseas operations of Japanese textile producers have not necessarily been successful. One illustration of unsuccessful overseas operations is withdrawal from overseas markets. Horaguchi (1992) compiles the number of firms which withdrew from Asia. In the textile industry, 222 affiliated firms withdrew between 1973 and 1986, accounting for 52.2 per cent of total firms that advanced into Asia in the same period (Table 6.10). This figure was extremely high compared with other sectors. The withdrawal from overseas operations was prominent at the individual firm level. For example, Teijin retreated from five overseas affiliates in the 1970s, and an additional 15 in the early 1980s.[71] Kanebo also withdrew from seven overseas affiliates in the 1970s and four in the 1980s.[72] As a consequence, the level of overseas operation in the textile industry remained almost unchanged through the 1980s, although it was relatively high in the late 1970s.[73] This is in a sharp contrast to the automobile and electronics industries which have steadily expanded overseas operations.

The high level of withdrawal from overseas operations in the 1970s

Table 6.10   Number of withdrawals of Japanese affiliates in Asia

Sector	A	B	100B/A
Food	393	75	19.1
Textiles	425	222	52.2
Wood and pulp	236	55	23.3
Chemicals	588	107	18.2
Metals, non-ferrous metals	446	148	33.2
General machinery	532	81	15.2
Electrical machinery	826	153	18.5
Transport machinery	252	36	14.3
Other manufacturing	865	221	25.5
Manufacturing total	4,563	1,098	24.1

Note: A denotes the number of inroads firms.
B denotes the number of withdrawn firms. The numbers are accumulated figures between 1973 and 1986.
Source: Horaguchi (1992, p.159).

and the early 1980s stemmed from factors relevant to the host countries as well as in the domestic market. In South Korea and Taiwan, local partners of joint ventures sought to expand business aggressively, and local governments supported this strategy. The Japanese partners, who were not keen on overseas business expansion, hesitated over new capital commitments and often retreated from the joint ventures.[74] In ASEAN countries, overall economic conditions were depressed until the mid-1980s, and most subsidiaries of Japanese textile firms incurred losses. For example, between 1974 and 1983, Toray's businesses in Thailand, Malaysia and Indonesia suffered operating losses except for the three years from 1978 to 1980.[75] The intensification of import restraints in advanced countries also led to a deterioration of profitability for Japanese affiliates in East Asia.

On the domestic front, Japanese parent companies were confronted with severe management problems in the 1970s and the early 1980s. The recession caused by the first oil shock in 1973 resulted in a protracted business slump in the textile industry. The first oil shock led to a sharp increase in prices of raw fibre materials. This increase, coupled with a rise in labour and fuel costs, contributed to rising production costs. In addition, the second oil shock in 1979 led to a sluggish demand for textiles. Accordingly, major textile firms were forced to implement drastic adjustment programs. Between 1973 and 1978, the number of employees in the seven major synthetic fibre companies fell from 93,000 to 53,000, while those in the nine major spinning companies fell from 99,000 to 56,000 (Okamoto 1988, p.79). Between 1970 and 1980, the number of textile workers decreased by approximately 359,000, 20.5 per cent of the total employed in the industry.[76] Efforts to retrench business by scrapping production facilities and laying off excess workers included curtailment in overseas operations. Major textile firms retreated from most of their overseas production bases. Teijin has retained only two plants in Thailand and one plant in Indonesia, while Kanebo has one plant in Indonesia, Malaysia and Australia. Toray alone maintained a large number of overseas production bases, six manufacturing plants in Indonesia, five in Malaysia, four in Thailand and one in South Korea.

A sharp yen appreciation after 1985 exacerbated the recession in the textile industry. The synthetic-fibre sector, in particular, was hit hardest because the sector exported half of its domestic production. The synthetic-fibre makers initiated a production cut in polyester filament in July 1986, but the price of polyester filament in late 1987 dropped to two-thirds of the price when the cutback started.[77] Major textile firms were forced to undertake restructuring programmes, mainly the dismissal and transfer of a redundant workforce. In the case of Teijin, for example, the total workforce was reduced from some 10,000 in 1985 to some 7,000 in 1988.[78] Between 1986 and 1989, the export ratio in total textile production decreased from 33 per cent to 24 per cent.

The synthetic-fibre sector recovered from the recession as a consequence of the *shingosen* boom starting in 1989.[79] *Shingosen* products, mainly used as materials for women's clothing, contributed to the expansion of the domestic market for synthetic fibres. During this period, synthetic-fibre makers made investments to expand production capacity. But Toray's investment was directed to overseas plants, and the company coped with the increase in demand by purchasing yarn at the market.[80]

The build-up of overseas production bases by textile companies resumed in 1992. Major synthetic-fibre companies have built joint ventures mainly in China. Kanebo, the most active investor in China, established two joint ventures in 1992, another two in 1993, and six in 1994. Teijin regards 1995 as the first year of globalization, and seeks to develop its overseas operations.[81] Toray also established a Trade Business Division in January 1995 whose objectives are to promote global operations as well as to deal with the import business.[82] The advance into China aims to supply yarns and fabrics to local apparel plants which suffer from losses of delivery time as well as from the cost of transport and tariffs. In addition, some companies have moved to build up integrated production systems from yarn production to the weaving and dyeing processes.

In brief, the curtailment in overseas operations during the 1970s and the early 1980s had a substantial effect on corporate attitudes in the textile sector. Toray alone has been able to maintain an integrated international production system from fibre production to spinning, weaving, and dyeing, and to divide its business between Japan and Southeast Asia. Toray feels little need for the introduction of the MFA on its own account, although it considers that application of the MFA is necessary for the textile industry as a whole.[83] In contrast, other textile producers which have not developed effective overseas operations have little or no interest in resisting protectionist measures.

The other factor that has induced textile firms to favour import restrictions is the direction of exports from the affiliates of Japanese textile firms in East Asia. Affiliates long avoided exporting to the

Table 6.11   Shares of exports to Japan by Japanese affiliates in Asia,
1980–95 (per cent)

Sector	1980	1983	1986	1989	1992	1995
Food	30.2	13.4	31.6	16.1	26.5	12.5
Textiles	4.0	5.3	10.3	14.9	14.2	20.9
Wood and pulp	30.8	39.1	25.5	35.9	47.2	13.6
Chemicals	8.9	9.3	3.8	10.3	4.9	4.1
Iron and steel	10.1	7.5	5.2	4.2	2.1	2.7
Non-ferrous metals	2.6	0.4	31.8	12.1	21.4	13.2
General machinery	5.5	15.2	31.4	18.2	23.6	28.5
Electrical machinery	16.2	21.0	22.2	26.9	27.2	28.7
Transport machinery	1.9	5.5	5.3	1.6	1.7	2.2
Precision machinery	9.1	30.5	21.9	22.2	51.8	51.5
Petro and coal	–	0.0	0.0	0.0	0.0	46.7
Others	6.0	7.9	7.7	12.1	9.4	15.8
Manufacturing total	9.8	10.8	15.8	15.8	15.8	18.8

Sources: MITI, *Kaigai toshi tokei soran* [Statistical Report on Foreign
Investment], No.1–No.6.

Japanese market. According to MITI survey data, the ratio of exports
to Japan by textile affiliates in Asia was 4.0 per cent in 1980 and 20.9
per cent in 1992 (Table 6.11). A 17 percentage point rise in this ratio
indicates that Japanese textile firms were to re-direct exporting to
Japan. However, the figure in 1980 was extremely low given that the
textile industry was relatively advanced in terms of foreign operations
at that time. The industry accounted for 13 per cent of cumulative
manufacturing investments between 1951 and 1980, and the 4 per
cent overseas production ratio in textiles in 1980 was higher than the
manufacturing average, at 2.9 per cent.[84] Even in the 1990s, the ratio
was relatively low considering that standardized textile products from
Asian countries are very competitive in price and the import volume
of textile products doubled between 1986 and 1992. This peculiarity
becomes clear if the textile sector is compared with the electronics
sector where reverse imports in consumer electronic goods have been
growing rapidly since the late 1980s.

The low ratio of textile exports to Japan is partly accounted for by
the tendency of Japanese textile producers to restrain reverse imports.
This propensity was first shaped by administrative guidance. When
Japanese textile producers decided to make inroads into overseas
markets in the early 1970s, they were encouraged by MITI not to
reimport the products manufactured there to Japan. In some cases,

firms were required to submit sworn documents that they would not reimport textile products to Japan.[85] There was no such guidance in the 1980s, but Japanese textile producers seem to have maintained a propensity against importing. For instance, Toray manufactures synthetic staple and filament in ASEAN countries and exports these products to various countries, but not to Japan until recently. Toray explained why it did not import cheap textile products from Asian plants as follows: 'If Toray imports such products to the Japanese market, it would lead to serious damage to the Japanese textile industry. We have to consider the balance of the whole economy, not the interests of consumers alone' (Ishizawa 1992, pp.169–70). Toray's action could be seen as an aspect of what Dore (1986) terms 'natural immunity'.[86]

Thus, major synthetic-fibre companies long avoided importing products manufactured in overseas markets. In the mid-1990s, this changed. In September 1994, Katsunosuke Maeda, President of Toray, created a stir in the industry by proclaiming that Toray would import polyester products from its overseas plants. In January 1995, Toray established the Trade Business Division whose major task was to import fibre and fabric manufactured in plants in Southeast Asia. The aim of reverse imports was to maintain the market share which was being lost to South Korean and Taiwanese makers.[87] Toyobo also decided to start reverse imports from its joint venture plant in Thailand. The company commenced production of polyester knit fabrics in April 1995, and plans to export all products to Japan.[88] In spite of this trend, major textile producers have not changed their stance on import restrictions. Other factors have also influenced the policy preferences of large textile producers.

Industrial structure and policy preferences

The structure of the textile industry influences the attitudes of large textile producers towards protection. The dual structure of the textile industry – a few big companies and a great number of small and medium-scale firms – is a widespread phenomenon in Japanese industry. In textiles, however, small-sized firms dominate the industry in terms of employment and establishments. More than 60 per cent in textile firms have between one and three employees, 20 per cent higher than the manufacturing average (Table 6.12). In terms of total employees, the share of these small-sized firms was roughly three times as large as that of the manufacturing average. These small-sized firms are family factories typically operated by three workers, the

Table 6.12   Shares of establishments with less than four employees, 1993 (per cent)

Sector	Establishments	Employees	Value added
Food	30.8	3.7	1.3
Textiles	61.1	15.3	6.9
Apparel	39.6	7.2	5.1
Wood	39.2	9.7	5.0
Chemicals	10.5	0.3	0.2
Petro and coal	11.3	1.0	0.4
Iron and steel	21.5	1.1	0.4
Non-ferrous metals	30.2	2.2	0.9
Metals	42.2	8.2	3.6
General machinery	41.1	5.3	2.5
Electrical machinery	21.4	1.1	0.5
Transport machinery	31.8	1.6	0.5
Precision machinery	38.0	3.7	1.7
Others	55.4	14.3	5.7
Manufacturing total	40.6	5.2	1.8

Sources: MITI, *Kogyo tokeihyo: Sangyohen* [Census of Manufactures: Report by Industry], 1993.

owner, his wife and another family member. Owing to their small corporate size, small firms had scant management resources to diversify their business or to relocate their operations offshore. They could only make adjustments to reduce excess capacity and to modernise machines and equipment. Large textile producers have assumed a leadership role in an industry with a majority of small-sized firms.[89] They have tended to resist measures which would undermine the interests of the majority of firms in the industry.

Big textile firms in the upstream stage also need to maintain close relations with firms in the mid- and downstream stages. The synthetic-fibre and spinning firms and weaving houses have been linked by service fee contracts since the 1950s. Under these contracts, yarn makers or trading houses supply yarns to weaving houses, which return the woven textiles to them in exchange for service fees based on the amount of woven textiles they produce (Itoh and Urata 1994, p.20). In the 1950s, weaving service fee contracts between major spinning companies and weaving houses expanded. Weaving production under service fee contracts enabled spinning manufacturers to ensure a stable market for yarn as well as to avoid risk arising from uncertainties about fluctuations in the price of raw materials and yarn and in the exchange rate (Fujii 1971, pp.113–14).

Service fee contracts have been prevalent in the synthetic-fibre sector as well. Synthetic-fibre makers produce two kinds of fibres: staple and filament. While most of staple is provided to spinning makers, filament is supplied to weaving houses. When synthetic-fibre makers succeeded in mass production of nylon and polyester in the 1950s, it was critical to ensure a stable market for these products. The fibre makers could select one of two options in ensuring a sales market. One was to integrate the weaving and dyeing process into their own operations. The other was to negotiate service fee contracts with weaving and dyeing houses. Since textile products are highly susceptible to movements in business cycles, and a division of labour between yarn producers and weavers had developed in the Japanese textile industry, synthetic-fibre makers selected the latter method (Uekusa and Nanbu 1973, pp.198–202). The synthetic-fibre makers actively invited weaving houses to enter their group in the late 1950s and the early 1960s.[90] Accordingly, the percentage of service fee contracts in the total synthetic-fibre weaving production continued at more than 60 per cent (Table 6.13).

As uncertainties in the market reduced, service fee contracts directly agreed with yarn makers declined, while those with local trading houses increased. However, yarn makers which invited major local trading houses into their group, assumed substantial responsibility for production development and risk (PFC 1990, p.116). The presence of excellent weaving houses is crucial for yarn makers. Synthetic-fibre makers have introduced new materials to the market. The quick transformation of new materials into new products has much to do with technical skills of weaving houses in dealing with new materials (Itoh and Urata 1994, p.21). The yarn makers retain a portion of yarns for their own brand products as 'maker chop' prod-

Table 6.13   Shares of service fee contracts in woven products, 1965–95 (per cent)

Product	1965	1970	1975	1980	1985	1990	1995
Cotton	42	44	48	45	49	50	48
Wool	49	63	71	76	77	72	73
Synthetic Fibre	64	61	63	65	67	66	63
Textile Total	50	54	58	58	60	60	59

Note: The figures are the share of productions under service fee contracts in total production.
Source: MITI, *Seni tokei nenpo* [Annual Report on Textile Statistics], each year.

ucts. The technical skills of weaving houses are particularly important for maintaining the competitiveness of 'maker chop' products. For example, it is often said that *shingosen* was produced as a consequence of the R & D efforts of synthetic-fibre companies. However, a key factor in the development of *shingosen* lay in the vertical planning and production systems which supported technology and cooperative relations in the process of yarn plying, weaving, dyeing and finishing.[91] *Shingosen* would not have emerged without the existence of the excellent weaving production teams and their cooperation. It is said that Japanese differentiated fibre products are ten years in advance of those from South Korea and Taiwan. This is because the Japanese fibre industry retains excellent weaving houses.[92]

The synthetic-fibre companies understand the importance of the weaving houses, as shown by the fact that Toray regards the production teams as its internal plants.[93] They have actively supported weaving houses to increase their technology level and develop new products.[94] At the same time, they sought to avoid policies that lower the competitiveness of the production teams. It is said that Toray decided to start imports from its overseas plants after it confirmed that its production teams could shift from standardized to differentiated production lines.[95]

In addition to the links to the midstream stage through service fee contracts, synthetic-fibre and spinning firms have promoted forward vertical integration for several reasons. First, the profit margin is higher in the downstream sector. In the case of men's suits, for instance, the value of the raw material is doubled in the yarn manufacture stage, increases five times in the fabric production stage, 25 times in the wholesale stage, and 75 times in the retail stage (Itoh 1994, p.16). Large textile firms have not only established divisions or subsidiaries to produce woven goods, apparel and made-up goods, but also promoted tie-ups with manufacturers of apparel and made-up goods. The second factor promoting forward vertical integration is the existence of a large uniform and quasi-uniform market in Japan (Itoh 1994, p.17). The large demand for school uniforms and company uniforms enable large spinning producers to enjoy economies of scale. The weaving divisions of large spinning producers have their own finishing facilities, and coordinate the weaving and finishing processes for such large volume products.

Recent pressure from rising imports has forced the Japanese textile industry to set up systematic production linkages among firms. Owing to production cost disadvantage, it is almost impossible for domestic manufacturers of standard textile products to compete with imported goods on price. They therefore seek to differentiate their goods in non-price areas. The development of differentiated products requires systematic linkages among the vertical stages, namely, the combination of skills and information in fibre production, spinning, weaving, dyeing, and apparel making enables textile makers to produce differentiated products.[96] Furthermore, as a measure to enhance efficiency, the industry sought to establish a quick response system.[97] Successful implementation of the quick response system requires collaboration between the up-, mid- and downstream sectors. Intense and systematic relationships among various subsectors make large textile producers less willing to adopt a policy stance which contradicts the interests of the majority in the industry.

Import pressure and policy preferences

The third factor pushing large textile producers to favour protectionist measures is that they faced a serious threat from rising imports in their core sector. Some big textile producers have diversified their business activities to new fields such as pharmaceuticals and biotechnology.[98] As a result, the share of non-textiles in total sales among nine major synthetic-fibre companies increased sharply from 6.8 per cent in 1964 to 57.8 per cent in 1994 (Sakura Research Institute 1995, p.4). However, the majority of these firms are still dependent on the textile areas for obtaining a stable corporate revenue. Toray, which is regarded as having successfully diversified its business, gained 43.2 per cent of total sales from textiles in 1993, while 24.4 per cent were from plastics and chemicals and 20.8 per cent from housing and engineering. Teijin gained 59.9 per cent from textiles, 16.9 per cent from plastics and chemicals and 7.8 per cent from pharmaceuticals and medical products in 1993. As capital-intensive industries, synthetic-fibre and spinning companies have to maintain a certain manufacturing level of standard products. Stable production of standard goods enables firms to maintain employment and profits, and stable profits from standard product sales support R & D expenditure on high-value-added products or the diversification to related business fields. It is also difficult to differentiate standard products and high-value-added ones in technology development. Technology which generates high-value-added products is created in the mass-production process of standard products.[99]

Since the mid-1980s, Japanese textile producers have been apprehensive about the rapid increase in the production capacity of their Asian neighbours. Japanese production capacity in synthetic fibres has been surpassed by Asian countries. Production capacity of polyester staple was exceeded by Taiwan before 1985 and by South Korea and China in 1991, and production in polyester filament was surpassed by China before 1985 and by South Korea and Taiwan in 1990 (JCFA 1993, p.1). Among the four major synthetic fibres, Japanese synthetic-fibre makers maintain an advantage in acrylic alone. The rapid build-up of production capacity in these countries is likely to be transformed into export pressure on the Japanese market. Japan, which has no quota under the MFA and is geographically close to Asian countries, will be a target for their exports.

Market conditions in the spinning sector are more acute. Owing to a decline in international competitiveness, the Japanese spinning sector has been obliged to reduce its operations. The number of firms fell from 84 in 1980 to 42 in 1994, and the number of plants fell from 168 to 88 in the same period (Table 6.14). The increase in production capacity in Asian countries is prominent in the spinning sector as well. Between 1985 and 1991, the number of spindles increased by 81.7 per cent in China, 95.7 per cent in Pakistan and 86.7 per cent in Indonesia, while that of looms increased by 44.1 per cent in China and 50 per cent in Indonesia during the same period (JSA 1993, p.3). The recent build-up in production capacity has contributed to a rise in imports to the Japanese market. Thus, a rapid build-up in production capacity in Asian countries is a critical factor encouraging large textile producers to take a stance similar to that of small and medium-sized firms.

Table 6.14   Major industrial indicators in the Japanese spinning sector, 1970–94

	1970	1980	1985	1990	1991	1992	1993	1994
Firms	103	84	71	53	52	50	45	42
Plants	208	168	148	122	120	110	99	88
Spindles ('000)	9,439	8,668	7,828	6,515	6,285	5,861	5,001	4,330
Employees ('000)	122	60	48	35	33	27	19	16

Note: The figures are concerned with firms which belong to JSA.
Sources: JSA (1993, p.13) and interview (JSA, Tokyo, September 1995).

CONCLUSION

While the cases in Chapter 4 and 5 belong to 'soft' cases which were selected in terms of their high degree of internationalization, this chapter sought to test the central hypothesis by taking up a 'hard' case. The Japanese textile industry, like that in other developed countries, has suffered from rising import pressure from developing countries since the 1980s. In order to cope with import pressure, textile circles have intensified their demand for import restrictions. Four out of seven anti-dumping and countervailing petitions in Japanese industry were lodged by the textile industry. The demand by the textile industry for invoking the MFA intensified over time. How did the internationalization of corporate activity affect firms' policy preferences towards rising import pressure? Did internationally oriented firms resist the demand for protectionst measures due to their international ties?

The answers to these questions are ambiguous. Several industrial associations were reluctant to support protectionist policies because of their international linkages. JAIC would not accept import restrictions at the downstream stage, although it accepted import restrictions at the up- and midstream stages. This was because the Japanese apparel makers had developed local production in East Asian countries, and they were also heavily involved in imports from production bases there to Japan. JTMA demanded restrictions on imports of towel products, yet the association opposed them on cotton yarn because its members were heavily dependent on imported cotton yarn as an input for production. JTIA has been a vocal opponent of import restrictions. It resisted the move to introduce the MFA, on the one hand, and opposed an anti-dumping suit, on the other hand. It has adopted an anti-protectionist stance because its members were importers. Thus, the policy stance of these industrial associations gives credence to the argument that firms with international ties prefer an open trade policy. Although basic characteristics are different between the hard and soft cases, greater international linkages have encouraged firms to change their preferences towards supporting an open domestic market.

The textile industry also included cases where industrial associations adopted a protectionist stance in spite of their international linkages. This was the stance of JCFA and JSA, the two major producer associations in the industry. Although they comprised big synthetic-fibre and spinning companies with international linkages, they stood in line with JKIA, JCSFWA, and JSRFWA, the associations of domestically oriented small firms. The degree of internationalization had a great bearing on their attitudes. The spinning and synthetic-fibre makers became the first investors in overseas markets in Japanese industry in the late 1960s and the early 1970s. However, their multinational operations did not develop, and there were successive withdrawals in the 1970s and the early 1980s. They also restrained imports from their overseas plants to Japan until recently in order to avoid unfavourable effects on domestic producers. Accordingly, they had little interest in resisting the demand for protectionist measures. Their stance favouring protectionst policies was also shaped by domestic linkages and the industrial structure in textiles. The synthetic-fibre and spinning firms that belong to JCFA and JSA have maintained service fee contracts with small and medium-sized weaving houses since the 1950s. They have also enhanced their interest in downward stage operations by promoting forward integration. Furthermore, rising import pressure urged the Japanese textile industry to strengthen systematic linkages among up-, mid- and downstream stages in order to enhance non-price competitiveness and to produce differentiated products. Thus, large textile firms maintain extensive domestic linkages, motivating them to incline towards a protectionist stance. The large textile firms, the most powerful actors in the industry, have regarded themselves as the leaders of the industry whose majority are small-sized firms. They are reluctant to push for measures which conflict with the interests of the majority in the industry.

7 Keidanren's Stance on Trade and Investment Policies

In the previous case study chapters, three industrial sectors – automobiles, electronics and textiles – were taken up in order to examine whether rising international corporate activities has affected firms' trade policy preferences. The case studies basically support the contention that firms with significant international operations prefer an open domestic market, with some exceptions to this in the textile industry. This chapter seeks to deepen our understanding of the relations between increased international business activity and corporate positions on commercial policy in Japan through an analysis of Keidanren. Keidanren is the leading organization through which Japanese big business influences policy making, and multinational corporations are its major members. The federation's stance and activities on various trade policies reflect the policy preferences of multinational corporations.

Several policy issues are examined to elucidate Keidanren's stance on commercial policy. The first set of issues concerns deregulation and inward investment in Japan. Deregulation became Keidanren's primary policy objective in the 1990s. Deregulation directly aimed to relax and eliminate government regulations on private business activities, and also had a great bearing on improving market access by foreign firms to Japan. Japan's regulated economic system fostered the image of a closed Japanese market. More business opportunities and the enhanced domestic demand created by deregulation led to better market access for foreign goods and firms and, more controversially, a reduction in Japan's trade surplus. Keidanren promoted deregulation through the submission of recommendations, negotiations with bureaucrats and politicians and cooperation with the Economic Reform Council, which was established with an eye to providing a blueprint for Japan's structural reform. Keidanren also published policy papers aimed at encouraging the government to offer a better environment for inward investment.

The second set of issues that this chapter focuses on in order to examine Keidanren's stance on trade policy is farm products trade and agricultural policy. The federation raised its voice in favour of the liberalization of agricultural imports after it established the Committee on Agricultural Policy (CAP) in 1980. Keidanren's stance on farm products trade evolved as Japanese manufacturing industries strengthened export dependence, and criticism of Japan's trade surplus became serious after the late 1970s. This chapter examines the reasons why Keidanren demanded liberalization of agricultural imports, and what influence its actions had on farm products trade and agricultural policy.

Keidanren was also committed to improving standards and certification systems in the early 1980s, as foreign firms and governments intensified their criticism of such Japanese trade-related administrative systems as non-tariff barriers. Not only did Keidanren release a number of recommendations for reform of the standards and certification systems, but it supported positively the activities of the Second Provisional Commission on Administrative Reform (*Daini Rincho*) which aimed to promote rationalization of administrative operations.

Before examining Keidanren's activities on these policy issues in detail, the first part of the chapter highlights organizational changes within Keidanren which had their origins in rising internationalization, in an attempt to investigate the changing influence of internationally oriented firms and sectors within Keidanren.

EFFECTS OF INTERNATIONALIZATION ON KEIDANREN'S INTERNAL ORGANIZATION

The central issue is whether Keidanren intensified its commitment to liberalization of the Japanese market as Japanese firms strengthened their international operations. In order to clarify causal relationships between the internationalization of corporate activities and Keidanren's commitment to an open domestic market, it is necessary to explore whether internationally oriented firms and sectors enhanced their status within the federation. There are three indicators of the rising influence of internationally oriented sectors and firms within Keidanren. The first is the composition of member companies. The number of corporate members of Keidanren has gradually increased from less than 800 in 1975 to 970 in 1994 (Table 7.1).[1] The composition of membership by sector reveals several features.

Table 7.1   Number of corporate members in Keidanren by sector, 1975–94

Sector	1975	1980	1985	1990	1994
Fishery	8	5	5	5	5
Mining	22	22	21	20	18
Construction	45	45	50	62	70
Food	31	31	34	36	34
Textiles	37	34	35	37	39
Wood and pulp	24	23	24	22	20
Chemicals	74	75	81	91	92
Oil and coal	14	15	16	15	15
Rubbers	12	12	11	10	10
Ceramics and cement	22	21	21	22	21
Iron and steel	29	28	28	27	26
Non-ferrous metals	15	16	14	15	17
General machinery	41	41	44	45	47
Electrical machinery	40	39	56	64	68
Transport machinery	29	29	32	32	35
Precision machinery	19	17	20	24	25
Commerce	54	67	76	78	81
Finance	179	186	178	186	184
Real estate	10	11	12	16	19
Transportation	37	36	37	45	46
Services	43	49	68	80	93
Others	2	2	3	5	6
Total	787	804	866	937	971

Sources: Compiled from *Keidanren Kaiin Meibo*, 1975, 1980, 1985, 1990, 1994.

One is the expansion of members in the services sector. Membership in the services sector increased significantly from 43 to 93 between 1975 and 1994. Membership in the commerce sector also expanded in the early 1980s as a result of the participation of large retail stores. Within the manufacturing sector, membership in the electrical machinery sector increased from 40 in 1975 to 68 in 1994, reflecting the strong growth of the sector.

The second indicator is the affiliation of Keidanren's executive personnel (Table 7.2). The executive personnel is decided with consideration to shifts in the structure of Japanese industry, coordination among financial *keiretsu* groupings and so on. Keidanren increased the number of vice-chairmen from seven or eight in the 1970s to 12 in the mid-1980s. This was partly because the federation accepted new members from the services sector. In the 1960s and 1970s, a consid-

Table 7.2   Posts of chairman and vice-chairmen of Keidanren by sector

Sector	5/1968	5/1974	5/1980	5/1986	12/1990	5/1994
Mining	–	1	–	–	–	–
Food	–	–	–	–	1	1
Textiles	–	1	–	–	–	–
Chemicals	1	1	1	1	1	1
Iron and steel	1	1	2	2	1	–
General machinery	–	–	–	–	1	–
Electronics	–	–	1	2	2	3
Transport equipment	2	*1*	1	1	1	–
Automobile	–	1	1	1	1	2
Trading	1	–	–	1	1	1
Distribution	–	–	–	–	1	1
Banking	1	1	1	2	1	2
Securities	–	–	–	–	1	–
Insurance	–	–	–	–	–	1
Oil and coal	–	–	1	1	–	–
Transport	–	1	1	–	–	–
Electric power	–	–	1	1	*1*	1
Keidanren's Secre.	2	–	1	1	–	–
Total	8	8	11	13	13	13

Note: Figures in italic include the post of chairman.
Source: Honjo (1993, pp.355–67); *Asahi Shimbun* (28 May 1994).

erable number of posts was allocated to leaders from the heavy and chemical industries. However, Keidanren accepted leaders from newly emerging industries such as the automobile and consumer electronics sectors to the executive posts, although the pace of change in representation was not as rapid as the change in the structure of Japanese industry. In May 1986, a second vice-chairman's post was allocated to the electronics industry and a third in May 1994. The automobile sector also obtained two posts from May 1984 to May 1986 and after May 1992. In contrast, the iron and steel sector, which dominated the chairman's post from May 1980 to December 1990, gained neither the post of chairman nor that of vice-chairman in the change of leadership of May 1994.

The shift of executive posts from the heavy and chemical to the automobile and electronics sectors is also reflected in the post of chairman. Akio Morita, Chairman of Sony, a representative consumer electronics company, was expected to be the eighth chairman of Keidanren. The seventh chairman, Gaishi Hiraiwa, considered Morita as the most suitable candidate because he was well known internationally and was expected to lead Japanese business from an international viewpoint. Morita's illness prevented his succeeding Hiraiwa. Instead, Shoichiro Toyoda, Chairman of Toyota, was selected as the head of Keidanren. The shift in the federation's executive personnel from the heavy and chemical to internationally oriented automobile and electronics industries implies that these internationally oriented sectors have an enhanced influence within Keidanren.

The shift in influence by sector is also reflected in the chairmanship of the policy committees. The number of policy committees increased from 30 in 1980 to 42 in 1995. In 1980, leaders from three sectors – iron and steel, trading and banking – chaired almost half the committees.[2] In 1995, the internationally oriented sectors became more important. Four policy committees were chaired by leaders from the automobile sector, while five committees were chaired by those from the electronics sector.

A third indicator is ranking in terms of membership fees. Although membership fees are confidential, *Mainichi Shimbun* published the ranking in 1992 (Table 7.3). The membership fees are calculated on the basis of a firm's total assets and ordinary profits. The top three companies – Toyota Motor, Tokyo Electric Power and Nippon Steel – are those that assumed the chairmanship after 1980. These firms are followed by Nissan and several major electronics companies. The companies that pay high fees assume Keidanren's executive posts, and play a leadership role.[3] In 1995, all the top ten companies except Kansai Electric Power and Sony assumed a post of

Table 7.3   Ranking of membership fees in Keidanren, 1992

Company	Industrial sector	Membership fee (million yen)
Toyota Motor	Automobile	32.8
Tokyo Electric Power	Electric power	31.4
Nippon Steel	Steel	31.0
Nissan Motor	Automobile	28.3
Hitachi	Electronics	27.3
Toshiba	Electronics	27.3
Matsushita Electric Ind.	Electronics	26.4
Kansai Electric Power	Electric power	23.8
Mitsubishi Heavy Ind.	Transport equipment	23.1
Sony	Electronics	21.0

Source: *Mainichi Shimbun* (2 March 1994).

chairman, vice-chairmen, or chairman, vice-chairmen of the Board of Councillors.

The influence of the internationalization of corporate activity is seen in Keidanren's internal organization. Not only did the number of policy committees increase between 1980 and 1995, their composition also reflects the rising internationalization of corporate activity and the Japanese economy (Table 7.4). In recent years, several policy committees dealing with external issues affecting Japanese corporations have been established. The Committee on Foreign-Affiliated Corporations was established in 1986. This Committee helps foreign-affiliated firms conduct business smoothly in Japan. In 1992, the Committee on *Kyosei* was set up.[4] This Committee aims to reform the corporate behaviour of Japanese firms as well as to examine the compatibility of Japanese institutions and conditions for competition with those in foreign countries. The establishment of the Committee is an indication of the shift in philosophy among Japanese big business from the pursuit of corporate growth to a broader concept including cooperation with society and foreign companies.

The number of bilateral relations committees has sharply increased from six in 1980 to 19 in 1995. These committees deal with bilateral relations with Japan's major trading partners and promote private diplomacy. The increase in the number of the committees reflects an elevation of Keidanren's concern with trade relations with foreign countries.

KEIDANREN'S STANCE ON INWARD INVESTMENT AND DEREGULATION

Keidanren issued recommendations aimed at facilitating investment in Japan in the 1990s. As broadly recognised, investment policy has a great bearing on trade flows and trade policy. An investment imbalance may impede the rectification of trade imbalances. Foreign-affiliated firms maintain a high level of imports.[5] An increased presence of foreign firms in Japan may lead to a reduction in the country's trade surplus. Whichever the case, the huge investment imbalance has intensified the foreign perception that the Japanese market is closed. The other issue that Keidanren took in the 1990s was the promotion of deregulation (*kisei kanwa*).[6] Deregulation has become a critical issue with respect to the Japanese market because a regulated social and economic system heightened the perception of

Table 7.4   Policy committees in Keidanren, 1995

Committee on Basic Strategy
Committee on Corporate Ethics*
Committee on Government Reform
Committee on Public Affairs
Committee on Business and Politics*
Ad-Hoc Committee on Nurturing Creative Human Resources*
Committee on Taxation
Committee on Economic Research
Committee on Fiscal and Monetary Policies
Committee on International Finance
Committee on Economic Structure*
Committee on International Taxation*
Committee on Statistics
Committee on Industrial Affairs
Committee on New Business*
Committee on Competition Policy*
Committee on Environment and Safety
Committee on Information and Telecommunication Policy
Committee on Energy and Resources
Committee on Quality of Life and Consumer Affairs*
Committee on Distribution
Committee on Transportation
Committee on Land Policy*
Committee on Housing and Urban Development
Committee on Concentration Problems in Tokyo*
Committee on Agricultural Policy
Committee on Industrial Technology
Committee on Oceanic Resources
Committee on Life Science
Committee on Corporate Finance
Committee on Economic Legislation
Committee on Corporate Management and Disclosure
Committee on Foreign Relations
Committee on Foreign Trade
Committee on Economic Cooperation
BIAC (Business and Industry Advisory Committee to OECD) Japan
Committee on Trade in Services*
Committee on International Industrial Cooperation*
Committee on Foreign-Affiliated Corporations*
Committee on Kyosei-Economic Symbiosis*
Committee on Corporate Philanthropy*
Committee on Promotion of Inter-Cultural Understanding*
Committee on Commodity Prices**
Committee on Coal Policy**
Committee on Atlantic Institute**

Note: * denotes the committees established between 1980 and 1995.
** denotes committees abolished between 1980 and 1995.
Sources: *Keidanren Jigyo Hokoku*, 1980; *Keidanren Annual Report*, 1995.

Japan as a closed society lacking transparency. Deregulation would also lead to the creation of new business opportunities and stimulate domestic demand. These factors contribute to better market access and the rectification of Japan's trade surplus.

Activities for promoting inward investment

In spite of the removal of formal restrictions on foreign investment, the rise in inward investment in Japan has been slow.[7] While outward investment from Japan has rapidly expanded since the mid-1980s, inward investment has remained at a low level. At the end of 1992, the ratio of outward to inward investment was 1.16 in the United States, 1.24 in the United Kingdom and 2.25 in Germany, while the ratio was 15.99 in Japan (OECD 1994, p.15). According to MITI (1994b, pp.4–15) survey data, in 1992 foreign-affiliated firms accounted for 1.1 per cent of total sales and 0.5 per cent of total employees in Japan. These figures are extremely low compared with other advanced countries.[8]

Keidanren expressed increasing concern about the lack of inward foreign investment in Japan in the 1990s. In order to identify impediments to foreign investment and to dismantle specific regulatory barriers to it, Keidanren took several initiatives. In June 1992, the federation set up an Ad Hoc Committee on Foreign Direct Investment in Japan under the Committee on International Industrial Cooperation and the Committee on Foreign-Affiliated Corporations. This Committee collected views from foreign embassies and companies on Japan's investment climate, presenting the results in a report entitled *Improvement of the Investment Climate and Promotion of Foreign Direct Investment into Japan*.[9] Issued on 27 October 1992, the report recommended nine detailed measures to facilitate the entry of foreign firms. It suggested some preferential incentives to entice foreign investment. The first measure related to taxation, cuts in corporate tax rates, the expansion of tax credits for investment and accelerated depreciation rates. The second measure was a boost to the ceiling of low-rate financing that the Japan Development Bank provided for foreign companies. The report also suggested revising problematic aspects of two private institutions: *keiretsu* groupings and industrial associations. The report pointed out that vertical *keiretsu* groupings, in spite of enhancing efficiency, make entry to intra-*keiretsu* dealings more difficult than that to general markets, while industrial associations create less transparent relations with relevant ministries and limit competition when they complement administration and implement some government functions.

A bold suggestion in the report was the liberalization of Japan's legal system. The Diet passed the Special Measures Law Concerning the Handling of Legal Business by Foreign Lawyers in May 1986, allowing foreign lawyers to practice in Japan at the beginning of April 1987. However, the Law imposed various restrictions on the activities of foreign lawyers. Based on the recognition that legal business cannot be exempted from the liberalization of trade in services, the report demanded the lifting of the regulations on the formation of partnerships with Japanese lawyers, the hiring of Japanese lawyers by foreign attorneys, the use of the name of the law firm to which they belong, and a five-year experience requirement of foreign lawyers.[10]

In 1993, Keidanren took a further step to boost foreign direct investment in Japan. It organised a Subcommittee for Improving the Climate for Foreign-Affiliated Firms under the Committee on Foreign-Affiliated Corporations. The Subcommittee, after exchanging opinions with the American Chamber of Commerce in Japan and the European Business Community, produced a report in December 1993 entitled *Improvement of the Climate for Foreign-Affiliated Corporations and the Reform of the Japanese Economy*. The report suggested 23 ways to improve access by foreign companies. A crucial recommendation was relaxation of the ban on holding companies.[11] The report proposed this on the grounds that there was little possibility that holding companies impede fair and free market competition, but that the ban hampered direct foreign investment in Japan by foreign firms. Revision of the regulations on discounts and prizes was another critical item. The maximum values of discounts and prizes, some of which were fixed over thirty years ago, did not reflect the rise in commodity prices and changes in firms' sales activities. Foreign firms, which had a limited name value in the Japanese market, saw revision of these regulations as valuable because discounts and prizes were an important incentive for expanding sales. Other issues in the report were the improvement in information on government procurement, and transparency and simplification of administrative operations, as well as strengthening of organization and authority of the Office of Trade and Investment Ombudsman (OTO).[12]

The third report on inward investment, entitled *Emergency Request for Expanding Inward Investment, Promoting Imports, and Deregulating Import-Related Administration*, was announced in March 1994. The report, based on previous recommendations as well as a questionnaire survey in October 1993, suggested deregulation aimed at expanding inward investment and promoting imports. Keidanren suggested eight measures to promote inward investment in Japan: deregulation of laws restraining inward investment; a cut in corporate tax rates; expansion of the ceiling of low-rate financing; reduction of land prices; revision of the public pension system; deregulation of construction permission processes; lifting the ban on holding companies; and deregulation of the conditions on issuing bonds.

In June 1995, Keidanren issued a fourth report, entitled *The Promotion of Foreign Direct Investment and Imports to Japan*. The report examined the government's response to the federation's December 1993 requests, and called on the government to consider further improvements. In addition, the report contained requests for rapid expansion of the import promotion zone, and extension of employment reference activities to private companies.

Activities for promoting deregulation

Deregulation has been one of Keidanren's major policy agendas since the early 1980s when the Second Provisional Commission on Administrative Reform (*Daini Rincho*) focused on it as a factor in administrative reform.[13] Keidanren's action in promoting deregulation in the 1990s has been even more comprehensive and decisive. Keidanren encouraged the government to implement deregulation by negotiating with the ministries and agencies involved and with ruling parties, and by critiquing government deregulation programmes.

The Japanese government took up deregulation especially after the LDP's single party reign ended in summer 1993. Eight coalition parties had formed the Hosokawa Cabinet that August, and on 16 September, the reform-minded cabinet announced an emergency economic package that encompassed deregulation in 94 areas. Prior to these events, Keidanren identified its priorities for deregulation items. In March 1993, Keidanren released a position paper entitled *Evaluation of Progress in Deregulation and Related Requests* and presented it at a session of the Third Provisional Council for Administrative Reform. By the end of August 1993, government ministries and agencies had laid out their initial deregulation plans. But 60 of the items in the various government plans did not include core issues because the bureaucrats had taken a 'wait-and-see' attitude in order to see what other agencies would sacrifice. Keidanren sought to prevent the ministries from omitting core areas from deregulation.[14] On 2 September 1993, the heads of the five business federations met with Koshiro Ishida, Director General of the Management and Coordination Agency, and requested that the government promote deregulation. At that time, Keidanren submitted a paper, *Emergency Requests Concerning Deregulation and Other Measures*, that called on the government to examine deregulation of 30 priority items across seven key sectors and areas of national economic concern.

On 21 January 1994, an Administrative Reform Promotion Headquarters, chaired by the Prime Minister, was set up. One month later, the government adopted a Cabinet Decision that would deregulate 250 items in the short term, and deregulate an additional 531 items to facilitate the coordination and streamlining of various procedures, such as the submission of notifications and reports in the long term. The Decision suggested drawing up a five-year action plan for deregulation by the end of the 1994 fiscal year.

The government recognised that the selection of specific fields and in-depth deliberation on these fields would be an effective way of promoting deregulation. For this purpose, working groups were set up under the aegis of the Headquarters in March 1994, charged with the job of considering deregulation in three areas: housing and land; information and communications; and import promotion, and improvement in market access and distribution systems.[15] The deliberations at the working groups led to a Cabinet Decision on 5 July 1994. Under this Decision, 279 items were listed for deregulation in those three fields, and also others in the finance, securities and insurance markets. The Decision also established seven principles for promoting deregulation during the five-year action plan.

Before the Cabinet Decision was announced, Keidanren submitted proposals on 13 May 1994 entitled *A Proposal for a Decisive Deregulation to Realise Political, Administrative and Economic Reform*. The proposals, which contained a deregulation list of 196 items relating to seven fields, suggested three principles for promoting deregulation: first, a zero-based principle which means that all regulations should be abolished and re-created on the basis of current needs; second, a sunset principle which would require automatic review or elimination within a certain time frame (five years at maximum) when the government enacts new rules or regulations; and third, a due-process principle which requires public hearings where affected parties would outline their views when new regulatory legislation is introduced in the Diet.[16]

In June 1994, the LDP, Japan Socialist Party, and New Party *Saki-*

gake had formed the Murayama Cabinet. This cabinet announced a five-year action programme for deregulation the following March 31, a long-awaited scheme that included deregulating 1,091 items. Keidanren had made its views public on this earlier in *A Proposal for a Deregulation Promotion Plan for Japan* on 17 November 1994. It recommended comprehensive deregulation, including 456 items across 19 areas. It also suggested that the five-year deregulation programme aim to cut economic regulations by half within five years.[17]

Keidanren also promoted deregulation through cooperation with the Economic Reform Research Council (the so-called Hiraiwa group), whose chairmanship was assumed by Gaishi Hiraiwa, Chairman of Keidanren. The 15-member council began its work on 16 September 1993 as a private advisory body to Prime Minister Hosokawa, following an example of the Maekawa panel in 1986. Its aim was to furnish a blueprint for structural reform policies of the Japanese economy from a medium- and long-term perspective. The panel submitted an interim report on 8 November 1993. The report stressed the need for a wholesale review of government regulations, stating that economic regulations should be abolished in principle, and social regulations on safety, health and the environment should be kept to a minimum, based on the principle of individual responsibility, with separate lists showing nearly 500 examples of regulations that could be eliminated or revised. The report also noted that a five-year plan for promoting deregulation should be enacted, and a powerful third party organization should be established in order to examine the deregulation plan, monitor the progress of deregulation, and issue recommendations to promote the efforts. Keidanren actively supported the panel. Two officials were appointed as full-time officials for the panel. In addition, Keidanren was prepared to write a draft of the report that the panel would publish.[18]

The demand for deregulation that would curtail the mandate of bureaucrats and lead to a change in the existing power structure has faced severe resistance from ministries and agencies. The Ministry of Finance's (MOF) attitude towards the elimination and reduction of tariffs on agricultural products and textiles presents a typical example. When Keidanren asked MOF to put tariffs in the five-year deregulation programme, MOF asserted that tariffs were not regulations and the items regarding tariffs were not listed in the scheme.[19] Frequently, when an issue arose that was relevant to several ministries, each of the ministries involved referred to it as relevant to one of its counterparts, and eventually no ministry took responsibility.[20] Resistance from bureaucrats was powerful in the deliberations of the Administrative Reform Promotion Headquarters' working groups. Isao Nakauchi, a vice-chairman of Keidanren, joined one working group as a headquarters specialist. He recalls that 'even if detailed suggestions were formulated at the headquarters, these were eventually overturned by opinions of former bureaucrat members. It was quite out of the question for representatives from the private sector to be allowed to participate in the final meeting.'[21]

Strong resistance to deregulation was apparent in the deliberations of the Economic Reform Research Council. In mid-October 1993, the secretariat of the Council, established in the Councillors' Office on Internal Affairs at the Prime Minister's Office, drew up a draft of the interim report. The draft was not only unclear and without detailed expression but it lacked a guarantee for implementation. In addition, regulations in banking, securities, and insurance, which were under the jurisdiction of MOF, were not included in the draft. This was allegedly because the director of the secretariat came from MOF.[22] The members from the private sector suggested rewriting the draft. Hence, concrete examples of regulations regarding electricity, gas, and international air fares were spelt out in the interim report. The report also referred to the creation of an independent agency to monitor a programme of deregulation, although a specific legal designation for the agency was not named. In addition, intensive debate occurred over the independent agency in the draft subcommittee.[23] The members were split over the authority of the agency, and requested the opinion of Chairman Hiraiwa. In spite of Hiraiwa's support for giving more authority to the agency, his opinion was not adopted because of strong objections from former bureaucrat members (Nakatani and Ōta 1994, pp.147–8).

The promotion of deregulation has been espoused generally by the business community. But there are important differences in stance between Keidanren and Nissho, which represents the interests of small business. Keidanren has argued for the abolition of economic regulations in principle. Nissho has adopted a more cautious attitude to regulatory reform. In December 1994, for instance, Nissho expressed the fear that the abolition of economic regulations might provoke excessive competition among firms, and eventually lead to market dominance by big companies with large capital and human resources.

The deregulation issue that divides Keidanren and Nissho most sharply is the Large-Scale Retail Stores Law.[24] Keidanren has demanded an amendment of the Law that would include the Law's incremental abolition.[25] Keidanren holds that reform of the Law will improve efficiency in the distribution system and create new business and job opportunities. In addition, reform is expected to increase imports of finished products by facilitating the business of large-scale stores which tend to import more than small-scale retailers.

Nissho's position is ambiguous. Originally Nissho was expected to coordinate interests between local small retailers and large-scale retailers.[26] However, Nissho has promoted the interests of small and medium-sized retailers. Not only have half of Nissho's management funds derived from local small and medium-sized retailers but also senior officials in certain local chambers of commerce and industry have been local retailers (Terada 1994, p.18). In addition, the Councils for Coordinating Commercial Activities played a role in coordinating interest in local areas until they disbanded in January 1992. Secretariats of the Councils set up in the local chambers of commerce and industry contributed the authority of chambers of commerce and industry, and maintained their influence on retail stores (Kusano 1992, p.240). The abolition of the Councils as a part of deregulation of the Law reduced the authority of chambers of commerce and industry. Hence, Nissho is unwilling to accept reform of the Law insofar as it threatens the management of small and medium-sized local retailers and would undermine Nissho's authority. Nissho has sought to prevent further reform of the Law. In April 1990, Chairman of Nissho, Rokuro Ishikawa, displayed his dissatisfaction with the amendment of the Law, stating that the Law's amendment and abolition would lead to a rush of large-scale stores, creating great uncertainty and disorder among small retailers.[27] When the abolition of the Councils for Coordination Commercial Activities was decided, Nissho suggested establishing the Councils for Commercial Issues, which had the substantially same function of the Councils for Coordination Commercial Activities (Kusano 1992, p.240).

Results of activities

Keidanren's attempts to promote inward foreign investment have led to changes in government policies.[28] In the second and third reports, Keidanren requested the lifting of the ban on holding companies. The Fair Trade Commission (FTC) had refused the lifting. For instance, it lodged its opposition with an Administrative Reform Promotion Headquarters and the tax reform panel of the coalition government

in June 1994.[29] However, opposition to the regulation has been gradually fostered.[30] The lifting of the ban on holding companies was
excluded in the preliminary report of the five-year deregulation programme. In the final programme announced on 31 March 1995,
however, the FTC agreed to exchange opinions with the private sector
and investigate the subject over the next three years.[31]

In February 1994, the functions of OTO were strengthened. Under
the revised system, the Prime Minister is the head of the Office of
OTO and the rank of member officials was raised from vice-ministers
to ministers. In addition, the OTO advisory council was transformed
into a Market Access Ombudsman Council. The Council, composed
of members selected directly by the Prime Minister, can initiate recommendations even when the Office of OTO does not ask it to do
so.[32] There have also been changes in the regulations on discounts and
prizes. The FTC was reluctant to revise the regulations on the grounds
that the costs of discounts and prizes would be transferred to sale
prices. However, the government incorporated revision of the regulations on discounts and prizes in the external economic reform plan
announced in March 1994.[33]

Keidanren's commitment to deregulation has led the debate and
pushed policy development. The five-year deregulation programme
announced in March 1995 was the first action programme for deregulation. This action programme was developed partially as a result of
Keidanren persistence. In March 1988, Keidanren's Committee on
Administrative Reform compiled a position paper entitled *Proposals
for Deregulation*. In this paper, Keidanren sought a government action
programme with a defined timetable for deregulation.[34] The need for
drawing up an action programme was repeated in a position paper
entitled *Basic Stance on Administrative Reform for the 21st Century*,
released in February 1993. Keidanren's demands were incorporated
in the Cabinet Decision in February 1994, and led to the five-year
deregulation programme in March 1995.

In the process of drawing up the five-year deregulation programme,
the Deliberation Committee on Deregulation, composed of representatives from business circles and academia, reflected the interests
of the private sector on the final programme. This committee was set
up as a consequence of Keidanren's successful pressure. The government at first had no intention of setting up an organization that would
include representatives from the private sector. Keidanren
approached New Party *Sakigake* and, in discussions with the party,
stressed the difference between the Hosokawa and Murayama Cabi-

nets. Under the Hosokawa Cabinet, the Administrative Reform Promotion Headquarters originally was expected to include representatives from the private sector. But strong resistance from bureaucrats prevented this, and the private sector representatives were instead accepted into working groups under the headquarters. Under the Murayama Cabinet, though, Keidanren persuasion was rewarded by strong support from *Sakigake*, which saw to the establishment of the deliberation committee.[35] This committee had a big impact on the five-year action programme. One hundred and twenty nine of the 172 items that the committee raised were accepted in the five-year action programme.[36] The committee's programmes contained Keidanren's major demands. Furthermore, Keidanren's commitment contributed to a strengthening of the five-year deregulation programme. The preliminary plans of the programme contained many items which did not have a time schedule for implementation. On 20 March 1995, Shoichiro Toyoda, Chairman of Keidanren, asked Prime Minister Murayama and major cabinet members directly to specify the date for implementation. By 31 March, the implementation schedule was specified in all plans.[37]

Government deregulation policies included many of the issues taken up by Keidanren. The emergency economic package that the government issued in September 1993 included 21 out of the 30 items on Keidanren's agenda.[38] The government's initial plans announced at the end of August 1993 covered only seven out of Keidanren's 30 items; active lobbying by Keidanren resulted in the inclusion of an additional 14 items in the final package. In the July 1994 Cabinet Decision on deregulation, exactly half of Keidanren's 196 requests were completely incorporated and an additional 14 items were accepted partially.[39] The five-year deregulation programme announced in March 1995 targeted 428 items across 15 fields, out of the 456 items across 19 fields that Keidanren requested. Out of 428 items, 130 were completely realised and another 79 were accepted in part.[40]

Although Keidanren has succeeded in getting its demands incorporated into government policies for deregulation, some qualifications are necessary to assess Keidanren's capability and influence. First, there are many deregulation measures which have been implemented with little or no involvement of Keidanren. A notable example is the amendment of the Large-Scale Retail Stores Law in May 1990. This amendment was largely a result of US pressure during the Structural Impediments Initiative (SII) talks (Terada 1994).

Second, Keidanren's commitment to deregulation is often supported by political initiatives. Where feasible Keidanren officials consulted with relevant ministries and agencies and sought commitment from politicians in support of their proposals.[41] Politicians have played a critical role in realizing Keidanren's requests. For instance, a critical reason why Keidanren's requests were largely accepted in the emergency economic package in September 1993 was that Masayoshi Takemura, the Chief Cabinet Secretary of the Hosokawa Cabinet, encouraged ministries to consider Keidanren's requests positively.[42] Third, Keidanren has experienced resistance to deregulation in the debate within Keidanren. Keidanren includes a wide range of companies and industries among its members, and its opinions tend to be the so-called *soron sansei kakuron hantai* ['endorse the general principle but reject specific measures for implementation'] because of difficulty in coordinating interests among members. Deregulation is not an exception to this general tendency. Industries that enjoy vested interests under existing regulations are likely to exert veto power to oppose measures to curtail the interests. The most notable example is the petroleum sector. The Natural Resource and Energy Agency put forward a plan in June 1994 to abolish the Special Temporary Law for Import of Specific Petroleum Products which regulated imports of petroleum products. Shoichiro Toyoda, Chairman of Keidanren, expressed his support for the reform, but he met strong resistance from the Petroleum Association of Japan.[43] In addition, when Keidanren drew up recommendations for deregulation in May 1994, proposals on the petroleum sector were omitted from the text due to strong opposition from that sector.[44] Another example is liberalization of the retail price of cigarettes. In spite of the appreciation of the yen, retail prices of cigarettes did not fall because of price regulation. When Keidanren sought to nominate cigarettes for deregulation, the tobacco industry strongly opposed it.[45]

Keidanren's motivations

Why has Keidanren become so active in promoting inward investment and deregulation in the 1990s? Keidanren's advocacy of inward investment derives largely from the management of international trade friction and the internationalization of corporate activity. A primary concern is that the huge Japanese foreign investment imbalance would foster a protectionist climate in foreign countries. The 1992 recommendation referred to this issue, observing that 'if investment friction is added to the current trade friction, a protectionist trend will be further fueled'.[46] The advanced multinationalization of Japanese corporations is likely to provide further background of Keidanren's commitment to promoting inward investment. Japanese corporations have made significant inroads into foreign countries and made efforts to be accepted in local markets. However, acceptance in those countries requires reciprocal acceptance of foreign firms in Japan.

The demand for deregulation has more complicated origins. First, Keidanren advocated deregulation in order to promote a change in the Japanese economic system away from a bureaucratic, centralised system towards a private sector-led, decentralized system. This was spelt out explicitly in a November 1994 position paper:

> Japan is now undergoing a period of radical reform. The era of the government-controlled socioeconomic system, the dynamo that has driven Japan's economic growth since the Meiji Period, is coming to a close. If we are to chart a new course of growth for the 21st century – and create a new society that fulfills its responsibilities to both the international community and its citizens – we must create a new social and economic system. The days for maternal protection are over. We must create this new, deregulated society now – one that is based on freedom of choice and supported by the principle of individual responsibility.[47]

Second, Keidanren sees deregulation as important in raising international competitiveness in the non-manufacturing sector. The Japanese economy is a mixture of export-oriented manufacturing industries and domestically oriented, mainly non-manufacturing industries. While the former have enhanced their competitiveness, the latter – transportation, telecommunications, distribution, construction, financing, and insurance – have long been protected by regulations. The regulations have dissuaded new entry and competition and left the industries less productive and less competitive.[48] The slow restructuring in non-manufacturing industries has created a high-cost economic structure, invited low-level imports and a high yen, and eventually imposed additional costs on manufacturing industries. Keidanren's demand for deregulation is an effort to alleviate the burden that is imposed on the manufacturing sector by the uncompetitive non-manufacturing sector. Although the Japanese economy grew with the expansion of the manufacturing sector until the 1980s, a rise in competitiveness in the whole of industry is indispensable in the 1990s (Takenaka and Miyoshi 1995, p.38). Reflecting Keidanren's concern about the non-manufacturing sector, it raised telecommunications, transportation, distribution as the primary fields for deregulation in its recommendations in September 1993, May 1994, and November 1994.

Third, Keidanren regards administrative reform and deregulation as indispensable for resolving trade friction. It is expected to promote imports and investment, narrow the gap between prices in Japan and abroad, and rectify Japan's trade surplus. More importantly, deregulation would make Japan's economic system more compatible with international norms. In Japan, 40 per cent of gross national product (GNP) is produced by industries under government regulation. This ratio is extremely high compared with those in other industrial countries (6.6 per cent in the United States). The internationalization of Japanese industry makes it important that Japan's corporations compete under conditions that obtain internationally. Deregulation is indispensable for creating equal and fair conditions for such competition.[49]

In brief, Keidanren has intensified its commitment to promoting inward investment and deregulation in the 1990s. Through the promotion of deregulation, the federation has aimed to change Japan from a bureaucracy-led economic system to a private sector-led system, as well as enhance the competitiveness of regulated non-manufacturing sectors. Equally important in promoting inward investment and deregulation is Keidanren's interest in preventing further trade friction and facilitating Japanese firms' multinational operations through the creation of a more open Japanese market. Keidanren's commitment to opening the Japanese market in the 1990s has involved an extension of its focus from trade policy itself to investment policy and the regulatory system as these factors significantly affect the closed nature of the Japanese economic system.

KEIDANREN'S STANCE ON AGRICULTURAL TRADE POLICY

Japan has long maintained a protectionist agricultural policy. The government has used quantitative import quotas, tariffs, and state trading in order to protect domestic agriculture. Keidanren, on the other hand, is a major advocate of the liberalization of agricultural trade.[50]

Table 7.5   Keidanren's recommendations regarding agricultural trade and policy

Date	Title
Feb. 1981	Problems of Agricultural Policy from the Food Industry Viewpoint
Jan. 1982	How Agriculture and Agricultural Policy Should Be Developed
Sep. 1983	The Food Industry in an Internationally Open Economic Society
Jun. 1985	A View on Food Security
Dec. 1986	White Paper on the Food Industry
Jan. 1987	Rice Deregulation: A Multistage Approach
May 1988	1987 White Paper on the Food Industry
Nov. 1988	A View on Raw Materials in the Food Industry and Agricultural Policy
May 1991	Third White Paper on the Food Industry
Mar. 1992	Japan's Agricultural Policy: Facing the 21st Century
May 1994	Demand for Deregulation on Agriculture and the Food Industry

Source: Compiled from Keidanren's internal documents.

It has made many recommendations for promoting the liberalization of farm product imports and the reform of administrative regulations on agriculture (Table 7.5).

Stance on agriculture before 1985

Keidanren's stance on agricultural policy and agricultural trade has evolved over time. Keidanren was, by and large, tolerant of agricultural protection before the mid-1970s for several reasons. First, Keidanren shared the popular view of the need to secure sufficient food supplies. Both Keidanren and the agricultural groups cited national security as a grounds for ensuring a domestically produced basic food supply (George and Saxon 1986, p.102). Furthermore, in the era of high economic growth, Japan had a limited capacity to purchase foreign food because of a shortage of foreign currency.[51] Second, big business recognized the conservative LDP government's dependence on rural support. Business circles represented by Keidanren recognized the conservative administration provided a stable basis for business activities. Accordingly, the federation did not advocate policies that would weaken the agricultural groups.

Keidanren changed its fundamental stance on agricultural trade policy in the 1980s. It intensified demands for liberalization of farm products trade after it established the Committee on Agricultural Policy (CAP) in January 1980. This committee was composed of the presidents of meat processors, beer producers, flour-milling firms, beverage producers and so on. The committee's February 1981 report, *Problems of Agricultural Policy from the Food Industry Viewpoint*, was based on the perception that expensive domestic agricultural raw materials robbed Japanese food processors of international competitiveness. It suggested that restrictions on imports of agricultural raw materials should be lifted to enable the Japanese food industry to procure them at international prices. It also proposed that the government should, instead of restricting imports, introduce deficiency payments in a major reform of domestic agricultural policy. The January 1982 report suggested that the market mechanism should be introduced into the agricultural sector both to alleviate the financial burden of Japanese agriculture and to strengthen its competitiveness. More significantly, it proposed the expansion of farm scale, improvement of agricultural infrastructure, the strengthening of research and development aimed at cost reductions, and creation of new agricultural technologies. The September 1983 report explained how the Japanese food industry was losing competitiveness against foreign suppliers due to its inability to import raw materials freely. It proposed swift liberalization of raw materials imports through a market-opening timetable for import quotas on farm products, and revision of the price support systems for agricultural and livestock items.

Several international and domestic factors had encouraged Keidanren to change its stance on agricultural trade liberalization in the 1980s. The increase in Japan's trade surplus with its major trading partners, especially the United States, from the second half of the 1970s was one. The US government demanded liberalization of Japan's beef and citrus market, and this demand intensified in the final negotiations of the General Agreement on Tariffs and Trade (GATT) Tokyo Round in 1978–9. For its part, the United States increased its pressure aimed at agricultural liberalization in late 1981 in the face of the impending expiration of the agricultural trade agreements between Japan and the United States reached in the Tokyo Round (George and Saxon 1986, p.106). The threat of retaliatory protectionism against Japanese manufacturing exports engendered a sense of crisis in Keidanren as export-oriented industries and firms were among its major members (George and Saxon 1986, p.106). Accordingly, Keidanren gradually shifted to an anti-protectionist stance on agricultural trade.

Keidanren's liberal stance on agricultural trade also derived from several domestic factors. First, the federation considered liberalization of farm products trade to be indispensable to the restoration of profitability and competitiveness in the Japanese food industry.[52] The high cost of domestic agricultural raw materials put Japanese food processors at a disadvantage in competition with foreign rivals who had access to cheaper raw materials.[53] The Japanese food processors that dominated Keidanren's Food Industry Policy Division under the CAP sought to ensure that their interests were reflected in the federation's approach. Their interests were incorporated into policy pronouncements in February 1981 and September 1983, protesting the need to pay high prices for domestic agricultural products and demanding easier access to inexpensive imported raw materials.

Second, Keidanren regarded reform of agricultural policy as vital to fiscal reform (George and Saxon 1986, p.106). Agriculture-related spending constituted a significant portion of the national budget. In 1970, the budget for agriculture, forestry and fisheries under the Ministry of Agriculture, Forestry and Fisheries (MAFF) accounted for 11.5 per cent of the general account, 42 per cent of which was used as subsidies and 48 per cent was carried over to the special account for food control. In 1980, the share of the agricultural-related budget in the general account was reduced to 8.4 per cent, but subsidies accounted for 65 per cent. In this year, the subsidization of rice amounted to US$5.2 billion, while that of other crops stood at US$1.4 billion (Balassa 1986, p.758). Keidanren attacked excessive subsidies to farmers and deficits in the special account for food control as major causes of the national deficit and the rise in corporate tax rates.

Stance on agriculture after 1985

The recommendations of Keidanren in the early 1980s tended to be general, but they increasingly contained detailed proposals criticizing agricultural policy including that on rice. In the June 1985 report, CAP criticised the time-honoured national food security tenet as narrowly focusing on improvement in self-sufficiency rates, and recommended an emphasis instead on improvement in self-sufficiency capacity. The report suggested that Japan should unload its food stockpiles when the opportunity arose, that people should change their eating habits and that the production of foods that generate higher calories such as grains and potatoes should increase.

In September 1985, Keidanren set up a Rice Problem Subcommittee under the CAP comprising experts from rice-related companies. The Subcommittee drew up a report on rice deregulation in January 1987.[54] The report was a landmark in that it was the first proposal from a business federation that spoke of reform of the food control system that regulated all aspects of Japan's rice market.[55] The report recommended that the food control system should be lifted in two phases within five years.[56] It also argued that rice imports for industrial processing should be deregulated and hinted at the possibility of opening up rice imports at those times when supplies fell below market intervention requirements or there was a need for special varieties of rice to meet diversifying demand.

Keidanren's demand for liberalization of rice imports grew louder in the 1990s. The federation released a report, *Third White Paper on the Food Industry*, in May 1991. The report pointed out that the price gap between domestic and imported food materials remained large in the food processing industry, and suggested that the market mechanism needed to come into play on Japan's rice market. The general meeting held 24 May 1991 adopted a resolution calling on the government to open partially the rice market and take the lead in reaching a successful conclusion at the GATT Uruguay Round of multilateral trade negotiations.[57] Keidanren was the first business federation to adopt such a resolution demanding liberalization of rice imports.[58] In its May 1994 paper, *Demand for Deregulation on Agriculture and the Food Industry*, the federation suggested drastic deregulation of rice production and retailing. The paper proposed selective rice acreage reduction and the diversification of sales channels for the grain.

Keidanren's demand for liberalization of agricultural trade has intensified since the mid-1980s. Not only did Keidanren demand open farm products trade, providing detailed proposals on farm products trade and agricultural policy, but it also called for the liberalization of the rice market after the late 1980s. Such changes can be explained by the internationalization of Japanese manufacturing corporate activities. The demand from Japan's trade partners for opening the Japanese market escalated in the second half of the 1980s as Japan's trade surpluses grew rapidly. The Uruguay Round, which had begun in September 1986, became the critical agenda in maintaining the free-trade system. In the negotiations, Japan's restriction on rice imports became a major issue. These factors motivated the intensification of Keidanren's opposition to agricultural protection.

The necessity to open Japan's agricultural market to maintain the international trade system was articulated vigorously by Keidanren's senior executives. At the annual meeting when the federation adopted the resolution calling for the partial rice liberalization in May 1991, Gaishi Hiraiwa, Chairman of Keidanren, stated that 'it's important for Japan to take the initiative in bringing the Uruguay Round of multilateral trade talks under the General Agreement on Tariffs and Trade to a successful conclusion. For that purpose, the rice issue could become Tokyo's trump card, and Japan's decision (to open its market to rice imports) will have no small impact internationally.'[59] In November 1991, Toshikuni Yahiro, a vice-chairman of Keidanren, also stressed the need for rice liberalization from an international point of view:

> The issue of food security, which the government and agricultural organizations have clung to as a way of justifying the ban on foreign rice, is selfish. It ignores the benefits that Japan has enjoyed over the past century by exploiting the world's free markets ... Japan has a duty to contribute to the preservation of international free trade, for which the success of the Uruguay Round is crucial. The opening of the rice market is symbolic from this perspective.[60]

The internationally oriented firms in the manufacturing sector have not directly been involved in the drawing up of Keidanren's recommendations on agricultural issues. This is because the agricultural group has always considered farmers to be victims of trade disputes which had been caused by export-oriented firms and industries.[61] If export-oriented firms had advocated the liberalization of agricultural products too actively, it would exacerbate the antagonistic feeling against them. However, their influence seems to have become critical in Keidanren's stance on agricultural trade, as shown by the fact that motivations demanding liberalization of agricultural trade have expanded from a measure to maintain international competitiveness of the food industry in the early 1980s to the broader objective of sustaining the free-trade system in the late 1980s. The driving force behind Keidanren's advocacy of agricultural trade liberalization was the deepening of its commitment to the multilateral trade system.[62]

Opposition to Keidanren's activities

In the process of demanding liberalization of farm product imports and removal of excess protection for agriculture, Keidanren was confronted with strong opposition from MAFF and agricultural groups represented by the Central Union of Agricultural Cooperatives (*Zenchu*).[63] MAFF intervened in the process of drafting the report of September 1983. In June 1982, the Food Industry Policy Division under Keidanren's CAP organised a special deliberation group composed of general managers of food processing companies. The preliminary draft drawn up one year later strongly criticized agricultural policy on import quotas and the system of a virtual monopoly on beef imports and distribution by the Livestock Industry Promotion Corporation. MAFF called on the members of the deliberation group to revise this report in part. The report's announcement was delayed for three months and passages critical of agricultural policy were revised.[64] *Zenchu* also criticized the report on the grounds that its implementation would strengthen dependence on imported raw materials, that its timing was inappropriate because the Japan–US talks on trade in beef and oranges were about to be held, and that US President Reagan was to visit Japan soon.[65]

In March 1984, the Hokkaido Farmers' Federation – with a membership of 78,000 – passed a resolution to boycott the products of Daiei, Japan's largest supermarket chain; Ajinomoto, a leading food maker; and Sony. Daiei and Sony were targeted on the grounds that senior executives of both companies had criticized publicly the excessive protection given to Japanese agriculture, while Ajinomoto was included because Bunzo Watanabe, an advisor to the company and Chairman of CAP, led the move for liberalization of agricultural product imports.[66] Watanabe eventually resigned as chairman and the president of Ajinomoto offered a formal apology, stating that Keidanren's recommendations lacked sensitivity towards Japanese agriculture.[67] Although a new chairman of CAP was selected soon, this incident influenced the activities of the Committee. The Committee held a meeting in October 1984 to discuss the direction of its activities, and decided to investigate rice issues, food security, and the improvement in the environment for the food processing industry taking into consideration the role of agriculture in the Japanese economy and the special character of agriculture. At the same time, the Agricultural Policy Affairs Division (*nosei bukai*) and the Food Industry Division (*shokuhin kogyo bukai*) were abolished, and the

Special Committee on Agricultural Policy Affairs (*nosei senmon iinkai*) and the Special Committee on Food Industry Policy (*shokuhin kogyo seisaku senmon iinkai*) were set up.[68]

Strong opposition from MAFF and agricultural groups can be seen in the 1990s. In July 1991, *Zenchu* and two other farmers' associations organized the 'Emergency National Rally for the Protection of Rice'. More than 50,000 farmers from all over Japan gathered in Tokyo to protest against any liberalization of the rice market. Following the rally, 200 farmers stormed Keidanren's headquarters building to protest the resolution that Keidanren adopted in May demanding partial liberalization of the rice market.[69] In 1994, MAFF summoned the President of Yamatane Corp., a rice distribution company, to dissuade him from criticizing the government's food policies. Yamatane Chairman Seizo Yamazaki, as head of Keidanren's Agricultural Policy Affairs Division within CAP, had criticized the government's food control system as impeding a stable food supply.[70]

MAFF's intervention in Keidanren's activities and opposition from *Zenchu* suggest that they regard the federation's activities as important and influential. In addition, Watanabe's resignation showed that Keidanren's advocacy of reform in agricultural policy and trade was accompanied by serious risk for business executives.

Influence on agricultural trade and policy

What influences have Keidanren's activities had on policy outcomes in respect of agricultural issues? The liberalization of agricultural trade has proceeded under strong pressure from foreign suppliers, especially the United States. The tariff reduction and removal of quotas on various agricultural products including beef, oranges, and citrus juice over the period for 1978 and 1988 were implemented in response to US pressure. In December 1993, the Japanese government agreed to convert all remaining agricultural import restrictions to tariffs, and to establish minimum access for rice. The deals over these issues were settled primarily in bilateral negotiations with the United States. Foreign pressure was, thus, a vital factor promoting liberalization of agricultural trade. Keidanren was a prominent domestic actor in promoting the liberalization of agricultural trade, but others were also important. For instance, the Policy Innovation Forum, a group of academic scholars, played a crucial role in publishing the costs of Japan's agricultural protection when the Uruguay Round broke down.[71]

Some argue that Keidanren failed to get its way on agricultural policy owing to strong resistance from MAFF, agricultural interest groups and LDP's agriculture and forestry *zoku*.[72] Some Keidanren officials admit that Keidanren's influence on agricultural trade may have been limited.[73] The limits to Keidanren's influence on agricultural trade were threefold.

First, agricultural issues were politically very sensitive. Many LDP politicians relied on rural support in gerrymandered election districts and accordingly had strong interests in agricultural issues.[74] Vital decisions affecting agricultural policy depended on internal politics within the LDP as well as the LDP's overall power in the Diet. This is evident in the changes in the policy stance of the LDP on agriculture in line with the results of national elections. In the 1980s, the LDP was in a position to adopt bold policies on agriculture when it gained an overwhelming majority in the Diet. The voice of agricultural reform was raised after the general election in July 1986 in which the LDP captured the biggest victory since its foundation in 1955, gaining 304 seats, 54 more than before the election. The Nakasone Cabinet drew confidence from this result in undertaking agricultural reform.[75] The policy stance of the LDP on agricultural issues changed dramatically in mid-1989, after a devastating defeat in the Upper House election on 23 July 1989, which led to its loss of a sole majority for the first time since the party's foundation.[76] One of the most serious causes of this setback was the dissatisfaction of farmers with the liberalization of imports of oranges and beef in June 1988 and the ambivalent attitude of the LDP on the rice issue. After the election, the LDP was obliged to adopt policies that appeased the agricultural group.[77] The LDP secured a clear majority in the Lower House election on 18 February 1990. After that, senior LDP politicians began to express the view that some form of rice liberalization was inevitable.[78]

The opening up of the rice market has been a national issue. A questionnaire survey by *Asahi Shimbun* in May 1990 revealed that 21 per cent of respondents supported liberalization of the rice market and 17 per cent were in favour of gradual liberalization. At the same time, 30 per cent of respondents supported the ban on rice imports and 27 per cent admitted minimum imports.[79] The major opposition parties as well as the LDP have been opposed to the liberalization of the rice market. The Diet three times passed resolutions opposing the opening of the rice market.[80]

The political sensitivity of agricultural issues made Keidanren sensitive to political factors in calling for the liberalization of farm products trade. After the LDP experienced its historical setback in the Upper House election in July 1989, Keidanren suspended its advocacy of agricultural liberalization until the party had obtained a secure majority in the Lower House election in February 1990. Between the two elections, Keidanren issued no reports on agricultural liberalization.[81]

Second, Keidanren's influence on the LDP with respect to agricultural issues was limited. The agricultural group and big business were the two wheels of the cart supporting the LDP administration. Agriculture contributed votes, while business provided money. Although the relative influence of these two sources of support for the LDP shifted over time and according to the issues, it was natural for the LDP to pay more attention to the interests of the agricultural group than to big business on agricultural issues. Furthermore, Keidanren's influence on the LDP with respect to agricultural issues was also limited in terms of access. Keidanren has maintained tight linkages with party bosses and top-ranking officials, but initiatives on agricultural policies are controlled by members of the LDP's agriculture and forestry *zoku*. These *zoku* members have often succeeded in achieving their objectives in spite of the opposition of party leaders.[82]

Third, Keidanren was not a directly interested party in the area of agricultural issues. Basic policies on agriculture have been determined by MAFF, the agricultural group and LDP's agriculture and forestry *zoku*. Even the food processing industry, which is often paired with farming as the two components that ensure a stable food supply, has seldom been involved in decisions on agriculture. Moreover, MAFF's Food Distribution Bureau, which has jurisdiction over the industry, has little power in the Ministry.[83]

Given the character of Keidanren's interest in agricultural matters, it is not surprising that its influence was limited. This does not mean that the federation's representation had no effect. One *Zenchu* official asserted that Keidanren's views had a critical influence on agricultural policies because not only did the government pay attention but the mass media also gave prominence to them.[84] A Keidanren executive also argued that the federation's representation had a body-blow effect on agricultural policy.[85] Keidanren became a harbinger challenging some of the tenets of agricultural policy, and spearheaded campaigns for the agricultural policy reform. In June 1985, the federation proposed a paper suggesting a suspension on the long-honoured tenet to improve self-sufficiency. This was a bold challenge to the agricultural groups, and forced *Zenchu* to publish a view rebuking it one week later. Keidanren was the first business federation to take a hard look at the food control system.[86] Other associations published views on the food control system after Keidanren's recommendations. Keizai Doyukai published a report, *Objectives and Policies for Rice Reform*, in October 1988. The Committee on the Food Control System, an advisory panel to *Zenchu*, produced a report titled *Future Directions of Rice Distribution and Control*. Keidanren's resolution calling for the partial liberalization of the rice market on 24 May 1991 had a big impact on business and political circles. It led the heads of other business federations to express similar views. Osamu Uno, Chairman of Kankeiren (the Kansai Economic Federation) and Takeshi Nagano, Chairman of Nikkeiren, called for the early liberalization of the rice market on 27 May and 29 May 1991, respectively.[87] Keidanren's resolution also helped sustain the trend to liberalization among LDP politicians with this explicit support from the business world.

More importantly, Keidanren's position papers – in parallel with the efforts of other business federations and scholars – often influenced policy guidelines on agriculture, especially those promulgated by the Agricultural Policy Advisory Council.[88] As an advisory panel to the Prime Minister, the Council issues reports on future agricultural policy every five years.[89] The 1980 report, *Basic Stance on Agricultural Policy in the 1980s*, paid attention to the food industry, spelling out that agriculture and the food industry are two wheels of the cart for ensuring a stable food supply. It also referred to the price gap between domestic and imported raw materials, and suggested structural, production, and price policies aimed at rectifying the gap. This sensitivity was a consequence of Keidanren's interim report of the recommendation of February 1981. The report drew attention to the crisis facing the food industry because of domestic agricultural policy, and suggested that agricultural import policy, which was complicated and lacked consistency across products, should be standardized and liberalized.

The emphasis on agriculture as industry in the 1986 report *Basic Stance on Agricultural Policy for the 21st Century* caught the eyes of many. The paper argued that agriculture should be established as an independent industry through productivity improvements based on cost performance. This mirrored the stance taken in Keidanren's recommendation of January 1982, which held that agriculture was an essential industry in which farmers could be independent and self-sustaining without massive government intervention.

In August 1994, the Council issued a report, *Directions for Agricultural Policy in a New International Climate*, that was particularly important because it provided a perspective on post-Uruguay Round agricultural policy. It argued that a new legal framework was needed to replace the Staple Food Control Law, which had governed production, distribution and prices of rice since 1942. It also recommended that rice growers decide how much to produce at their own discretion, and that punitive measures on farmers who do not abide by government-set production schemes should be abolished. Regarding distribution regulations, it stressed the need to introduce market mechanisms, promoting the entry of new rice wholesaling and retailing businesses in place of the system dominated by agricultural cooperatives. Keidanren's advocacy of reform of the food control system went back to its recommendations on rice deregulation in January 1987. In May 1994, Keidanren suggested the introduction of a selective rice planting system in which rice growers could decide whether they accept rice planting limits or not. The Council's report thus can be seen largely as having incorporated Keidanren's recommendations.

In summary, Keidanren's capability to affect directly the decisions on changing the basic of agricultural policy was limited. The agricultural issues are too politically sensitive, and detailed policies have been worked out among MAFF, the LDP, and the agricultural groups. However, Keidanren spearheaded the campaign for agricultural reform and liberalization of agricultural trade, and the federation's views have played a catalytic role in beginning the transformation.

KEIDANREN'S STANCE ON THE IMPROVEMENT IN STANDARDS AND CERTIFICATION SYSTEMS

Keidanren actively committed itself to improving standards and certification systems, and achieved considerable success in the 1980s.[90] Japan's complicated standards and certification systems were held up by foreign firms and governments in the 1970s and 1980s as proof of the closed nature of the Japanese market, and their application led to successive trade disputes between Japan and its trade partners.[91]

Keidanren expressed its concern about foreign criticism of the systems and actively lobbied the government to revise them.

The 1983 Gotoda Decision

The first substantial and comprehensive improvement in standards and certification systems was implemented in 1983. On 13 January 1983, the government held a cabinet meeting on economic measures, and announced a third package of external economic measures.[92] This package included the reduction of tariffs on 86 items, the relaxation of import quotas on six farm products, the promotion of imports, and an improvement in standards and certification systems. A Liaison and Coordination Headquarters on Standards and Certification Systems was set up to discuss and promote the improvement in standards and certification systems. The Headquarters – comprising vice-ministers of relevant ministries – collected opinions from relevant organizations, and discussed detailed measures for improving standards and certification systems.[93] On 26 March, the Headquarters announced the so-called Gotoda Decision.[94] According to the principle of domestic and external non-discrimination in the process of certification, the government decided to amend 17 laws regarding MITI, MAFF, the Ministry of Health and Welfare, the Ministry of Transport and the Ministry of Labour. The omnibus package amending these laws was adopted on 18 May 1983, and came into force in August 1983.

Keidanren was at the forefront of the movement to revise standards and certification systems in 1983 through collecting detailed examples, publishing them in recommendations and negotiating with the responsible government agencies and the LDP. On 27 April 1982, Keidanren's Committee on Foreign Trade made public a statement entitled *For Better External Economic Relations with Our Trading Partners*. In addition to further tariff reductions and liberalization of the 27 remaining quota items, the statement demanded drastic simplification of complicated approval systems, including export and import inspection procedures.

In autumn 1982, the Committee on Foreign Trade collected approximately 1,000 complaints on trade-related regulatory issues, mainly from foreign firms. Then, a panel of experts on trade procedures was set up under the Committee, along with three specialized subcommittees. The panel groups discussed 300 detailed trade-related complaints at the meetings where some 250 specialists in total gathered 12 times.[95] Based on intensive discussions over the improvement in trade regulatory procedures, Keidanren adopted a position paper entitled *A New Look at Trade-Related Regulatory Administration* on 21 December 1982, and submitted it to the Nakasone Cabinet and the LDP. This paper requested that 'various regulatory agencies be abolished except where they are indispensable from the standpoint of national policy and for securing the safety of citizens', and suggested that the current trade-related regulatory systems should be internationalized by accepting foreign standards and by abandoning double inspection and testing.[96] This recommendation also included detailed examples for improving licensing, approval and other trade regulatory systems.

Keidanren obtained a response from concerned ministries on every item it raised in its recommendation of December 1982, and recognized that many of the problems regarding trade regulatory administration sprang from the way that laws and ordinances were administrated, but there were cases where improvement was difficult without amendment of the legislation itself.[97] Accordingly, Keidanren decided to establish another subcommittee consisting of experts on trade-related laws and ordinances. Four research groups were also organized under the panel of experts to study the Customs Law, the Foreign Exchange and Foreign Trade Control Law, the Pharmaceutical Affairs Law and the Food Sanitation Law.[98] In order to accumulate more cases and examples and to explore the irrational aspects of existing systems, Keidanren conducted another questionnaire survey among its members in February 1983, and compiled a list of complaints from foreign governments and organizations.[99]

Based on these various surveys and discussions in the subcommittee and in the research groups, the Committee on Foreign Trade drew up a statement entitled *Reforming Trade-Related Regulations and Improving Their Application*. Keidanren submitted this to the government and the LDP on 22 March 1983, and explained this at the OTO advisory council the next day.[100] The statement included 207 detailed examples for revision concerning 43 laws and ordinances ranging from the revision of the custom system to the promotion of transparency in administrative procedures.

In addition to direct commitments to concerned ministries and agencies, Keidanren cooperated with the LDP's Special Committee for International Economic Measures chaired by Masumi Esaki. The Committee, established in December 1981 as a direct organization of the President of the LDP, was a substantial body to promote market-opening measures including the improvement in import administrative procedures in the early 1980s.[101] Keidanren supported the Committee's initiatives. It is said that the data the Committee used in revising standards and certification systems were based largely on the responses to a Keidanren questionnaire (Funabashi 1987, p.57). Keidanren also maintained close communication with the Committee by exchanging views over revising standards and certification systems. For example, when Keidanren drew up its December 1982 position paper, it had the opportunity to cite major examples for improving trade-related regulatory administration before the Committee. Esaki then requested that the relevant agencies discuss the responses to the issues Keidanren raised.[102]

The Action Programme in 1985

The improvement in standards and certification systems became a major issue in the Action Programme of July 1985.[103] Following a meeting in Los Angeles in January 1985 between Prime Minister Yasuhiro Nakasone and US President Ronald Reagan, the Japanese government decided to formulate further market liberalization measures as well as to launch market-oriented sector-specific (MOSS) negotiations in pharmaceutical and medical devices, telecommunications, electronics, and forestry products. On 9 April 1985, the government received a report from the Advisory Committee for External Economic Issues chaired by Saburo Okita. The report advocated six sets of measures for easing trade friction including an action programme to improve market access, economic expansion centred on the domestic demand, and the expansion of economic cooperation. On the same day, the government announced a seventh package of external economic measures, and decided to draft the framework for the Action Programme by July. The Government-Ruling Parties Joint Headquarters for the Promotion of External Economic Measures, headed by the Prime Minister himself, was established on 19 April.

On 30 July, the government issued an *Outline of the Action Programme for Improved Market Access*. This outline addressed the matter of opening the market in six areas: tariffs; import restrictions; standards, certification, and import procedures; government procurement; capital and financial markets; and service imports. The Programme included the reduction and elimination of tariffs on 1,853 items, 1,790 of which were cut by 20 per cent. In the area of government procurement, 16 government-related organizations were added to the scope and coverage of the GATT agreement on government procurement. With respect to the improvement in standards and certification systems, 88 items covered by 31 laws were expected to be amended. Although the overall assessment of the effectiveness of the Programme was rather low, the improvement in standards, certification, and import procedures received a relatively favourable assessment.

Although Keidanren initiated the move towards the improvement in certification systems and inspection procedures, it was not satisfied with the amendment of 16 laws in 1983, and there was still foreign discontent with Japan's system of trade regulation. In addition, economic relations between Japan and the United States deteriorated as the US trade deficit with Japan climbed from US\$19 billion in 1983 to over US\$33 billion in 1984.

Keidanren submitted a proposal entitled *Smoothing the Way for Imports* on 4 February 1985. It recommended that the administration make a deliberate commitment to reassess and reform both its policy objectives and the means used to give effect to them, responding to the growth of the national economy, advances in science and technology, and changes in lifestyles.[104] This paper included 44 detailed proposals for the revision of 18 laws. Keidanren focused particularly on the Food Sanitation Law and the Pharmaceutical Affairs Law because many grievances about non-tariff barriers related to food and drugs. The Committee on Foreign Trade had conducted another questionnaire survey in May 1984 dealing with food and drugs, and had extensive talks with the relevant ministries.[105] The results of this survey were incorporated into the recommendations. Twenty-one out of 44 cases taken up in the recommendations were relevant to the Food Sanitation Law and the Pharmaceutical Affairs Law. Keidanren pushed for the improvements through negotiations with the ministries and agencies responsible on a case-by-case basis and through the commitments to the Cabinet Special Assignment Office, and the LDP's Committee for International Economic Measures.

In February 1985, Keidanren published another position paper entitled *Toward Rebuilding and Strengthening the Free Trade System*. It stressed the need to open the Japanese market from a broader standpoint. It called for immediate reduction and elimination of tariffs on wood products, alcoholic beverages, boneless chicken and so on, reform of trade-related regulatory procedures, and action on such long-term issues as the promotion of a new multilateral trade negotiation round, and elimination of restraints outside the GATT framework.

In addition to the submission of the position papers, senior executives of Keidanren called directly on the government and the LDP to promote market liberalization. On 21 March, senior executives of Keidanren asked the LDP's top-ranking officials to promote the reduction of tariffs on boneless chicken and plywood.[106] On 8 April, Yoshihiro Inayama, Chairman of Keidanren, had a meeting with executive officials of MAFF including the Minister, and suggested reducing the tariffs on boneless chicken and plywood.[107]

Results of activities

Keidanren's requests concerning the improvement in standards and certification systems were widely incorporated into government policies. Particularly important in the Gotoda Decision in March 1983 was the acceptance of foreign inspection data. Several Japanese laws did not admit acceptance of foreign inspection data on the grounds that it might cause security and health problems. Keidanren called on the government to accept foreign standards and foreign inspection data in the statement of December 1982 and of March 1983 with the objective of promoting the compatibility of the domestic legal system with international norms. In the March 1983 statement, amendment of a dozen laws relating foreign inspection data was advocated. The Gotoda Decision suggested accepting foreign inspection data with respect to 17 laws including the Pharmaceutical Affairs Law, the High-Pressure Gas Control Law, the Agricultural Chemicals Control Law; 11 out of those had been taken up in Keidanren's March 1983 proposals.

The other important revision in the Gotoda Decision and the omnibus package in May 1983 concerned the Road Vehicles Law. Keidanren called on the Ministry of Transport to revise 13 items of this Law including the acceptance of inspection data conducted by recognized foreign automakers as well as the amendment of safety regulations. The package incorporated most of Keidanren's requests, including that for an improvement in type designation procedures and handling procedures for motor vehicles imported in small batches, as well as the revision of safety regulations for headlights, turn signals, rear reflectors, headrests, and rear bumpers.

Keidanren failed to realize its objectives for market opening in some areas in the Action Programme of July 1985. For instance, the reduction in tariffs on plywood was excluded from the Programme due to strong resistance from MAFF and agriculture and forestry *zoku*. However, in the areas of improvement in the standards and certification systems, many items for which Keidanren had requested revision were included in the Programme. The Programme incorporated Keidanren's 27 requests concerning seven laws, including ten and nine items with respect to the Food Sanitation Law and the Pharmaceutical Affairs Law respectively.[108] An important case was the permission for passage of high-cube containers within Japan. The Japanese government prohibited the domestic use of high-cube containers on the grounds that the Japanese highway system was structurally unable to handle such loads and their use would cause safety problems. The importers had to change high-cube containers widely used in the Pacific line to the domestic ones. However, the passage of high-cube containers for exports was allowed on the grounds that these were inseparable freight, and this double-standard treatment had been criticized as unfair. In responding to foreign criticism, Keidanren had maintained since spring 1983 that the issue could be resolved even under present conditions by using permits to transport the containers at specific times along specific routes.[109] Keidanren also called for the revision of the Load Law and the Load Traffic Law in the position papers of March 1983 and February 1985.

Keidanren's motivations

Why did Keidanren so actively commit itself to improving standards and certification systems? The federation's motivations had much to do with the establishment of the Second Provisional Commission on Administrative Reform (*Daini Rincho*). *Rincho* started with nine members and 21 special members on 16 March 1981. Keidanren and other business federations provided both foundation of *Rincho* and momentum of its activities. A clue to Keidanren's interest in administrative reform was the new seven-year economic and social plan announced in August 1979. This plan spelt out the need to correct fiscal deficits by tax increases. Keidanren, anxious to avoid tax increases, demanded administrative and fiscal reform. In September 1979, the federation released a position paper entitled *Opinions on the Future Tax System*, which opposed tax increases and urged the government to develop detailed plans for fiscal reconstruction. Two months later, Keidanren released another position paper, *Hope for*

Decisive Implementation of Administrative and Financial Reform, which contained detailed measures for administrative and financial reform (Heiwa Keizai Kenkyū Kaigi 1982, pp.85–6). Furthermore, the federation repeatedly required the LDP and MOF to refrain from introducing policies leading to tax increases. These initiatives led to the establishment of *Rincho*.

Leading *zaikai* supported the activities of the commission. Keidanren dispatched Toshio Doko, who had just finished a six-year term as Chairman of Keidanren, as the head of *Rincho*. Three out of nine commission members were selected from business circles. In addition, when the Commission was established, the Chairmen of the five business federations – Keidanren, Keizai Doyukai, Nikkeiren, Nissho and Kankeiren (the Kansai Economic Federation) – organized the Five Member Committee for Promoting Administrative Reform. However, the common front on administrative reform by *zaikai* lasted only for one year because differences among the major business federations – especially between Keidanren and Nissho – began to emerge. Nissho, whose members are small and medium-sized firms, favoured the expansion of public expenditure, as the Japanese economy plunged into recession. In July 1982, Shigeo Nagano, Chairman of Nissho, backed away from the line advocated by *Rincho* calling on the government to stimulate the economy by expanding public expenditure.[110] This was incompatible with Keidanren's stance favouring cuts in public expenditure. Nagano confronted Keidanren, proclaiming that he would organize a political association composed of small and medium-sized firms.[111] Thus, although the common front by *zaikai* lasted only for a short time, Keidanren remained as a pivotal supporter of *Rincho*.

Rincho had two objectives. One was to resolve the fiscal bind by simplification and rationalization of administrative operations. Business circles, which had successfully overcome the problems of the two oil shocks by restructuring and rationalization efforts, expected bureaucrats to make similar efforts by cutting excess intervention in private activities as well as by rationalizing administrative operations (Maki 1982, p.65). The improvement in standards and certification systems promoted administrative reform in trade-related areas.

The other objective of *Rincho* was to resolve problems resulting from internationalization of the Japanese economy (Doi, Hayakawa and Yamaguchi 1985, p.206). Japanese manufacturing industries had intensified their dependence on exports since the late 1970s. On the one hand, rising dependence on overseas markets meant that big business did not have to rely so heavily on the public expenditures that *Rincho* sought to curtail (Heiwa Keizai Kenkyū Kaigi 1982, p.83). On the other hand, rising dependence on exports meant that Japan's trade surpluses rose. *Rincho* sought to resolve trade friction through rationalization of administrative operations and elimination of non-tariff barriers to trade.

The improvement in standards and certification systems aimed to achieve the second objective of *Rincho* through directly removing non-tariff barriers to trade. Around 1983, foreign governments voiced stronger criticisms of the closed Japanese market. In March 1982, the European Community proposed to initiate consultations with Japan under the provisions of GATT Article 23. The Community raised the complicated and exclusive import inspection, standards and certification systems as evidence of the closed nature of the Japanese market. Criticism against the domestic structure of the Japanese economy was also voiced by the US government. The US Trade Representative submitted a report on *Japanese Barriers to US Trade and Recent Japanese Government Trade Initiatives* to Congress in November 1982, pointing out that the Japanese standards and certification systems ran counter to domestic and external non-discrimination.[112] Keidanren feared that the deterioration of relations with major trading partners would jeopardize the free-trade system.

Tatsuzo Mizukami, Chairman of the Committee on Foreign Trade, made the point as follows:

If we ignore foreign criticisms of Japan . . . there is the serious danger that the forces of protectionism [will be] set loose to destroy the liberal trading system. What we must appreciate more than anything else is the fact that freeing our market to foreign imports is in our own interest in the sense that the Japanese people can have access to products of the best quality available in the world at the cheapest price.[113]

That Keidanren positively committed itself to improving the standards and certification systems to preserve the free-trade system is also shown in various recommendations.[114] For example, in February 1985 it urged:

Japan must now assume a major role in rebuilding and strengthening the free-trade system. We must work even harder than other countries to open our domestic market wider still, and we should be ready to shoulder our share of the costs. At the same time, we must redouble our efforts to carry forward the administrative reform program and put a stop to excessive government intervention. And administrative policy must be made more transparent.[115]

The improvement in standards and certification systems attracted only minor interest. This was partly because it contained a wide variety of very detailed amendments in laws, and partly because it did not necessarily lead to any immediate increase in imports. However, the systems of trade regulations constituted the major non-tariff barriers, and were regarded as a symbol of a closed Japanese market. Keidanren's efforts improved these systems considerably, and the main target of trade friction shifted away from the trade regulation system to other issues after the late 1980s.

Keidanren played a crucial role in improving the standards and certification systems. Not only did it identify problematic aspects of these systems in its various recommendations, but it also demanded their revision through direct negotiations with government agencies responsible for the administration and with the ruling party. Keidanren's actions were spurred by the desire to promote administrative reform in trade-related areas. Equally important was the concern to maintain the free-trade system on which Japanese manufacturing industry depended by showing Japan's willingness to remove non-tariff barriers.

CONCLUSION

The analysis here has explored the development of Keidanren's open trade stance, especially since the early 1980s. The federation expressed an anti-protectionist stance on agricultural trade and took the initiative in improving standards and certification systems. Significantly, Keidanren over time strengthened its open trade stance. The evolution of Keidanren's policy stance can be seen in its commitment to farm products trade and agricultural policy liberalization. The federation was not a vocal opponent of protectionist agricultural policy until the late 1970s. This stance changed in 1980 through the establishment of CAP. Although the attack on agricultural trade protectionism came from the perspective of the food processing industry in the early 1980s, it became more comprehensive, including a demand for liberalization in the rice market in the late 1980s. The evolution of

Keidanren's stance was also apparent in other commercial policy areas. Keidanren made serious efforts in the early 1980s to improve standards and certification systems, so-called border measures directly impeding the entry of foreign goods. The federation aggressively advocated deregulation after the late 1980s. The demand for deregulation was linked to the revision of the economic system that impeded better market access. Keidanren's interest also took in investment policies in the 1990s as a factor affecting perceptions of a closed Japanese market. Keidanren called on the government to create a better environment for foreign investment in Japan through the removal and relaxation of regulations on investment-related policies, and the provision of incentives to attract inward investment. Keidanren's commitment to achieving better market access expanded from trade policies proper to related investment policies and reform of the economic system that created a closed market.

Several of the factors that encouraged Keidanren to adopt an open trade stance were domestically based. A critical factor urging the federation to promote administrative reform through the activity of *Rincho* and to demand reform of the food control system was the need to restore sound public finance, and avoid tax increases. The demand for deregulation also involved commitment to the change from the bureaucracy-led centralized social and economic systems to private-sector-led decentralized systems. Central to all of these was the internationalization of Japanese corporate activity and its influence on the character of Keidanren's commitment to an open market. The evaporation of the group's tolerance for agricultural protectionism provides insight into the increased importance attached to Japanese industry's linkages with overseas markets. While Japanese manufacturing industries increased their dependence on overseas markets through exports, Japan's surpluses with trade partners mushroomed and raised the serious possibility of retaliation against Japan's exports. Keidanren's commitment to improve standards and certification systems can also be understood in this context. Moreover, Keidanren's concern about the lack of foreign investment in Japan increased as the investment imbalance grew due to the huge expansion in the multinational operations of Japanese corporations. The demand for deregulation sprang from the perception that Japan's trade surplus would not decrease and Japan's trade relations would remain unstable unless there was reform of a regulation-dominant economic system.

Keidanren's policy influence differed case by case. In the area of agricultural policy, its influence was limited in spite of the persistence of its representation. Agricultural issues were politically extremely sensitive, and Keidanren was not a full participant in the policy process on agricultural issues. However, the federation played a role in initiating the campaign for agricultural reform and helped to shape the long-term agenda for reform. Keidanren has not influenced all measures for market liberalization, either. There are numerous market-opening measures in which other factors such as foreign pressure seem to be more influential. However, in the area of standards and certification systems and deregulation, Keidanren's influence was conspicuous. Keidanren, cooperating with politicians and other business federations, took the lead in trying to influence policy making, and was successful in getting its voice heard and its recommendations accepted.

8 Conclusions

This study has looked in detail at the automobile, electronics, and textile industries, and at Keidanren to explore the influence of rising international corporate activity on firms' policy preferences. The case studies suggest that as Japanese corporations have extended their multinational operations and international corporate alliances, they have become more interested in promoting the liberalization of the Japanese market, except for some cases in the textile industry. The study also reveals several distinctive features of the relationship between greater international interdependence of corporate activity and firms' trade policy preferences in Japan. In Japanese industry, vertical linkages affect the preferences of large corporations for opening up the home market. Divergent views among corporations within an industry are also less common in Japan. Moreover, multinational operations and corporate preferences for an open domestic market often develop concurrently in Japan. The preferences of the private sector influence changes in trade policy, and the effectiveness of commercial policy depends on the explicit or implicit preferences of the private sector in other cases.

The first section of this chapter examines how the central hypothesis that firms with extensive multinational operations and corporate alliances prefer an open domestic market applies to Japanese industry, and draws out the salient features of the formation of corporate preferences peculiar to Japan. The second section reviews how corporate preferences have affected Japanese policies on market liberalization. The third section discusses the limitations of this study and explores future research issues.

FIRMS' POLICY PREFERENCES

The central question of this study was 'how has the internationalization of corporate activity changed Japanese firms' preferences on trade policy?' The hypothesis is that as firms strengthen their international linkages in the form of multinational operations and international corporate alliances, they have more interest in the openness of the global market including the market at home. This corporate policy preference is expected to have an important influence on trade policy. The findings in this study, by and large, support the internationalization hypothesis. In the three sectoral case studies, the internationalization of corporate activities has played a pivotal role in changing corporate preferences for open trade, with the exception of some areas in the textile industry. Multinational operations have been a crucial factor motivating Japanese automakers in the opening up of supplier *keiretsu*, and in expanding market access for foreign products by increasing the purchase of foreign auto parts and vehicles. Growing multinational operations have led to economic and political pressures to increase purchases from local suppliers, and made international procurement policies indispensable for creating efficient global procurement. These considerations led to the opening of supplier *keiretsu* relations to foreign parts makers. Multinational operations have also made Japanese automakers more sensitive to foreign criticism of the closed Japanese market. In order to dissuade foreign industries from demanding retaliatory restrictions on the local operations of Japanese automakers, and to ensure access to foreign markets, Japanese automakers have been keen to facilitate the access of foreign products to the Japanese market. The major automakers have changed their stance on free trade and market access. In the past, they considered that free trade was necessary to expand their market share in the world market. As their operations shifted from exports to local production, they were required to be insiders in local markets. They came to regard the expansion of market access of foreign products to Japan as necessary to their acceptance in foreign markets.

Growing multinational operations have also affected the stance of Japanese electronics producers on market access issues. As they extended their multinational operations, electronics producers reconsidered their pattern of aggressive competition, and paid more attention to cooperation with their competitors, as well as promoting the harmonization of Japanese institutions and customs to international norms. These changes in strategy in 1989 encouraged major electronics firms to draw up international cooperation programmes designed to expand market access for foreign products to Japan. The influence of multinational operations is also revealed in the stance of electronics firms on market access issues in the US–Japan Semiconductor Arrangement. Although their cooperative action on market access for foreign semiconductor suppliers can be accounted for by the benefits from the arrangement, successful pressure by the US Semiconductor Industry Association (SIA), and persistent encouragement of the

Ministry of International Trade and Industry (MITI), changes in corporate preferences on market access were also of importance, especially in explaining the behaviour of consumer electronics producers. These producers were not major semiconductor producers and were highly dependent on the production of consumer electronic goods. As they expanded their multinational operations, they became more sensitive to foreign criticism of their corporate behaviour and of the closed Japanese market.

In the electronics industry, multinational operations also dampened the protectionist movement. Rising imports of electronic products did not encourage electronics firms to demand import restrictions. The industry experienced growing intra-industry trade as imports grew, and there continued to be a large trade surplus in this sector. Importing was largely carried out by Japanese multinational electronics firms themselves, as they implemented internal business rationalization policies. While high-value-added electronic goods continued to be manufactured in Japan, the production of standardized consumer electronic goods was increasingly transferred to overseas plants. These efforts diminished firms' interest in, and need for, import restrictions.

In the textile industry, which faces rising import pressure, international corporate activity can also be expected to encourage firms to resist the temptation to press for import restrictions. The Japan Apparel Industry Council (JAIC) opposed import restrictions at the downstream stage, but supported import restrictions at the upstream and midstream stages. This is because apparel makers developed local production in East Asian countries, and were heavily involved in imports from these production bases to Japan. Other textile industry associations were reluctant to endorse protectionist policies because of their international links. The Japan Towel Manufacturers' Association (JTMA), whose members were users of imported cotton yarn, opposed restrictions on imports of cotton yarn, despite demand for restrictions on imports of towel products. The Japan Textiles Importers' Association (JTIA), whose members were engaged in the import business, resisted the move to activate the Multi-Fibre Arrangement (MFA) and opposed an anti-dumping suit.

International corporate alliances have also contributed to the opening of the Japanese market. In the automobile industry, corporate alliances are a crucial factor promoting the opening of distribution *keiretsu*. Japanese automakers, through their distribution channels, sell vehicles that their alliance partners manufacture. In the electronics industry, some alliances have provided an environment in which close mutual understanding and communications have developed. This has contributed to the increased penetration of foreign semiconductors into the Japanese market. Alliances also motivated some electronics firms to implement market access activities more seriously in order to maintain stable relationships with alliance partners.

The case studies suggest that multinational operations and international corporate alliances have been key factors in changing the preferences of Japanese corporations in favour of an open domestic market. A preference for greater market liberalization led to action to facilitate market access for foreign products and to resistance towards protectionist measures. This is not, of course, to suggest that the internationalization of corporate activity has been the only dominant factor encouraging firms to change their stance on market access for foreign products. The rapid appreciation of the yen after 1985 was another critical factor motivating Japanese corporations to use more imported products. In the automobile and semiconductor cases, US pressure was important in making the Japanese government and firms take action. The real and potential pressure from the US government motivated its Japanese counterpart to encourage automakers to announce programmes for expanding market access of foreign products. Furthermore, political pressure from the Liberal Democratic Party (LDP) constituted a reason why Nissan announced an international cooperation programme in 1989.

Japanese business has a different institutional setting from its US counterpart, through the representation of interests by peak business federations, especially Keidanren. Keidanren has intensified its demand for an open Japanese market as Japanese corporations have expanded their international operations. The evolution of Keidanren's stance is evident in its commitment to liberalization of trade in farm products. Previously Keidanren was not a vocal opponent of the protectionist agricultural policy. This stance changed in 1980 through the establishment of the Committee on Agricultural Policy. Although Keidanren's attack on agricultural trade protectionism was moderate and general in the early 1980s, it became stronger and more comprehensive in the late 1980s, including a demand for liberalization in the rice market. The evolution of Keidanren's stance is also evident on other trade policy issues. In the early 1980s, the federation sought to improve standards and certification systems, so-called border measures directly impeding the entry of foreign goods. Keidanren intensified its advocacy of deregulation from the late 1980s, attempting to revise domestic systems that impeded better market access. The federation also directed attention to policies affecting inward investment in the 1990s, perceiving them as a factor fostering perceptions of a closed Japanese market. Keidanren's commitment to opening the Japanese market extended from border measures to reform of the domestic system, and from trade policies proper to related investment policies.

Keidanren's actions can be explained by several domestic factors. An important factor encouraging the federation to promote administrative reform, including improvement in standards and certification systems, and to demand reform of the food control system was its desire to restore sound public finance, and thereby avoid tax increases. Deregulation aimed to change a bureaucracy-led, centralized economic system to a private sector-led, decentralized economic system. Liberalization of agricultural trade was also demanded in order to strengthen international competitiveness in the food processing industry. However, the internationalization of corporate activity is clearly an important factor motivating Keidanren to advocate liberalization of the Japanese market. Keidanren took a stronger antiprotectionist stance on agricultural trade because the Japanese manufacturing sector had increased its dependence on foreign markets and its involvement in overseas manufacturing, and Japan's surpluses with its trading partners raised the likelihood of retaliation against Japan's exports. The Japanese manufacturing sector accelerated its multinational operations after 1985. This led to a rise in the investment imbalance as well as to increased vulnerability to potential foreign retaliation. Keidanren focused on investment policies and deregulation in order to change the system that had created a closed Japanese market. Thus, Keidanren, the organization representing the interests of internationally oriented big business, has also intensified its open trade stance as Japanese corporations have extended their international corporate activity.

The case studies here basically support the hypothesis that firms with greater multinational operations and international corporate alliances prefer an open domestic market. In the textile industry, however, there are qualifications to the argument. The Japan Chemical Fibres Association (JCFA) and the Japan Spinners' Association (JSA), comprising big synthetic-fibre and spinning companies with international links, demanded protectionist measures on textile imports. Their stance is partly explicable in terms of the main hypothesis of this study. Although their members were among the first over-seas investors in Japanese industry in the late 1960s and the early 1970s, multinational operations did not expand and there were suc-cessive withdrawals from overseas investment in the 1970s and the early 1980s. They also restricted imports from their overseas plants to Japan to avoid unfavourable effects on domestic producers. Hence, they had little interest in resisting the demand for protectionist mea-sures. The international linkages of these textile producers are less sig-nificant than those of automobile or electronics producers. In contrast to their weak international links, they had strong domestic links. The textile producers were linked to small and medium-sized firms through service fee contracts after the 1950s. They also concentrated their interests in downstream operations by promoting forward inte-gration. The large textile firms, potentially the most powerful actors in the industry, assumed the role of leaders of the Japanese textile industry. The majority of firms in the industry are, however, small scale. Large companies tended to resist measures that undermined the interests of the majority in the industry. They suppressed their own interests in favour of those of the majority.

The exceptional case of the textile industry suggests that domestic linkages are also a crucial factor affecting firms' trade policy prefer-ences.[1] Why, however, was there a difference in the case of the textile industry and not in the automobile and electronics industries? In these three industries, vertical *keiretsu* relations are present between large and small-sized firms. Large producer firms encourage small sub-contracting firms to organize cooperative associations, and provide various assistance and information to their members. However, there are subtle differences in the business relations in each industry. In the textile industry, small-sized weaving houses are a significant source of the non-price competitiveness of Japanese textile products. Japanese textile producers have difficulty in finding weaving houses with the same quality overseas, and few Japanese weaving houses have been able to relocate abroad successfully. Accordingly, large textile pro-ducers have sought to preserve the competitiveness of these subcon-tracting firms.

The automobile industry is similar to the textile industry in the sense that subcontracting firms are a source of competitiveness. However, major parts suppliers have been able to go abroad with their assembly makers or on their own, and auto assemblers have been compelled by economic and political pressures to find parts suppliers in local markets. The internationalization of corporate activity has functioned to loosen the vertical relations between auto assemblers and parts suppliers. In the electronics industry, unlike the automobile sector, major producers manufacture numerous parts in-house; the ratio of in-house manufacturing is higher than in the automobile industry. In addition, electronics producers procure a portion of parts from suppliers' catalogues in the market, not from subcontracting firms. In respect of semiconductors, core devices are manufactured in-house, and supplementary devices are supplied by other semiconductor producers, not by subcontracting firms. Accordingly, when electronics producers sought to purchase more foreign semiconductors, it was easier to switch from in-house production to procurement from other firms, and from domestic to foreign suppliers. In these three industries, the strength and form of vertical linkages diverge. The degree of internationalization of subcontracting firms is also different. Vertical linkages do affect the preferences of large producers for opening the home market. But the detailed characteristics of linkages have greatly influenced company preferences in different sectors.

In addition to strong domestic linkages, there are at least two other noteworthy features of the relationship between the internationalization of corporate activity and its influence on firms' preferences for commercial policy in Japan. The first is that multinational operations and corporate preferences in favour of an open domestic market often occur concurrently. Multinational operations among Japanese manufacturing industry have been rather recent phenomena compared with industries in other western countries. The share of overseas to domestic sales was only 3 per cent in 1985 for Japan compared with 18.1 per cent for the United States and 19.3 per cent for West Germany. Although Japan's share rose to 8.6 per cent in 1994, this ratio was still below the share of the United States (26.0 per cent) and Germany (23.0 per cent).[2] Furthermore, multinational operations by Japanese manufacturing firms began as a result of external factors rather than internal corporate strategies. Rising trade friction with other industrial countries after the late 1970s and a sharp appreciation of the yen after 1985 were crucial factors encouraging Japanese manufacturing firms to promote overseas operations. These factors simultaneously highlighted Japanese firms' concerns about the openness of the home market. The preference in favour of open trade developed with multinational operations rather than after them. The crucial point is that the firms that developed multinational operations before the mid-1980s were the most active in opening the Japanese market. This was shown in the case of Nissan and Matsushita which took the initiative in drawing up international cooperation programmes in 1989.

The second feature relates to the resolution of intra-industry divisions of views. Internal divergence of views on trade issues within an industry often prevents that industry from developing a unified position on trade policy. Milner (1988, p.248) attributes these divergent views to a difference in the degree of internationalization, that is, the largest firms have tended to become internationalized, while the smaller ones have often remained dependent on the domestic market.

These studies of Japanese industry add to the understanding of intra-industry divergence of position on liberalization in subtle ways. There are several cases where intra-industry divisions emerged over trade issues. The most prominent example was in the textile industry. The Japan Textile Industry Federation (JTIF), the peak organization of the industry, called on the government to introduce the MFA as the collective will of the industry. Yet JTIA strongly opposed import restrictions, and this disagreement had the effect of weakening the demands of the textile industry for government action. There were also divergences at the firm level. Toray, the leading synthetic-fibre producer, decided to begin importing textile products manufactured in its overseas plants. This decision broke a tacit consensus within the industry that products manufactured in overseas plants should not be imported into Japan. Toray did not accept the agreement among synthetic-fibre makers to cut production capacity, either. Toray, which had established an integrated production system in Southeast Asia, could send yarn in oversupply in Japan to its overseas plants instead of cutting production in Japan.

Divisions among companies were evident in other sectors. In the electronics industry, NEC, the leading semiconductor producer, did not accept MITI's injunction to cut semiconductor production. NEC's resistance lasted for half a year and this defection undermined the effectiveness of MITI's administrative guidance of the industry. Although there are only 11 producers in the automobile industry, the cohesion of the industry has not been strong. For instance, when the extension of voluntary export restraints (VERs) became an issue in 1985, the companies failed to reach a common position, and this was a crucial reason why the Japanese government decided on the extension of VERs. The relatively weak cohesion in the automobile industry is partly because Toyota, which did not have its headquarters in Tokyo until 1991, was less interested in maintaining cohesion in the industry. In the case examined here, Nissan's international cooperation programme was greeted cynically by other automakers in 1989.

These cases are in line with the argument that leading companies with intensive international linkages often take actions that contradict the interests of other firms in their industries. It also suggests the importance of examining individual firms' preferences and behaviour.

In the cases examined here, disagreements among firms were less prevalent and cases where internal divisions made it difficult to develop a unified position on trade issues were rare. Industries were likely to develop a common position. In the textile industry, JTIA opposed import restrictions, but JTIA was not an association of textile producers. Textile producer associations maintained a common position on import restrictions. Despite its reluctance to support the introduction of the MFA on imports of cotton yarn, JTMA demanded the introduction of the MFA on towel imports. Toray broke an industry consensus not to import products manufactured in overseas plants, but not until 1994. Toray had avoided reverse imports for twenty years in order to maintain industry solidarity. In the automobile industry, all the major automakers announced similar programmes in 1989, following Nissan's example. In the 1992 Action Plan, all the major automakers eventually announced plans to increase the purchase of US-made parts and vehicles. A common front among firms was also evident in most instances in the electronics industry. The major electronics firms made concerted efforts to expand market access for foreign semiconductors. This is shown by the fact that some 60 members of the Electronic Industries Association of Japan (EIAJ) joined the Users' Committee of Foreign Semiconductors (UCOM) when it was founded. All the major electronics firms, including those that were not involved with the dumping problems in the US market, attained the 20 per cent market share target of foreign semiconductors by 1992.

Two factors explain the tendency of Japanese corporations to adopt a similar position on trade issues. The first factor is similarity of international operations. Originally, Japanese corporations tended to follow a leader's example due to their strong sense of equal level competition, and an industrial structure that is not heavily concentrated (Encarnation 1986, pp.130–2). In addition, unlike US corporations which have engaged in international operations over a long period, Japanese corporations generally entered international operations recently and at the same time as a consequence of the appreciation of the yen and rising trade friction. In the automobile industry, eight out of the nine passenger car producers established production plants in North America in the 1980s. In the electronics industry, 186 out of 455 firms belonging to EIAJ as full members had overseas manufacturing facilities in 1993, and 356 out of 924 manufacturing facilities were set up between 1985 and 1989 (EIAJ 1993b). These common moves into international operations reduced the possibility of intra-industry conflict over trade policy issues.

The second factor is the existence of powerful industrial associations. Some scholars argue that associations that link state and societal actors have over time played an increasingly important role in policy formation and policy implementation (Gourevitch 1986, pp.229–32). Other scholars who specialize in Japanese politics and political economy assert that Japanese industrial associations have played an important role in reflecting their members' interests in policy making as intermediaries between government agencies and individual firms (Lynn and McKeown 1988; Shindō 1992). The findings of these case studies confirm these points. The leadership of industrial associations is apparent in the textile industry in which all major sub-sectors organize an association. These associations are bases for political activities, and their lobbying was a crucial factor in changing the government's stance on import restrictions. EIAJ also played a crucial role in promoting market access in the semiconductor sector. Market access activities became prominent after EIAJ discussed with SIA detailed measures for expanding the sales of foreign devices in March 1988, and established UCOM two months later. EIAJ and UCOM took the initiative in promoting market access for foreign semiconductors by suggesting measures for market access and providing opportunities for Japanese semiconductor users and foreign suppliers to meet. In the automobile industry, the Japan Automobile Manufacturers' Association (JAMA) organized design-in seminars and conferences and undertook various public relations activities in order to promote market access. These associations played a key role in representing preferences of member firms on trade issues to the government, and initiating activities for market liberalization. The strong leadership of industrial associations minimized the possibility of intra-industry divisions on trade issues among member firms.

THE INFLUENCE OF BUSINESS ON POLICY MAKING

One of the most critical issues regarding the Japanese political economy is whether business interests are a crucial factor in determining economic policy and affecting policy outcomes. Previous studies of this issue referred to Japan as a strong state, and emphasized the dominant role of the bureaucracy in shaping and implementing economic policy. While Katzenstein (1978b) characterizes the Japanese political economy as statist because Japan enjoys a high degree of centralization of both state and society, symbiotic relations between business and the state, and a wide range of administrative tools, Johnson (1982, pp.20–1) argues that 'the elite bureaucracy of Japan makes most major decisions, drafts virtually all legislation, controls the national budget, and is the source of all major policy innovations in the system'.[3] According to the strong state thesis and the bureaucracy-dominant model, the central bureaucracy has the capability to determine economic policy goals autonomously from political parties and interest groups. The bureaucrats pursue these goals with a wide range of policy tools, by varying formal industrial, monetary and fiscal policies, and by informal administrative guidance. The private sector is responsively dependent on the bureaucrats and follows their policies and guidance.

In recent years, a growing number of scholars have challenged the strong state thesis and the bureaucracy-dominant model. The major criticisms come from two directions. The first is that relative importance in policy making has gradually shifted from bureaucrats to LDP politicians. More than 30 years in power enabled the LDP to enhance the function of the Policy Affairs Research Council (PARC), the LDP's deliberation organ, in formulating government policy. The power of the LDP also strengthened as the LDP's *zoku* played a larger role in the policy-making process. *Zoku* field requests from local governments and interest groups and lobby the central government to incorporate their requests into public policy (Sakakibara 1991, p.73). The shift of importance in decision making from the bureaucracy to the LDP could be considered merely a sideways shift *within* a still-strong state (McKean 1993, p.80). However, this has much to do with the rising influence of the private sector in policy making. As Calder (1988a) finds, the policy stance of the LDP has been strongly influenced by the interests of its supporting clientele and interest groups. Insofar as the LDP's power derives from the support of various interest groups, its strength *vis-à-vis* the bureaucracy implies that private interests permeate the policy process more strongly by restraining the influence of bureaucratic power (McKean 1993, pp.80–1).

Second, quite a few scholars who have accumulated empirical research demonstrate that interests of societal actors permeate the policy process. They argue that there are quite a few cases where private business has played a critical role in formulating government policy (Rosenbluth 1989; Mason 1992; Calder 1993; Uriu 1996). These empirical studies reveal subtle relations between the state and business in which the latter's interests often impinge on the policy-making process, and indicate the limitation of an over-generalized typology of weak and strong states or an over-simplified interpretation of bureaucratic dominance.

What insight does this study, focusing on corporate preferences in trade policy formation, provide into the role of business in Japanese policy making? The influence of Keidanren's commitment to the opening of the Japanese market was important in the improvement in standards and certification systems and the promotion of deregulation. Keidanren identified problematic aspects of regulation systems in trade-related areas and in other areas of the economy, and suggested detailed measures to rectify them. Strong lobbying of the government and the ruling parties often led to the incorporation of its demands into government policies. Even in agricultural issues, where Keidanren is not a primary member of the policy formation group, it played a role in initiating a campaign for reform of agricultural trade policy and in suggesting a long-term strategy on reform. The difference in the results the federation's commitments achieved between agriculture and other commercial areas also shows the importance of politicians in the ruling parties. Keidanren was successful in getting its demands incorporated into government policies when it both provided supporting data and business lobbying and obtained cooperation from ruling parties' politicians. Indeed, the political influence of Keidanren declined compared with the 1960s when Yanaga (1968) argued that *zaikai* was the most influential element among the power group consisting of the ruling party, the bureaucracy, and big business. However, Keidanren still maintains privileged access to political circles and exerts influence on policy changes.

The influence of business interests on policy outcomes was also apparent in the textile industry. There was a serious confrontation between the textile associations and the government over the introduction of the MFA, and the government softened its attitude towards the introduction. The most critical factor in this case was strong pressure from textile circles, reflected in a 1994 textile report document which recommended that the government should examine the conditions for introducing the MFA. These cases provide evidence of the direct influence of business preferences and commitments on changes in trade policy direction.

In the automobile and electronics cases, government policies were rarely formed or changed as a direct result of firms' or industries' commitments. The Japanese government, especially MITI, requested firms and industries unilaterally to adopt measures to promote market access for foreign firms and products. This does not necessarily mean that MITI autonomously promoted the opening of the Japanese market and industrial actors were responsively dependent on MITI.

The statist thesis posits that the Japanese state can utilize a wide range of effective policy instruments. For example, Katzenstein (1978a, p.20) argues that Japanese policy makers are provided 'with a formidable set of policy instruments which impinge on particular sectors of the economy and individual firms'. However, in the case studies, policy instruments available to MITI were limited and less powerful. MITI launched several policies designed to open the Japanese market and to attract foreign products and firms. However, policy instruments directly aimed at the private sector have been limited. MITI pressured firms into accepting its guidance by hinting at the possibility of invoking legal authority such as the regulation of exports under the Export Trade Control Ordinance, but these cases were exceptional. In addition, these instruments were not necessarily powerful enough to direct the private sector towards the state's policy objectives. This is shown by MITI's failure to make major manufacturers abide by its administrative guidance. In October 1989, the Minister of MITI requested automakers to refrain from making large capital investments. Nissan ignored this request on the grounds that the capital spending would not lead to a further export drive.[4] MITI also failed to persuade NEC to cut production of DRAMs by 20 per cent in 1986.

Although MITI appeared to implement market-opening policies unilaterally, these policies often followed activities and interests of the private sector. In 1989, for example, MITI hoped to promote imports in a medium-term time frame, yet it did not have any plausible pretext for requesting the private sector to do so. After Nissan announced an international cooperation programme, MITI formally asked 50 firms to draw up similar programmes. Nissan's programme gave substance to MITI's intention and offered a pretext to take this issue up with industry. Similar relations between MITI and the private sector were seen in the Business Global Partnership Project that MITI announced in November 1991. The uniqueness of this project lay in the promotion of industrial alliances. The private sector had already been engaged in extensive joint ventures and technical tie-ups, and MITI's policy followed these moves. Some companies asked MITI to consider import promotion not only directly but also through providing global industrial alliances. MITI adopted these views and made the promotion of industrial alliances a pillar of the project.

Market access in semiconductors was promoted effectively after EIAJ's active involvement. MITI's encouragement to promote market access was certainly an important factor that led the electronics industry to consider market access seriously. However, concrete measures such as the establishment of a task force on consumer electronics, the promotion of design-in and the use of distribution channels originated in the electronics industry. Moreover, when the relations between MITI and the electronics industry were difficult, MITI failed to attain its policy objective. The unstable relationship between MITI and the electronics industry was a vital factor in provoking US sanctions. The case studies are not consistent with the assertions of recent studies of Japanese political economy in the sense that industrial actors have not always played a leading role in shaping government policies. However, they suggest that although the Japanese government seemed to lead the private sector to expand market access forcefully, the effectiveness of such initiatives often depended on the explicit or implicit preferences of the private sector. This subtle relationship between bureaucrats and business actors is consonant with the argument that industrial development in Japan was not attained by strong government leadership but by negotiations between bureaucrats and firms based on 'reciprocal consent' (Samuels 1987).

Through the 1980s, the Japanese government announced a series of market liberalization measures, but these measures were regarded as 'too little, too late', far below the expectations of foreign governments. If these inadequate measures are explained by focusing on government action alone, the cause of the limited outcome is simply negligence by the Japanese government. If the preferences of private business are taken into account, this result stems from private actors' inadequate recognition of the necessity for expanding market access. This illustrates the importance of preferences and activities of industrial actors in analysing industrial policy development.

The firms and government agencies have developed various forms of communication channels in the 'network' state (Okimoto 1989). In each of the case studies, MITI had various channels, including advisory councils, close relations with industrial associations, and direct connection to companies and industrial leaders. These networks enabled MITI to intervene in the activities of private business such as investment plans, advertising, and import expansion programmes. However, intervention does not necessarily mean influence. Internationally competitive firms have sufficient resources to formulate and pursue their own corporate strategies. Even if firms take action that the government encourages, this does not necessarily mean that they do so by abiding by the government's guidance. Their actions may spring from their own preferences or from a desire for cohesion within the industry.

By the early 1980s, MITI's influence on industry had gradually declined as Japanese industry enhanced its international competitiveness and accumulated corporate power. When the internationalization of corporate activities grew rapidly in the 1980s, Japanese corporations became embroiled in political problems. This was because they tended to pursue market share single-mindedly, paying little attention to the political effects of their behaviour. MITI gradually regained some influence on internationally competitive sectors by intervening to seek solutions to trade friction caused by firms in areas where MITI's involvement had in the past been limited.[5] The study suggests that internationally oriented firms are more likely to formulate corporate strategies taking into consideration political as well as economic factors. If this tendency is strengthened, MITI's influence on internationally competitive sectors is likely to decline once again.

ISSUES FOR FUTURE RESEARCH

The study sought to exhibit the influence on trade policy of changed corporate preferences. However, it still needs more detailed examinations of how changed corporate preferences are transformed into trade policy. In addition, the study is not free from the inherent limitations of case studies, in particular the problem of uniqueness. The study does not show that all Japanese MNCs take a position supporting market liberalization in Japan. However, as major Japanese industries such as electronics and general machinery, in addition to automobiles, have promoted international operations, they are likely to find more interest in open trade. Given that these manufacturing industries are influential in Japanese business, policy trends for market liberalization are expected to strengthen in Japan. At the same time, large textile producers adopted a protectionist stance, and this evidence suggests the need to undertake studies of firms' trade policy preferences in other sunset industries.

The research also has implications for broader international comparative research. The Japanese evidence confirms the main conclusions of work on the United States and France but also suggests subtle differences from the US and French cases, mainly because of close links in Japan among domestic firms, the existence of powerful industrial associations, and the difference in institutional setting. The study highlights the value of conducting research on countries with different industrial characteristics and different institutional settings. Further research can also be done on the influence of international corporate alliances on government policy. The study suggests that corporate alliances in the electronics and automobile industries contributed to the change in corporate preferences towards more open trade. Research on other industries and other countries on this issue may strengthen confidence in this conclusion.

Notes and References

1 Introduction

1. An MNC is defined as a corporation that 'controls and manages production establishments – plants – located in at least two countries' (Caves 1996, p.1).
2. For the depiction of the trade policy formation in Japan, see Higashi (1983). For an examination of interactions among actors on trade policy in Japan, see Kusano (1983), NIRA (1989) and Mikanagi (1996).
3. For instance, see Aggarwal, Keohane and Yoffie (1987), Milner (1987, 1988), Milner and Yoffie (1989), and Goodman, Spar and Yoffie (1996).
4. Seven major market-opening programmes were implemented between 1982 and 1985. The Japanese government announced four deregulation programmes between 1993 and 1995.
5. The import promotion tax system for manufactured products introduced in 1990 allows manufacturers to deduct 5 per cent tax of increase in import amount, and wholesalers and retailers are allowed to deduct 20 per cent tax. In 1984, the Japan Development Bank began low rate loans for companies establishing distribution institutions and other equipment for imports. The Export–Import Bank of Japan also commenced special loans for Japanese importers, users of imported goods and foreign exporters in 1984.
6. For a similar argument, see Vogel (1978) and Pempel (1982).
7. The US demand for market opening has escalated since the early 1980s both because US trade deficits with Japan grew and because the Japanese market has become a profitable large market as a consequence of the sharp yen appreciation.
8. The major examples are the Market Oriented Sector Specific (MOSS) negotiations in 1986 and the Structural Impediments Initiative (SII) in 1989 and 1990.
9. In the SII talks, the Japanese and US governments identified several issue areas for reform. Six areas were raised on the Japanese side: the price mechanism, the distribution system, the savings–investment balances, land policy reform, exclusionary business practices, and *keiretsu* relationships.

2 The Rise of Multinational Corporations and Policy Preferences

1. Some economists, employing regression analysis, have examined the correlation between multinational operations, resultant intra-firm trade, on the one hand, and trade policy outcomes, on the other. Pugel and Walter (1985) conduct a micro-political test of a company's position on trade

217

policy issues, examining the relationship between US firms' positions on trade liberalization and three factors: the intensity of import competition, the benefits deriving from foreign markets, and the capabilities for adjustment during the 1970s. They conclude that a firm that gains more benefits from access to foreign markets or that has more product diversification is more likely to favour trade liberalizing legislation, while a firm facing stronger import pressure tends to oppose liberalising legislation. Other studies at the aggregate industry level differ subtly in their results regarding the effects of multinationality or intra-firm trade on policy outcomes. While Baldwin (1985, pp.150–72) finds that policy outcomes were little influenced by the level of FDI, Lavergne (1983, pp.153–4) suggests that intra-firm trade had little effect on tariff levels.

2. *Survey of Current Business*, vol. 75, no.6, June 1995, p.39.

3. For the argument that demands for protection are less pervasive among export-dependent firms, see Baldwin (1985, pp.150–72), Destler and Odell (1987), and Milner (1988). For the argument with respect to the preferences of firms that import a substantial portion of their intermediate input, see Destler and Odell (1987).

4. Corporate alliances refer to cooperative arrangements made between firms for mutual advantages, including joint ventures, cooperative R & D, marketing and distributorship agreements, and other business link-ups (Starr 1991, p.138).

5. Ostry and Nelson (1995, p.78) refer to this kind of friction as 'system friction'. Exclusionary business practices and firms' *keiretsu* groupings, which became the major issues at the Japan–US Structural Impediments Initiative (SII) talks, are examples.

6. There are numerous studies concerning Japanese MNCs and their FDI. For the early stage of FDI, see Tsurumi (1976) and Yoshihara (1978); for FDI in the United States, see Graham and Krugman (1991); for FDI in ASEAN countries, see Phongpaichit (1990); and for FDI in Europe, see Thomsen and Nicolaides (1991). For a recent trend of Japanese FDI, see Chen and Drysdale (1995).

7. Japanese FDI has been accelerated by several factors. First, sharp appreciation of the yen has encouraged Japanese firms to invest in foreign markets. After the Plaza Agreement of 1985, the value of the yen against the US dollar almost doubled within two years. Japanese firms were obliged to relocate their operations overseas so as to restore competitiveness by reducing production costs. Second, FDI has been promoted as a means of mitigating the trade surplus with the United States and Western Europe and circumventing increased protectionism. In addition to these external factors, changes in corporate strategy have stimulated overseas activities. Japanese firms have to meet two contradictory demands in global corporate competition: to supply differentiated products which respond to differences in local needs and tastes; and to reduce production costs. Growing interdependence in a 'borderless' world does not result in one amorphous mass of universal taste. On the contrary, the provision of goods which are exactly suited to local preferences is indispensable to survival in fierce corporate competition. Internationally ori-

ented firms have, therefore, increasingly shifted R & D institutions and marketing bases to local subsidiaries and have made efforts to become insiders in each market. Japanese firms are pursuing this corporate strategy.

8. MITI, *Kaigai toshi tokei soran* [Statistical Report on Foreign Investment], No.6 (1998), p.37.

9. Owing to the dominant role of general trading companies (*sogo shosha*) in Japanese trade, intra-firm trade has been high in Japanese firms. In 1988, for example, trade between MNCs and their affiliates accounted for 79.4 per cent of US imports from Japan and 57.2 per cent of US exports to Japan, while such trade accounted for 40 per cent of US exports to Europe and 48.5 per cent of US imports from Europe (Lawrence 1991a, p.39). The difference in the trade between US–Japan and US–Europe lay in the role of Japanese *sogo shosha*.

10. MITI, *Kaigai toshi tokei soran* [Statistical Report on Foreign Investment] No.2 (1985), pp.74–7; No.6 (1998), pp.95–7.

11. The number of reverse imports of the Accord increased from 5,395 in 1988 to 50,694 in 1995.

12. Patrick and Rosovsky (1976), Trezise (1983), and Adams and Ichimura (1983) stand in line with this view. Patrick and Rosovsky (1976, p.47), for example, argue that 'while the government has certainly provided a favorable environment, the main impetus to growth has been private – business investment demand, private saving, and industrious and skilled labor operating in a market-oriented environment of relative prices. Government intervention generally has tended (and intended) to accelerate trends already put in motion by private market forces – the development of infant industries, the structural adjustment of declining industries, and the like.'

13. Kaplan (1972), Pempel (1982), and Johnson (1982) adopt this view. Kaplan (1972, p.10) contends that '[i]t is the special and unique way in which the Japanese government has guided the economy's development and the interaction of government and enterprise which is the peculiar hall-mark of the Japanese economy. Japan's economic destiny has not been left to the free play of market forces. The government has undertaken from the beginning of Japan's modernization and industrialization to identify objectives and priorities for the Japanese economy.'

14. The revisionists contend that since the Japanese system is organised on fundamentally different economic principles from those in other western countries, different rules and treatments should be applied to Japan. For the argument of the revisionists, see Johnson (1982, 1995), Fallows (1989), Prestowitz (1988) and van Wolferen (1989).

15. The Chamber of Commerce, founded in 1912, comprises 180,000 member companies and several thousand state and local chamber and trade association members. The National Association of Manufacturers, established in 1895, consists of 13,000 companies, 150 state and local associations of manufacturers and 110 manufacturing trade associations (Lynn and McKeown 1988, p.81).

16. The role of *zaikai* will be discussed in detail in Chapter 3.

17. For instance, the Ministry of Finance holds a meeting with *zaikai* leaders in the budget compilation process (Yamakawa 1984, p.114).
18. Senior *zaikai* members have chaired most of the advisory councils on economic policy such as the Economic Council, the Industrial Structure Council, the Financial System Council, and the Foreign Exchange Council. In 1995, for instance, the Industrial Structure Council and the Financial System Council were chaired by Shoichiro Toyoda, Chairman of Keidanren, and the Economic Council and the Foreign Exchange Council were chaired by Gaishi Hiraiwa, the former chairman of Keidanren (*Nihon Keizai Shimbun*, 14 July 1995).
19. These data, collected by MITI, are not necessarily suitable for comparisons between years and industries because the number of companies surveyed is different from year to year. Nonetheless, it is useful to know the general trend in intra-firm trade in Japan.
20. MITI, *Kogyo tokeihyo: Sangyohen* [Census of Manufactures: Report by Industry], 1980; 1993.
21. *Seni Nenkan*, 1995, p.68.

3   The Influence of Business on Japanese Policy Making

1. For a comprehensive depiction of Keidanren, see Honjo (1993). For a historical survey of Keidanren through the appointments of chairmen and vice-chairmen, see Allinson (1987).
2. The figures are from 1994. Keidanren also has 46 special members composed of public corporations and 50 recommended individual members.
3. Sub-governments are defined as 'small groups of political actors, both governmental and nongovernmental, that specialize in specific issue areas' (Ripley and Franklin 1984, p.8). *Zoku* (tribe, clan) are 'LDP Diet members who exert, formally or informally, a strong influence on specific policy areas mainly at the LDP's PARC' (Inoguchi and Iwai 1987, p.20). The LDP politicians, who have had positions such as political vice-minister (*seimujikan*), chairman and vice-chairman of the PARC divisions, and chairman of the Diet standing committees, have accumulated special expertise and influence concerned with policy implementation as well as formulation.
4. Industrial associations are normally rendered in Japanese as *gyokai dantai*. The term *jigyosha dantai* used in the Antimonopoly Law indicates the same meaning.
5. Although some industrial associations were established before the Second World War, the majority of manufacturers' associations were organized as *toseikai* (control associations) during the war. *Toseikai* aimed to cooperate with war plan execution by deploying technical and manufacturing expertise of the private sector for the government's material procurement plans. *Toseikai* was reorganized as industrial associations after the war.
6. Fair Trade Commission, *Kosei torihiki iinkai nenji hokoku* [FTC Annual Report] 1996, p.188.

7. This questionnaire survey was conducted in September 1993, targeting 844 industrial associations, including 432 in the manufacturing sectors.

8. In 1996, there were 217 advisory councils under Article 8 of the National Administrative Organization Act, 33 of which were attached to MITI. In addition to these official councils, there are a number of unofficial private advisory bodies in Japan. Since these bodies are not organizations with legal authorization, it is difficult to know the exact number. One survey estimates that there were 284 bodies in 1985 and 1986, some 140 bodies established per year (Ryū 1995, p.109).

9. For instance, Okimoto (1989, p.160) raises advisory councils as one of intermediate institutions bridging public and private spheres. However, there is a controversy over the assessment of advisory councils. Although they are often criticized as *kakuremino* ('an invisible fairy's cloak'), Schwartz (1993) assesses their functions positively as mediating conflicting interests and shielding decision-making bodies from disputes over conflicting interests.

10. Through 1962 to 1963, MITI drafted the bill of the Special Measures Law, which aimed to provide certain industries with tax and monetary incentives for rationalization and consolidation in an effort to prepare for the coming liberalization. Although the draft of the bill was submitted to the Diet three times, it was eventually discarded owing to an anxiety about the strong administrative control, especially the administrative restriction on capital supply. For the Special Measures Law, see Johnson (1982, pp.255–60) and Ōyama (1996, ch. 5).

11. *Keizai dantai rengokai 30 nenshi* [The 30-year history of Keidanren], 1978, pp.363–76.

12. Keidanren set up the Economic Reconstruction Association (*Keizai Saiken Kondankai*), a fund-raising institute in 1955, after a big political funding scandal occurred in the shipbuilding industry. The institute was transformed into *Kokumin Seiji Kyokai* in March 1975 (Hanamura 1994, pp.88–9).

13. *Jichi no ugoki*, no.262, November 1993, p.11.

14. *Mainichi Daily News*, 22 November 1989.

15. The Administrative Management Agency, *Gyosei kikozu* [Organizational chart], 1980, p.143; The Management and Coordination Agency, *Gyosei kikozu* [Organizational chart], 1995, p.163.

16. The Administrative Management Agency, *Gyosei kikozu* [Organizational chart], 1980, p.144; The Management and Coordination Agency, *Gyosei kikozu* [Organizational chart], 1995, p.164.

17. Administrative guidance is defined as an administrative action that, without any coercive legal effect, 'encourages regulated parties to act in a specific way in order to realize some administrative aim' (Young 1984, p.923). For the discussion of the role of administrative guidance, see Haley (1986), Shindō (1992) and Ōyama (1996).

18. Ōyama (1989, pp.34–5) regards the advisory council system in policy making and the administrative guidance system in policy implementation as playing complementary roles in coordinating industrial interests.

19. Interview, Users Committee of Foreign Semiconductors, Tokyo, September 1995.

20. *Shukan Toyo Keizai*, 15 October 1994, pp.80–1.
21. *Jichi no ugoki*, no.132, September 1978, pp.14–15.
22. The number of interest groups in Japan increased from 17,413 in 1966 to 20,614 in 1975 and to 33,668 in 1986 (Tsujinaka 1988, p.19). The emergence of new interest groups is prominent in policy areas such as welfare, education and consumer affairs.
23. *Mainichi Daily News*, 14 April 1990.
24. According to the FTC survey, 67.6 per cent of the respondent foreign-affiliated firms operating in Japan joined some industrial associations in 1993 (FTC 1993c, p.20).
25. *Yomiuri Shimbun*, 16 June 1994.

4 The Japanese Automobile Industry and Market Liberalization

1. According to the Motor Industry of Japan in 1996.
2. *Jidosha sangyo hando bukku*, 1996, pp.305–7.
3. Most late starters opted for joint ventures with their US partners. Mazda established AutoAlliance International Inc. (AAI), a 50/50 joint venture with Ford in 1985, starting production in September 1987. The joint venture provides half of its output to Ford. Mitsubishi Motors built up Diamond-Star Motors (DSM) with Chrysler in October 1985. DSM started production in September 1988 with a capacity of 240,000 a year. Although Chrysler retreated from DSM in October 1991, DSM continues to supply vehicles to Chrysler. While Fuji and Isuzu established Subaru-Isuzu Automotive Inc. (SIA) in 1987, Suzuki established CAMI Automotive Inc. with GM in Canada.
4. *Jidosha sangyo hando bukku*, 1994, pp.140–51.
5. *Jidosha sangyo hando bukku*, 1995, pp.310–19; Toyota, *Kaisha gaiyo* 1995, p.11; Nissan, *Nissan jidosha no gurobarizeishon*, 1994, p.5; Honda, Annual Report 1993, p.6.
6. GM established the Geo brand in the Chevrolet division in 1989, which was solely composed of Japanese original equipment manufacturing (OEM) vehicles (*Soken Chosa*, October 1991, p.13).
7. *Nihon Keizai Shimbun*, 25 July 1994.
8. *Soken Chosa*, October 1991, p.13.
9. The term *keiretsu* broadly means various forms of inter-firm relationships, but its real meanings are diverse. Sheard (1993, pp.5–6) identifies five common usages: first, the six enterprise groups composed of firms in different markets which are connected through common financial affiliation, interlocking shareholdings and director ties; second, sets of firms that have common financial links (financial *keiretsu*); third, a group of firms comprising a large parent company and its subsidiaries and affiliates; fourth, a group of firms composed of a parent firm and its subcontracting suppliers (supplier *keiretsu*); and fifth, a group of firms comprising a core manufacturer and its affiliated wholesalers and distributors (distribution *keiretsu*). The first and second types are referred to as horizontal *keiretsu*, while the third and fourth are vertical *keiretsu*. The automobile industry has a bearing on all *keiretsu* groups, yet sup-

plier *keiretsu* and distribution *keiretsu* have been the primary source of trade disputes. The present discussion is directed to these two *keiretsu* in the automobile industry.

10. See, for instance, Balassa (1986), Lawrence (1991b), and Bergsten and Noland (1993). Lawrence (1991b), for instance, argues that while vertical *kereitsu* improves efficiency by reducing imports and promoting exports, horizontal *keiretsu* only reduces imports and inhibits new entrants.

11. *Asahi Shimbun*, 7 January 1992.

12. *Nikkei Sangyo Shimbun*, 13 February 1992.

13. The design-in for automobiles refers to 'a process in which engineers from suppliers work together with design and development engineers from car manufacturers in the early stages of vehicle development' (*JAMA Information Update*, July 1991, p.1). In design-in, suppliers are required to select appropriate materials, perform self-evaluation and implement most of the development work on their own initiative, while assemblers offer guidance and support as necessary.

14. JAMA, *Important Facts about the Japanese and U.S. Auto Industries*, n.d., p.8.

15. Interview, Toyota, Tokyo, April 1994.

16. VA is the effort to reduce costs through proposals on improvements after the start of mass production, while VE is such effort prior to mass production (Asanuma 1989b, p.20).

17. For example, Toyota decided to purchase air-bag sensors and controls from an American maker, TRW Technic Inc., instead of from Nippon Denso. TRW surpassed Nippon Denso, an affiliate of Toyota, by producing a new design and a finished product from conception to production within 14 months (*Los Angeles Times*, 25 February 1992).

18. Interview, Toyota, Tokyo, April 1994.

19. Interview, Nissan, Tokyo, April 1994.

20. Although it is often considered that parts suppliers are divided according to *keiretsu* makers, they participate in several associations. According to an FTC survey, parts suppliers join an average of 3.5 supplier associations (FTC 1993a, p.32).

21. *Nihon Keizai Shimbun*, 27 April 1994.

22. *The Japan Economic Journal*, 18 May 1991.

23. Relation-specific skills are defined as skills required of parts suppliers to maintain and develop relations with core firms through the supply of intermediate products, responding appropriately and efficiently to their specific needs (Asanuma 1989a, p.74).

24. As long as long-term transactions have an economic rationale – and 'exclusionariness' is almost a definition of a long-term contract – it is misleading to consider them in terms of closure of markets (Sheard 1993, p.34; Drysdale 1995, p.278).

25. There are at least two factors other than those explained above that promoted the breakup of supplier *keiretsu* groups. The first is technological innovation. As parts production puts weight on high function, electronically-controlled auto parts and systematization, and assembly

makers seek to differentiate their products from their rivals through high-quality auto parts, they are forced to deal with parts producers with high technology and high development ability regardless of *keiretsu* links. A symbol of this was the commencement of deals between Toyota and Hitachi in January 1992. Toyota decided to purchase electronically-controlled fuel injection sensors from Hitachi, which had previously dealt mainly with Nissan (*Nihon Keizai Shimbun*, 20 January 1992). The second is the severe recession of the 1990s. On the one hand, assembly makers cut back on model variations and used more common auto parts in order to curtail production costs. On the other hand, major suppliers sought new customers irrespective of *keiretsu* links in order to improve scale economies further. According to an FTC survey, 71 per cent of parts suppliers conduct activities to expand their deals to new companies (FTC 1993a, p.26).

26. *Nikkan Kogyo Shimbun*, 4 February 1994.
27. *Nihon Keizai Shimbun*, 22 April 1994.
28. *The Japan Economic Journal*, 18 May 1991.
29. For an analysis of the Japan's car distribution system, see Shimokawa (1987), Ishibashi (1991), and Shioji (1992).
30. The survey suggests that the US car sales would increase by 37,000 annually, if the impediments of *keiretsu* links between automakers and dealers were removed (*Nihon Keizai Shimbun*, 14 February 1994).
31. *The JAMA Forum*, vol. 12, no.2, December 1993, p.4.
32. *Nikkei Sangyo Shimbun*, 23 March 1994.
33. Several research reports point to tight relationships between Japanese automakers and dealers. For instance, the final report for the MOSS Motor Vehicle Study issued in February 1994 points out that 33 per cent of domestic car dealers accept equity participation from automakers, while 25 per cent borrow short-term operating funds from automakers, and 40 per cent have long-term debts. FTC survey data on the distribution also show that 12.9 per cent of dealers accept executives from automakers (FTC 1993b, p.23).
34. Interview, Nissan, Tokyo, April 1994. In reality, according to an FTC survey, all dealers who undertook prior consultation with their producers in handling imported cars could attain the objective (FTC 1993b, p.41).
35. *Asahi Shimbun*, 9 November 1991.
36. *Asahi Shimbun*, 20 November 1991.
37. *Nihon Keizai Shimbun*, 7 May 1994.
38. Ford Japan became an equity partner in the Autorama channel in 1989.
39. In the case of Nissan's dealers, Kushiro Nissan handles Mercedes-Benz, Volkswagen, and Audi, Sunny Miyagi sells Mercedes-Benz, and Tochigi Nissan sells Mercedes-Benz, Audi. There are many other cases (Interview, Nissan, Tokyo, June 1994).
40. *Nihon Keizai Shimbun*, 1 October 1994.
41. Interview, Honda, Tokyo, April 1994.
42. *Nihon Keizai Shimbun*, 16 April 1991.
43. *Nihon Keizai Shimbun*, 16 April 1991.
44. *Nihon Keizai Shimbun*, 31 August 1994.

45. *Nikkei Sangyo Shimbun*, 24 March 1994.
46. *The Economist*, 1 July 1995, p.68.
47. These measures include seven major market opening programmes between 1982 and 1985, new tax systems and financial loans programmes designed to promote inward investment as well as imports, and import promotion activities through the Japan External Trade Organization (JETRO).
48. *The Japan Economic Journal*, 9 December 1989. Nissan's response contrasted sharply with that of Mazda. Mazda, whose president was a former MITI official, accepted MITI's guidance to curtail planned production capacity at its new plant.
49. *Nihon Keizai Shimbun*, 14 December 1989.
50. These were US$51.4 billion in 1986, US$52.1 billion in 1987, and US$47.6 billion in 1988.
51. *The New York Times*, 26 May 1989.
52. In 1989, commodity taxes, which were imposed on standard cars at a rate of 23 per cent and on compact cars at 18.5 per cent, were transformed into a 6 per cent consumer tax on all kinds of vehicles.
53. *The Japan Economic Journal*, 6 May 1989.
54. *Nikkei Sangyo Shimbun*, 26 May 1989.
55. *Nihon Keizai Shimbun*, 19 June 1989.
56. Interview, Nissan, Tokyo, April 1994.
57. The ratio of the Japanese in total employees at the Japanese manufacturing plants operating in the United States was 2.5 for Toyota, 5.0 for Honda and 1.9 for Mitsubishi, and only 0.7 for Nissan (Ishii 1990, p.14).
58. Interview, Nissan, Tokyo, April 1994.
59. *Mainichi Shimbun*, 21 September 1989.
60. *The Japan Economic Journal*, 9 December 1989.
61. For instance, Shoichiro Toyoda, President of Toyota, commented on Nissan's programme that 'it is natural that exports will decrease as local production increases. We have referred to this direction many times' (*Asahi Shimbun*, 23 September 1989).
62. *Nihon Keizai Shimbun*, 21 October 1989.
63. *Nihon Keizai Shimbun*, 21 October 1989.
64. *Nihon Keizai Shimbun*, 31 October 1989.
65. While Honda planned to increase the value of imports in 1988 by 2.5 times to 160 billion yen by 1992, Mitsubishi's import figure was 100 billion yen in 1992, up 3.6 times on 1988 (*Nihon Keizai Shimbun*, 25 November 1989; 18 January 1990).
66. *Nihon Keizai Shimbun*, 21 October 1989.
67. *Nihon Keizai Shimbun*, 20 November 1989.
68. MITI expected that the industry would coordinate orderly exports with a volume of less than 2.3 million after VER was abolished, but the industry failed to coordinate their interests. MITI's hearing revealed that the total export volume amounted to more than 2.7 million (NIRA 1989, chap.1).
69. *Nihon Keizai Shimbun*, 27 December 1991.
70. *Yomiuri Shimbun*, 5 January 1992.

71. *Nihon Keizai Shimbun*, 26 December 1991.
72. *Yomiuri Shimbun*, 5 January 1992.
73. He censured Toyota for considering its own company alone without understanding Japan's situation (*Mainichi Shimbun*, 8 March 1994).
74. *Mainichi Shimbun*, 8 March 1994.
75. *Nikkei Sangyo Shimbun*, 9 January 1992.
76. For instance, Yutaka Kume emphasized the need for the programmes as follows: 'The cooperation between Japanese and US firms is important for the solution to trade friction regarding auto parts. For this purpose, each firm has to draw up a program for purchases of US-made parts as soon as possible' (*Nihon Keizai Shimbun*, 25 September 1991).
77. *Nihon Keizai Shimbun*, 20 November 1991.
78. MITI requested the major firms in automobiles, electronics, steel, and machine tools to submit plans for purchasing foreign-made equipment and materials as well as plans for subsidiaries abroad to purchase parts and materials from foreign companies. These firms were also required to draw up plans for establishing joint ventures and technical tie-ups with foreign companies.
79. Nissan and Mazda would double the purchase of parts between 1990 and 1994, while Toyota and Mitsubishi would increase them by 75 per cent.
80. *Ekonomisuto*, 28 January 1992, p.29.
81. *Nikkan Jidosha Shimbun*, 6 January 1992.
82. *Yomiuri Shimbun*, 10 January 1992.
83. *Asahi Shimbun*, 9 January 1992.
84. *Purejidento*, January 1985, p.311.
85. *Nihon Keizai Shimbun*, 26 December 1991.
86. *Yomiuri Shimbun*, 29 December 1991.
87. *Nihon Keizai Shimbun*, 7 January 1992.
88. *Nihon Keizai Shimbun*, 12 January 1991.
89. *The New York Times*, 1 June 1991. The Big Three asserted that the import expansion of the Japanese minivan at a low price harmed the US auto industry. Although the Department of Commerce found that the prices of Japanese minivans were a case of dumping in May 1992, the International Trade Commission, which was responsible for determining whether there had been a damage to the US industry, decided in June 1992 that this was not the case. However, the market share of Japanese minivans in the United States had fallen sharply from 14.2 percent in August 1991 to 6.7 percent in May 1992 because the Japanese makers refrained from active sales advertisement.
90. *Nikkei Sangyo Shimbun*, 3 June 1991.
91. *The Washington Post*, 21 December 1991; *JEI Report*, No.2B, 17 January 1992.
92. *Nihon Keizai Shimbun*, 8 December 1991; *Tokyo Shimbun*, 10 January 1992.
93. Interview, JAMA, Tokyo, March 1994.
94. *Nihon Keizai Shimbun*, 1 January 1992.
95. This strategy was adopted by President Eiji Toyoda in January 1978 when the market share of Toyota in the world was 7 per cent. Although the 'Global 10' was an abstract slogan at first, it became an explicit target

in Toyota's growth process such as the start of overseas production in 1984 and 2 million domestic sales in 1988. The objective was attained in 1990 when the market share grew from 8.6 per cent in the previous year to 10.3 per cent (Fourin 1991, p.9).

96. *Nihon Keizai Shimbun*, 21 September 1991.
97. *Nihon Keizai Shimbun*, 25 August 1991.
98. *Nikkei Bijinesu*, 27 April 1992, p.67.
99. *Keizaikai*, 14 April 1994, p.30.
100. *Nihon Keizai Shimbun*, 29 January 1991.
101. *Sentaku*, February 1992, pp.76–7.

5 The Japanese Electronics Industry and Trade Policy

1. Other industrial associations in the electronics industry have been formed according to product category. The Japan Electrical Manufacturers' Association (JEMA) covers heavy electrical apparatus such as prime movers and boilers, motors and generators, electrical systems for industrial facilities and plants, as well as home electrical appliances including washing machines, refrigerators, and air-conditioners. The Japan Electronic Industry Development Association (JEIDA) covers computers and related equipment. The Communications Industry Association of Japan (CIAJ) covers communication equipment such as terminal and network equipment and parts and components.

2. *Nihon no denshi kogyo* [The electronics industry in Japan] 1993/94, p.1.

3. This is a common feature of the semiconductor business internationally, with the exception of the United States. The major semiconductor producers in Europe such as Philips, SGS-Thomson, and Siemens, and Korean makers such as Samsung are vertically integrated producers. In the US case, while Motorola and Texas Instruments belong to the above category, National Semiconductor, Intel, and Advanced Micro Devices are producers that specialise in semiconductor production.

4. According to a report of the Integrated Circuit Engineering, the share of internal transfers in the total Japanese integrated circuit market was roughly 35 per cent (EIAJ 1989, p.8).

5. The ratios of R & D in total sales for the semiconductor sector and the manufacturing average were 14.9 per cent and 1.91 per cent in 1981, 17.1 per cent and 2.69 per cent in 1985, and 15.9 per cent and 3.36 per cent in 1990 (EIAJ 1994a, p.23).

6. For example, capital investment for a plant with a capacity of 20,000 units per month rose from US$300–400 million for one megabyte dynamic random access memory (1M DRAM) to US$400–600 million for 4M DRAM to US$600–850 million for 16M DRAM, and to US$900–1,200 million for 64M DRAM (EIAJ 1994a, p.92). The development and production of next generation products such as flash memories and 256M DRAM are expected to cost more than US$1 billion.

7. The National Research Council (1992, p.10) mentions the following examples: R & D alliances which include licensing and cross-licensing

agreements, technology exchange, and joint development; manufacturing alliances which contain original equipment manufacturing (OEM) agreements, second sourcing agreements whereby a company is given permission to manufacture products developed by another company; marketing and service alliances which consist of procurement agreements, sales agency agreements and servicing contracts; and general purpose tie-ups represented by joint ventures.

8. *Nikkei Sangyo Shimbun*, 2 June 1994; *Nikkan Kogyo Shimbun*, 7 June 1994.

9. For example, the export value of 11.1 trillion yen in 1994 was four times as large as the import value of 2.7 trillion yen, leading to a trade surplus of 8.4 trillion yen.

10. *Nikkei Sangyo Shimbun*, 8 May 1992; *Nihon Keizai Shimbun*, 24 December 1994.

11. Matsushita has the largest number of retail outlets, some 23,000 shops. Toshiba, Hitachi, Sanyo, Mitsubishi Electric, and Sharp have 10,000, 8,600, 6,000, 4,500, and 4,000 shops respectively (*Shukan Toyo Keizai*, 23 April 1994, p.114).

12. *Keidanren Geppo*, February 1992, p.65.

13. For instance, Matsushita reorgansied its *keiretsu* shops into the MAST (Market Oriented Ace Shop Team) system in April 1992. This system sought to support selected shops with active sales promotion (*Keizaikai*, 14 April 1992, pp.32–5). Other electronics firms are also trying to restructure their distribution *keiretsu* channels.

14. It is also incorrect to argue that the distribution *keiretsu* system is a major factor impeding market access of foreign products in the electronics industry. It needs to focus on regulatory controls which limit outlets and increase distribution costs (Drysdale 1995, p.278).

15. For instance, Besuto Denki, the leading large-scale retail store, is owned by Matsushita, Toshiba, Hitachi Sales, Mitsubishi Electric and Sharp, while that of Daiichi Corp., the second largest store, is owned by Matsushita, Toshiba and Hitachi (Nikkei Ryūtsū Shimbun (ed.) 1993, p.87).

16. A close relationship between electronics producers and large-scale retail stores has been revealed in the control of retail prices by electronics producers. In March 1992, for instance, the Fair Trade Commission (FTC) investigated the sales subsidiaries of Matsushita, Sony, Toshiba, and Hitachi on the suspicion that these companies had pressured retail stores to accept predeterminded retail prices for audio-vidual products (*Nihon Keizai Shimbun*, 26 March 1992). In February 1993, the FTC issued a retraction order to the four companies (*Nihon Keizai Shimbun*, 11 February 1993).

17. *Nihon Keizai Shimbun*, 11 December 1991.

18. *Nikkei Sangyo Shimbun*, 18 September 1990.

19. *Tsusan Janaru*, October 1991, p.18.

20. *Nihon Keizai Shimbun*, 21 June 1989.

21. *Nihon Keizai Shimbun*, 11 May 1989.

22. *Nihon Keizai Shimbun*, 28 July 1989.

23. *Nikkei Bijinesu*, 13 August 1990, pp.14–15.

24. Interview, Matsushita, Osaka, May 1994.
25. *Nihon Keizai Shimbun*, 13 January 1989.
26. *Nihon Keizai Shimbun*, 8 July 1989.
27. *Nihon Keizai Shimbun*, 29 May 1989.
28. *Tokyo Business Today*, April 1991, p.51.
29. Although yield rates were often less than 25 per cent when new devices were introduced, the rates would climb to 90 per cent as the devices matured. Companies tend to manufacture high-volume products in order to raise yield rates (Yoffie 1988, p.84).
30. In this process, the Japanese TV makers seemed to coordinate their export plans by notifying each other of their intended quantity of shipments and prices, and allocating US customers among themselves. The coordination was implemented through the Japan Machinery Exporters Association and the Television Export Council attended by top executives of TV exporters. (Yamamura and Vandenberg 1986, p.259).
31. The ratio of capital investment to total sales by twelve Japanese semiconductor producers surpassed 20 per cent between 1979 and 1985 (EIAJ 1994a, p.132).
32. In the second period, Japanese chip producers drastically increased capital spending. Capital investment by twelve Japanese semiconductor producers was 763 billion yen in 1984, 42 per cent of total sales, and 478 billion yen in 1985, 35 per cent of total sales, in spite of a worldwide semiconductor recession in these years (EIAJ 1994a, p.132).
33. As evidence that Japanese semiconductor producers conducted aggressive price competition, the memorandum that Hitachi sent to its distributors of EPROM in February 1985 is put forward. This memorandum said: Win with the 10 per cent rule. . . . Find AMD and Intel sockets. Quote 10 per cent below their price . . . If they requote, go 10 per cent again . . . Don't quit till you win.
34. Merchant producers are companies that manufacture and sell semiconductors to other firms for installation in their products. They are distinguished from captive makers that use all their semiconductors for in-house consumption.
35. Japan's trade surplus was US$96.4 billion in 1987, US$95 billion in 1988, and US$76.9 billion 1989.
36. *Nihon Keizai Shimbun*, 8 July 1989.
37. *Zaikai*, 26 June 1990, p.55.
38. Interview, Industrial Policy Bureau, MITI, Tokyo, May 1994.
39. *Nihon Keizai Shimbun*, 10 July 1991.
40. Interview, Matsushita, Osaka, May 1994.
41. For the Japan–US semiconductor dispute before 1985, see Prestowitz (1988, pp.46–55).
42. SIA was founded in 1977 by five merchant semiconductor producers – Advanced Micro Devices, Fairchild, Intel, Motorola and National Semiconductor – with an eye to strengthening members' interests as well as to coping with the Japanese challenge. By 1985, the association had increased its membership to 48, including IBM with combined revenues of more than US$100 billion (Yoffie 1988, p.86).

43. Section 301 empowers the US President to decide which countries carry out unfair trade practices and to take appropriate action against them.

44. The first part included four items: (1) the Japanese government would encourage its semiconductor users to purchase more foreign semiconductors, while the US government would encourage its semiconductor manufacturers to strengthen their marketing efforts; (2) the governments of both countries agreed that the expected improvement in access should be gradual and steady during the coming five years; (3) the Japanese government would establish an organization for helping foreign producers increase sales in Japan, evaluating product quality, and promoting long-term relationships between Japanese and US firms; and (4) the governments of both countries would exercise voluntary control to prevent excessive production capacity.

45. *Nihon Keizai Shimbun*, 6 March 1987.

46. *Asahi Shimbun*, 21 April 1987.

47. *UCOM News*, 20 June 1993, p.8.

48. *UCOM News*, 26 January 1993, p.8.

49. *UCOM News*, 26 January 1993, p.8.

50. For example, see EIAJ (1987, p.1).

51. These are as follows: promoting long-term relationships between producers and users; increasing the design-in of foreign products; increasing Japanese purchases of existing foreign products; broadening the base of users and suppliers engaged in market access efforts; and accelerating the commencement of foreign participation in the consumer electronics and automobile sectors (SIA 1990, pp.7–8).

52. The design-in in semiconductors is defined as 'a process by which certain semiconductors are newly designed or redesigned (custom/semi-custom semiconductors), or end products themselves are newly designed or redesigned with the use of specific semiconductors in mind from the design stage of developing these end products' (EIAJ 1993a, p.29).

53. UCOM has carried out various activities such as purchasing promotion seminars, design-in seminars, and dispatch of overseas trade missions. The missions were sent eight times and gathered a cumulative total of 283 foreign suppliers by 1993.

54. The consumer electronics task-force examined the market conditions of consumer electronics and recommended an action plan suggesting the promotion of design-in and cooperation of US and Japanese semiconductor suppliers.

55. According to survey data by UCOM, the number of semiconductor users that established special internal sections for market access expansion increased from 8 in 1986 to 61 in 1992 (*UCOM News*, 20 June 1993, p.8). In addition, the number of seminars on purchasing promotion of foreign devices or the exchange of technical information held by semiconductor suppliers doubled between 1986 and 1992, whereas those by semiconductor users grew by ten-fold in the same period. In 1992, 84 per cent of seminars were sponsored by semiconductor users (UCOM 1993, p.7).

56. A report on consumer task-force activities issued in February 1990,

shows that six major US suppliers, on average, produced 6 per cent of existing chips meeting the need of five major Japanese consumer electronics makers (A report of EIAJ/SIA consumer task-force activities).

57. These characteristics lead to a difference in product category between Japanese demand and US supply. Foreign share is the highest in bipolar digital devices, a very small share of the Japanese chip market, while it is meagre in discrete devices which constitute a considerable segment of the total Japanese market. In 1990, foreign share of bipolar digital devices was 29 per cent but the share was 5 per cent of the total Japanese chip market. In contrast, only 5 per cent of discrete devices, which accounted for 22 per cent of the Japanese market, were supplied by foreign firms, and the share was decreasing. Without discrete devices, the foreign market share would rise by 5 per cent (EIAJ 1994c, p.2.4).

58. Interview, EIAJ, Tokyo, September 1995. The semiconductor divisions, which had long accumulated operating losses, were regarded as a 'burden' in the electronics firms.

59. The average share of in-house parts production for auto producers is 30 per cent. The share of in-house parts production for electronics producers varies by company and by production item. A study shows that in TV production at Matsushita, 60 per cent of the parts are manufactured in two parts companies in the Matsushita group (Chen 1994, p.70).

60. 'Marketed goods' are those 'which are offered to the public irrespective of the will of the core [manufacturer] firm and are therefore purchasable by merely selecting from the catalog' (Asanuma 1989b, p.11). This makes a contrast with 'ordered goods' (*gaichuhin*), which are supplied accordingly to specification provided by the core firm.

61. For example, in the case of the TV division of Matsushita, 36 subcontracting parts suppliers that provide custom products such as cabinets and transformers organise *TV kyoei-kai*. Twelve independent makers such as NEC, Mitsubishi Electric which offer ordered goods also organise *meka-kai*. Matsushita organises a trade meeting with the members of *TV kyoei-kai* each month, and with the members of *meka-kai* every six months (Chen 1994, pp.77–80).

62. For example, consumer electronics companies operate an 'approval system for non-inspection'. The suppliers which obtain this qualification are exempt from inspection of their parts. It is common for electronics producers and parts suppliers to implement value analysis (VA, activities for cost reduction after entering mass production) and value engineering (VE, activities for reducing costs before starting mass production) in order to reduce production costs (Wu 1991, pp.71–2).

63. Interview, UCOM, Tokyo, September 1995.

64. For instance, although there were interactions between SIA and EIAJ, shown in the submission of the rebuttal papers, EIAJ was discouraged by MITI from reacting against SIA after MITI decided to negotiate with the US government (Fujiwara 1988, p.130).

65. *Purejidento*, May 1988, p.189.

66. Several critical points were agreed on at the talks: first, the 11 major

semiconductor firms would raise the purchase rate of US semiconductors; second, the Japanese government would encourage other semiconductor users and industries to increase the share of US semiconductors; third, a price-monitoring system under which semiconductor producers would report prices would be introduced in order to prevent exports of cheap semiconductors to the US market (*The Washington Post*, 29 May 1986; *Electronic News*, no.1604, 2 June 1986). Watanabe allegedly recognised that the US government expected to increase its market share in Japan to 20 per cent within five years. The side letter on market access seemed to be based on this talk (Shimura 1993, p.287).

67. *Nikkei Bijinesu*, 26 March 1990, p.19.
68. Tomio Matsumura, a managing director of NEC asserted that 'it is natural for semiconductor users to prefer cheap, high quality products under a reliable supply system. To expect them to ignore these preferences is an unreasonable demand' (*Asahi Shimbun*, 3 June 1986). Semiconductor producers also criticised the price monitoring system, arguing that it is difficult to control semiconductor prices because not only do prices fluctuate with supply and demand but production costs fall sharply due to technological innovation and a rise in yield rates (*Asahi Shimbun*, 3 June 1986).
69. In addition to the side letter, the two governments allegedly exchanged confidential chairman's notes in which the Japanese government suggested controlling sales prices in third countries (*Purejidento*, May 1988, p.191; Fujiwara 1988, p.134).
70. *Nikkei Bijinesu*, 26 March 1990, p.21.
71. *The Washington Post*, 29 July 1986.
72. For example, Soichi Saba, President of EIAJ, criticised the urgency of the US government to obtain a substantial result, contending that 'it is premature and even irrational to attempt an assessment of the impact of the agreement and our efforts to comply with it only 6 months after concluding the agreement' (*Electronic News*, no.1649, 6 April 1987). Atsuyoshi Ouchi, Vice-Chairman of NEC, also argued that 'we have made efforts to provide more services than the arrangement anticipated such as production cuts and the establishment of INSEC. We expected gratitude from the US, but instead we got the criticism of non-compliance. The US action is like returning evil for good' (Ōuchi 1987, p.98).
73. For analysis of political interactions on the side letter, see Ōyane (1997).
74. *Nikkei Bijinesu*, 26 March 1990, p.21.
75. *Purejidento*, May 1988, pp.187–8. In the early 1980s, the Japanese and US governments sought to resolve the trade disputes over semiconductors by governmental agreements. Both governments reached the first agreement in November 1982. It was designed to seek to ensure equivalent opportunities for US firms in Japan to those enjoyed by Japanese firms in the US market (Prestowitz 1988, p.52). The second agreement, concluded in November 1983, contained a commitment by the Japanese government to promote US access to the Japanese market as well as the establishment of the data collection system to prevent dumping by Japanese firms. The second accord worked for a while, but Japanese

electronics firms introduced low-priced DRAMs and EPROMs, and the US share in the Japanese market began to decline in 1984 when market conditions changed.

76. *Wall Street Journal*, 30 January 1987; *Electronic News*, no.1640, 2 February 1987.
77. *Purejidento*, August 1987, p.81.
78. *Purejidento*, May 1988, p.189.
79. Interview, Machinery and Information Industries Bureau, MITI, Tokyo, February 1994.
80. After the production cut, the price of 256K DRAM began an unprecedented increase. The price increased from US$2.25 in the first quarter of 1987 to US$3.5 in the fourth quarter of 1988 (Tyson 1992, p.115).
81. Interview, UCOM, Tokyo, September 1995.
82. *Nikkei Bijinesu*, 26 March 1990, p.13.
83. *Nihon Keizai Shimbun*, 8 August 1989.
84. Interview, Toshiba, Tokyo, February 1994.
85. There are several episodes which reveal this stance. When the continuation of the sanction became an issue at the renewal of the arrangement, the US semiconductor industry was passive. At the hearing of the US Senate, for instance, Jerry Junkins, President and Chairman of Texas Instruments, expressed the stance of the US semiconductor industry as follows: 'Now, we, the SIA and the CSPP [Computer Systems Policy Project], do not advocate a punitive approach toward Japan. Instead, we believe the positive efforts toward compliance that the Japanese have undertaken in the last 2 1/2 years should be encouraged to continue' (US Senate 1991, p.10).
86. *Nikkei Sangyo Shimbun*, 6 April 1991.
87. Interview, UCOM, Tokyo, September 1995.
88. More than 60 projects including electron-beam exposure and large-scale integration production equipment, discrete devices, and low-power, high-performance semiconductors received public support between 1971 and 1977 (Tyson 1992, p.95). In addition, the Japanese government sponsored the joint research association for VLSI operating from 1976 to 1979. This association generated more than 1,000 patents and laid the foundation of future development in the semiconductor and computer sectors (Anchordoguy 1989, pp.137–45).
89. MITI and executives of major semiconductor firms have unofficial meetings periodically. EIAJ organises the semiconductor executive division, which comprises ten major semiconductor producers, and its trade committee functions as a communication body with MITI (Fujiwara 1988, p.129; *Nikkei Bijinesu*, 26 March 1990, p.7).
90. In 1992, Matsushita and Sony were the fifth and ninth largest Japanese semiconductor producers, but the primary and fourth biggest semiconductor users (EIAJ 1993a, pp.75–6).
91. The ratio of semiconductors used in the consumer electronics fields was 55 per cent in Matsushita and 75 per cent in Sony in 1993.
92. *Nihon Keizai Shimbun*, 30 July 1991.
93. *Nihon Keizai Shimbun*, 6 June 1991.
94. While NEC started DRAM production in 1984, eight other Japanese

producers – Fujitsu, Hitachi, Matsushita, Mitsubishi Electric, NMB, Oki Electric, Sony, and Toshiba – began production between 1989 and 1991 (Dohlman 1993, table D15).

95. Interview, UCOM, Tokyo, September 1995.

96. *Nikkei Sangyo Shimbun*, 7 June 1994.

97. In the case of Matsushita, there was another factor which encouraged the company to tackle market access issues. While Akio Tanii, President of Matsushita, assumed the chairmanship of EIAJ between 1989 and 1990, Hiroshi Mizuno, an executive director of Matsushita, served as the head of UCOM from June 1989 to June 1990. As the chairman company of EIAJ and UCOM, Matsushita made serious efforts to expand market access (Interview, Matsushita, Osaka, May 1994). UCOM established the consumer electronic task force in June 1989, and the joint committee on high-definition TVs in November 1989. EIAJ also made constructive proposals regarding US semiconductor access to Japan in December 1989. Matsushita took the initiative in these activities.

98. Interview, Sony, Tokyo, March 1994.

99. *Nihon Keizai Shimbun*, 12 April 1990.

100. Interview, Sony, Tokyo, March 1994.

101. Their first alliance was the collaborative development of 16M DRAM in December 1988. The two companies have evolved this partnership in various forms. They agreed to cooperate in the development of 64M DRAM in November 1991 and 256M DRAM in January 1993. In addition, the targeted product also expanded from DRAM to SRAM. Texas Instruments gave Hitachi a licence to design SRAM, whereas Hitachi offered the know-how of SRAM production to Texas Instuments (Higashi and Ōkawa 1993, p.94). Furthermore, they agreed in August 1994 to set up a joint venture to manufacture 16M and 64M DRAM in the United States.

102. There are several examples of this type between Japanese and US firms. Micron Technology and Sanyo concluded a sales agency agreement in October 1989. Sanyo made Japanese catalogues and technical documents of devices of Micron to sell them in Japan through its own distribution channels. Matsushita and Intel concluded a sales agreement in February 1990 (*Nihon Keizai Shimbun*, 6 February 1990). Not only does Matsushita use Intel's EPROM in its group but it also offers them for other users such as game makers under the Intel brand. Intel would expand its sales in Japan by utilising Matsushita's powerful distribution network.

103. A typical example of this type is the Hitachi–Gold Star alliance in July 1989, the first Japanese and Korean alliance in the semiconductor sector. Hitachi offered 1M DRAM production technology to Gold Star, and procured it under OEM contracts (*Nihon Keizai Shimbun*, 27 July 1989). Not only did this alliance enable Hitachi to concentrate its management resources on the development of next generation devices, but it allowed Gold Star to enter the Japanese market. Mitsubishi Electric and Texas Instruments also concluded alliances for exchanging DRAM in December 1989. Mitsubishi provides Texas Instruments with 1M DRAM, while

Texas Instruments offers 64K DRAM to Mitsubishi (*Nikkei Sangyo Shimbun*, 13 December 1989). Both companies sell the received products under their own brand name.

104. The number of design-ins increased seven times or at an annual rate of 32 per cent between 1986 and 1993 (EIAJ 1995, p.4–1).
105. *Far Eastern Economic Review*, 22 March 1990, p.74.
106. *Purejidento*, November 1993, pp.288–291.
107. The company exported four numerically controlled machine tools to the Soviet Union in violation of a degree of the COCOM. These machines are said to be capable of cutting submarine propeller blades, which makes submarines quieter and more difficult to detect.
108. He recalled the then situation as follows: 'We were convinced that the parent company [Toshiba] had nothing to do with the incident that the subsidiary provoked. I, at once, told my friends in Toshiba that we would not change our attitude and behaviour towards Toshiba at all. This was as if we reconfirmed friendly relationships when a member of a friend's family caused trouble' (Ōtani 1989, p.44).
109. *Nikkei Bijinesu*, 16 December 1991, p.18. Toshiba's case reminds us of Toyota which recognised the importance of further cooperation with US auto producers as a result of the minivan dumping incident.
110. Motorola's sales of semiconductors in Japan increased from US$113 million in 1986 when the alliance was agreed and to US$497 million in 1991 (National Research Council 1992, p.96).
111. *Nikkei Bijinesu*, 16 December 1991, p.17.

6   Trade Policy Preferences in the Japanese Textile Industry

1. The share of imports in total domestic demand jumped from 16.3 per cent in 1980 to 50.8 per cent in 1993.
2. The number of employees per establishment was 221.3 in the synthetic-fibre making sector and 71.7 in the spinning sector in 1991. The figures in weaving, knitting and garment manufacturing sectors were 4.5, 10.8 and 12.3, respectively (*Seni Nenkan*, 1995, p.66).
3. Textiles usually include primary processing and secondary processing, and fibre production is excluded from textiles proper. However, the discussion in this chapter includes fibre production in textile activities because preferences and activities of major synthetic-fibre companies have a great influence on the textile industry as a whole.
4. The current discussion includes the spinning sector in the upstream stage due to similarities between fibre production and spinning as a capital intensive industry as well as the role of both major spinning and synthetic-fibre producers as yarn suppliers.
5. Even in 1950, the industry accounted for 19.1 per cent of manufacturing output and 37.3 per cent of manufacturing exports (*Seni Nenkan*, 1981, p.105).
6. *Seni Nenkan*, 1995, p.65.
7. MITI, *Kogyo tokeihyo* [Census of Manufactures] 1993.

8. In 1994, there were 204 national associations relevant to the textile industry (*Seni Nenkan*, 1995, pp.16–17).
9. These are Toray Industries, Teijin, Asahi Chemical Industry, Kuraray, Unitika, Mitsubishi Rayon, and Toho Rayon.
10. The nine major spinning companies are Toyobo, Kanebo, Fuji Spinning, Daiwabo, Nisshinbo Industries, Omikenshi, Nitto Boseki, Kurabo Industries, and Shikibo.
11. The small and medium-sized firms are either corporate enterprises with capital funds of less than 100 million yen or with less than 300 employees, or individual enterprises with less than 300 employees.
12. The Japan Export Clothing Manufacturers Association, *JECMA Bulletin* 93, December 1994, p.24.
13. *Seni Nenkan*, 1981, p.105; 1995, p.65.
14. *Seni Nenkan*, 1995, p.86.
15. For a description of structural adjustment policies in the Japanese textile industry, see Ike (1980) and Yamawaki (1992, pp.94–105).
16. These laws are the Law on Temporary Measures for the Structural Improvement of Specified Textile Industry (1967–73), the Temporary Special Measures for the Textile Industry (1971–73), the Law on Temporary Measures for the Structural Improvement of Textile Industry (1974–present), and the Law on Temporary Measures for the Adjustment of Industry Structure (1987–present).
17. *Seni Nenkan*, 1975, p.111.
18. For restraints on raw silk imports, see Zhao (1993, chap.2, 3).
19. When a dumping file is petitioned, MITI and MOF decide whether to start a dumping investigation within two months. Then, within one year of the investigation, both ministries decide whether dumping duties should be imposed or not.
20. The number of anti-dumping suits in Japan is very small compared with other developed countries. For instance, between 1980 and 1987, there were 263 anti-dumping actions in the European Community, 11 of which were related to the textile industry (Hamilton 1992, p.137).
21. *Textile Asia*, February 1983, p.81.
22. *Nihon Keizai Shimbun*, 28 December 1982.
23. *Textile Asia*, January 1983, pp.63–4.
24. *Asahi Shimbun*, 21 October 1988.
25. *Asahi Shimbun*, 24 June 1988.
26. *Nihon Keizai Shimbun*, 13 September 1988.
27. Interview, JTIF, Tokyo, March 1994.
28. *Asahi Shimbun*, 20 August 1988.
29. Miyazaki maintained that 'this anti-dumping would be a model case for other industries which have similar trade issues. The redress of unfair trade is a responsibility of industrial associations' (*Nihon Keizai Shimbun*, 22 October 1988).
30. *Senken Shimbun*, 22 October 1988.
31. For example, Eiichi Tamori, Deputy Director-General of MITI's Consumer Goods Industries Bureau, expressed the view that in the resolution of knitted sweater dumping, it was desirable that the relevant industrial associations should pursue the matter independently in order

to prevent the politicization of the issue in South Korea (*Seni Nenkan*, 1989, p.56).

32. *Asahi Shimbun*, 21 January 1989.
33. *Nikkei Sangyo Shimbun*, 10 June 1993.
34. *The Nikkei Weekly*, 27 December 1993.
35. *Senken Shimbun*, 2 August 1995.
36. The first duties were imposed on the imports of ferrosilicon manganese from China in February 1993.
37. The LTA allowed an importing country to limit international trade in cotton textiles which would 'cause or threaten to cause disruption in the market of the importing country'. It allowed bilateral consultations and import increases of 5 per cent a year in the absence of agreements.
38. The MFA was renewed in 1978, 1982 and 1986. The MFA IV, which expanded coverage to textiles made of vegetable fibres, blends of vegetable fibres and blends containing silk, was extended twice in 1991 for one year and five months and in 1993 for one year.
39. In the process of the GATT Uruguay Round negotiations over textiles, the Japanese government sought to play a bridging role between the developed and developing countries by presenting a proposal in February 1990. The major textile associations did not object to the government's intention to phase out the MFA. Not only did they find it highly improbable that the Japanese government would actually introduce the MFA in the meantime but regarded the MFA as a source of the growth of imports in Japan due to quotas under the MFA in other developed countries. For interactions between the Japanese government and textile circles over the Japanese proposal on the GATT textile negotiations, see Ōyane (1992).
40. Interview, JCSFWA, Tokyo, February 1994.
41. In 1984, imports of cotton yarn climbed by 58 per cent, while imports of knitted products increased by 50 per cent.
42. *Nihon Keizai Shimbun*, 26 March 1985.
43. *Nihon Keizai Shimbun*, 23 January 1988.
44. *Textile Asia*, July 1988, p.70.
45. *Senken Shimbun*, 5 June 1985.
46. In the deliberation process at the subcommittee on trade issues from 1993 to 1994, the Consumer Goods Industries Bureau persuaded other bureaus to understand the introduction of the MFA by stressing the necessity for ensuring administrative transparency (*Senken Shimbun*, 18 May 1994). Yukio Doi, after retiring from the post of Director-General of the Consumer Goods Industries Bureau, published an article entitled 'Defending the Textile Industry' in which he stressed the significance of the industry, and referred to MITI's policy to refrain from introducing the MFA as unfair to the industry (Doi 1995).
47. *Nihon Keizai Shimbun*, 23 January 1988; *Textile Asia*, July 1988, p.70.
48. MITI publishes the textile industry report entitled *Toshin: Kongo no seni sangyo oyobi sono sesaku no arikata* [Report on the future of the textile industry and its policy measures] every five years. The reports are deliberated and drawn up in the joint advisory committee of the Textile

Committee of the Industrial Structure Council and the Textile Industry Council. Recent reports were issued in 1983, 1988, and 1993.

49. *Toshin: Kongo no seni sangyo oyobi sono sesaku no arikata* [Report on the future of the textile industry and its policy measures], November 1988.

50. These associations are JCFA, JSA, JCSFWA, JSRFWA, JKIA, JTMA, JAIC, JTIA, and the Japan Chain Stores Association.

51. For instance, Reiichi Yumikura, Chairman of JCFA, commented that the recommendation was epoch-making because it set the basis on which import restraints could be triggered (*Nikkei Sangyo Shimbun*, 18 May 1994).

52. The guidelines stipulate that MITI decides whether to commence investigations within two months after receiving a request from textile associations. MITI then judges whether to set in place negotiations with the export countries within one year after starting the investigation. In February 1995, JSA requested the introduction of transitional safeguards against imports of 40-count cotton yarn, and JSA and JCSFWA against imports of poplin and broadcloth. MITI decided to start investigations in April 1995.

53. *Seni Nenkan*, 1989, p.56.

54. *Kasen Geppo*, December 1993, p.49.

55. Interview, JTIA, Tokyo, September 1995.

56. *Kasen Geppo*, June 1993, pp.60–1.

57. *Senken Shimbun*, 22 May 1993.

58. Interview, JTMA, Tokyo, September 1995.

59. Interview, JTMA, Tokyo, September 1995.

60. Interview, JTIF, Tokyo, September 1995.

61. Interview, JTIA, Tokyo, September 1995.

62. *Asahi Shimbun*, 22 October 1988.

63. Interview, JTIA, Tokyo, September 1995.

64. Interview, JTIA, Tokyo, September 1995.

65. *Asahi Shimbun*, 10 September 1988.

66. Interview, JCFA, Tokyo, February 1994.

67. *Nihon Keizai Shimbun*, 14 March 1988.

68. *Textile Asia*, July 1988, p.70.

69. Interview, Toray, Tokyo, April 1994.

70. Interview, Teijin, Tokyo, September 1995; Interview, Kanebo, Tokyo, September 1995.

71. Interview, Teijin, Tokyo, September 1995.

72. Interview, Kanebo, Tokyo, September 1995.

73. For instance, the ratio of overseas production in textiles in the 1980s was similar to or lower than the ratio in 1980.

74. Interview, JCFA, Tokyo, February 1994.

75. Interview, Toray, Tokyo, March 1994.

76. *Seni Nenkan*, 1981, p.105; 1993, p.65.

77. Japan Economic Almanac, 1988, p.163.

78. Interview, Teijin, Tokyo, September 1995.

79. *Shingosen* is referred to as 'new polyester' which covers a whole group

of products made by complex, high-tech processing of polyester fila-
ments (*Japan Economic Almanac*, 1991, p.151).

80. *Keizaikai*, 29 March 1994, p.29. This strategy had a crucial outcome in
1993 when the demand for yarn shrank. While synthetic-fibre makers
agreed with the production cut, Toray alone did not abide by the cut on
the grounds that the company did not increase its production capacity
during the expansion period (*Nikkei Bijinesu*, 20 February 1995, p.27).
Toray could cope with the reduced demand by decreasing the yarn purchased at the market and by exporting excess yarn to its mid-stream
plants in Southeast Asia.
81. *Senken Shimbun*, 22 February 1995.
82. *Senken Shimbun*, 27 February 1995.
83. Interview, Toray, Tokyo, March 1994.
84. The accumulated value of FDI between 1951 and 1980 was US$1,637
billion in textiles out of US$12,573 billion in total manufacturing.
85. Interview, Toray, Tokyo, March 1994.
86. The natural immunity means 'a dense web of "relational contracting"
between firms specializing in different parts of the production process,
or between manufacturers and trading companies, between trading
companies and retailers – relationships which are backed not only by
their foundation in trust and mutual obligation, but by all the things that
trust means, quality guarantees and security of supply' (Dore 1986,
p.248).
87. Although Japanese synthetic-fibre makers dominate differentiated polyester markets, commodity polyester markets have been penetrated by
South Korean and Taiwanese products. In 1993, imported polyester
reached 71 per cent, 67 per cent, and 40 per cent of the domestic demand
for ladies' trousers, sweaters, and blouses, respectively (*Shukan Daiyamondo*, 26 November 1994, p.13).
88. *Nihon Keizai Shimbun*, 5 April 1995.
89. The past four chairmen of JTIF came from large spinning and synthetic-
fibre producers such as Toyobo, Asahi Chemical, and Teijin.
90. Synthetic-fibre makers often refer to relevant weaving houses as 'production teams'. In the case of Toray, the first production team was
organised in September 1959, and the number of the teams increased
to 337 by April 1964 (Toray 1977, pp.116–18).
91. *Kasen Geppo*, February 1992, p.71.
92. *Shukan Daiyamondo*, 26 November 1994, p.13.
93. *Senken Shimbun*, 10 May 1994.
94. According to Itoh and Urata (1994, pp.43–4), weaving houses in the
Fukui and Ishikawa prefectures regarded support from synthetic-fibre
makers or trading companies as the most useful sources for improving
technical skills and developing new products.
95. *Shukan Daiyamondo*, 26 November 1994, p.13.
96. The necessity for promoting systematic linkages was explicitly shown
in the 1988 textile report. The report suggested establishing 'link-
age production units' which meant linkages among many firms for
mutual supplementation of information collection, product planning,

and response to the demand for many kinds of textile products in small quantities.

97. The quick response system seeks to deliver products with a shorter turn-around time by using information networks. This system, developed in the United States in the 1980s, not only reduces the loss of the stock but also speeds up the flow of information about the market. The Japanese textile industry organized the Council for Promoting Quick Response in September 1994 with the participation of 203 groups from upstream to downstream stages (*Senken Shimbun*, 27 September 1994).

98. While Asahi Chemical and Kanebo have become the leading companies in housing and cosmetics, respectively, Toray and Teijin are major international manufacturers of base films for magnetic tape (*Japan Economic Almanac*, 1990, p.171).

99. Interview, Toray, Tokyo, March 1994.

7   Keidanren's Stance on Trade and Investment Policies

1. Although no special qualifications to become a corporate member of Keidanren are written into the articles of association, Keidanren's member companies are members of industrial associations composed of big companies, or one of the major members of industrial associations which include medium and small-sized firms (Honjo 1993, p.196).

2. Of 30 policy committees, three were chaired by leaders from iron and steel, four by trading, and six by banking.

3. The main organs of Keidanren are the Board of Councillors, the Board of Governors, the Executive Council and the Chairman and Vice-Chairman Meeting.

4. *Kyosei* is referred to as 'symbiosis' or 'living together' in English but its main idea is 'mutually beneficial co-existence'. *Kyosei* became a central issue after Keidanren espoused a commitment to the concept in its *Basic Guidelines for the 1990s* in 1991 (*Keidanren Review*, no.137, October 1992, pp.4–6).

5. According to MITI (1994b, p.6) survey data, while foreign-affiliated firms imported goods worth 4.72 trillion yen in 1992, accounting for 16 per cent of Japan's total imports, they exported products from Japan worth 1.84 trillion yen, 4.3 per cent of Japan's total exports. They ran trade deficits of 2.88 trillion yen.

6. There were 508 regulatory laws and 10,945 government authorizations or licences at the end of March 1994 in Japan (Management and Coordination Agency 1995, pp.14–20). As much as 40 per cent of Japan's gross national product (GNP) is produced by industries under some form of government regulation. There are two kinds of regulation. One is economic regulation which imposes restrictions on new entrants, prices and fares and controls on service and investment from a viewpoint of supply–demand adjustments. The other is social regulation which aims to ensure health, security and environmental protection (Etō 1994, p.8). Isao Nakauchi, a vice-chairman of Keidanren as well as Chairman of Daiei, a representative retailing company, explains the burden of excess

regulations as follows: 'Seventeen laws, 45 administrative requirements, 200 pages of application documents – this is what it takes to open one sales outlet. All this costs the distribution industry sales as much as 50 billion yen a year' (*The Nikkei Weekly*, 30 August 1993).

7. The liberalization of capital investment in Japan was implemented mainly in the period from 1967 to 1971 through a four-stage liberalization programme. In 1980, while the Foreign Investment Law was abolished, the Foreign Exchange and Foreign Trade Control Law was modified, changing the basis of the foreign investment system from approval to prior notification, and allowing foreign investors to acquire full ownerships of existing firms. Now Japan has no restrictions on foreign investment except reservations under the OECD Code of Liberalization of Capital Movements in agriculture, forestry and fisheries, oil, mining, and leather and leather products, and sectors related to national security (MITI 1994a, p.204).

8. The share of foreign-owned firms in total sales was 10 per cent in the United States and 18 per cent or higher in the United Kingdom, France and Germany in 1986 (Graham and Krugman 1991, p.33). Limited inward investment in Japan results from several home market factors. First, fierce corporate competition and high land and labour costs have discouraged foreign investors from advancing into Japan (MITI 1994a, p.205). Second, such Japanese business and social practices as close long-term business relations and the difficulty of finding quality labour in the face of the life-time employment system have made it difficult for foreign investors in Japan. Third, the incompatibility of many Japanese standards, regulations and inspection practices as well as the lack of transparency and administrative guidance have placed foreign firms at a disadvantage *vis-à-vis* local firms (Mason 1995, p.138).

9. The Committee held hearings from the American Chamber of Commerce in Japan, the European Business Community, and relevant embassies in order to collect opinions with respect to Japan's investment climate. Then it received explanations from representatives of related government agencies about the conditions of Japan's investment climate. Parallel to these activities, the Committee conducted a questionnaire survey of the members of the Committee on Foreign-Affiliated Corporations about Japan's investment climate (*Gekkan Keidanren*, December 1992, p.23).

10. The Japan Federation of Bar Associations (*Nichibenren*) criticised the report as lacking consideration of the Japanese legal system and the Japanese system for lawyers, established to protect people's basic rights (*Nihon Keizai Shimbun*, 28 October 1992).

11. The establishment of companies that have the sole purpose of controlling another company is prohibited in Japan under Article 9 of the Antimonopoly Law. This ban resulted from the bitter lesson that the pre-war Japanese economy had been dominated by a handful of *zaibatsu* (conglomerates), which were allegedly a factor that led Japan into the Second World War.

12. OTO was established in January 1982 as a consequence of a recommendation in 1981 by the Japan–US Economic Relations Advisory

Group (the so-called Wisemen's Group). Its primary objective is to deal promptly and efficiently with complaints from foreign businesses with respect to access to the Japanese market. For the details of OTO, see Komine (1986, pp.135–43) and *Boeki Nenkan* (1989, pp.150–5).

13. A detailed explanation of *Rincho* will be provided later.
14. *Nihon Keizai Shimbun*, 30 August 1993.
15. *Nikkei Bijinesu*, 12 September 1994, p.117.
16. *Keidanren Shuho*, no.2213, 23 May 1994, pp.2–5.
17. *Keidanren Review*, no.148, February 1995, pp.4–7.
18. *Nihon Keizai Shimbun*, 9 October 1993.
19. Interview, Keidanren, Tokyo, September 1995.
20. *Gekkan Keidanren*, June 1994, p.17.
21. *Nikkan Kogyo Shimbun*, 17 June 1994.
22. *Nihon Keizai Shimbun*, 20 October 1993.
23. The panel set up a subcommittee composed of four members – two former bureaucrats, one business leader and one scholar – in order to draw up the draft of the report.
24. The Law came into force in March 1974. Its aim is to promote the proper development of retail business and to insure business opportunities for small and medium-sized retailers by regulating the retail activities of large-scale stores in the area concerned with care for protecting consumer interests. The Law has been amended many times. The amendment in May 1979, February 1982, and February 1984 aimed to strengthen the regulation on large-scale stores. The amendments in the 1990s – in May 1990, January 1992, and May 1994 – aimed to make it easier for large retailers to own a larger number of outlets and to strengthen their businesses.
25. Keidanren recommended deregulation in the distribution sector in February 1988, March 1990, December 1993, and September 1995. In its recommendations, it demanded that the Law should be amended to expand business opportunities of large retail stores. In the recommendations that referred to deregulation as a whole, Keidanren has also raised the amendment of the Law as a primary interest.
26. Reflecting this character of Nissho, the Large-Scale Retail Store Council has an executive director of Nissho as one of its seven members (Kusano 1992, p.240).
27. *Nihon Keizai Shimbun*, 6 April 1990.
28. For the details of overall government policies for promoting inward investment, see MITI (1995b).
29. In a position paper, the FTC raised three reasons for the ban on holding companies: first, holding companies become a means to control business, leading to the impeding of free and fair competition; second, removal of the ban would strengthen Japanese *keiretsu* groupings which would stimulate criticism from foreign countries; and third, corporate restructuring is possible within the framework of the existing antitrust statutes (*Nihon Keizai Shimbun*, 7 June 1994).
30. Keizai Doyukai released a report in October 1992, urging the government to abolish the ban on holding companies in order to bring Japan's corporate system into alignment with western countries (*Nihon Keizai*

Shimbun, 28 October 1992). The advisory panel to Director-General of MITI's Industrial Policy Bureau also announced a report in February 1995. The report maintained that the ban on holding companies had lost rationality, and concrete deliberation to lift this should be set forth (*Nihon Keizai Shimbun*, 23 February 1995).

31. *Nihon Keizai Shimbun*, 28 March 1995.
32. *Nihon Keizai Shimbun*, 1 February; 25 February 1994.
33. In March 1995, the FTC announced that it would ease the regulations on discounts and prizes. The maximum value of discounts to all buyers was set at 10 per cent of the regular price of a product or up to a maximum of 50,000 yen. The new regulations left the 10 per cent rule but lifted the 50,000 yen ceiling. The FTC also agreed to increase the maximum of 50,000 yen of prizes to selected customers, and to raise the maximum allowed value of prizes awarded to winners from a pool of entrants from 1 million to some 10 million yen (*Nihon Keizai Shimbun*, 29 March 1995).
34. *Keidanren Geppo*, May 1988, p.9.
35. Interview, Keidanren, Tokyo, September 1995.
36. *Gekkan Keidanren*, June 1995, p.31.
37. *Gekkan Keidanren*, June 1995, p.31.
38. *Keidanren Review*, No.142, October 1993, p.6.
39. *Asahi Shimbun*, 9 August 1994.
40. *Gekkan Keidanren*, June 1995, p.31.
41. Interview, Keidanren, Tokyo, September 1995.
42. *Nihon Keizai Shimbun*, 9 October 1993; Interview, Keidanren, Tokyo, September 1995. In the Hata Cabinet, Hiroshi Kumagai, Cheif Cabinet Secretary, was the key politician who promoted deregulation, while Koichi Kato, Chairman of the LDP's Policy Affairs Research Council (PARC), played a similar role in the Murayama Cabinet (Interview, Keidanren, Tokyo, September 1995).
43. *The Nikkei Weekly*, 20 June 1994.
44. Although Kozo Uchida, a managing director of Keidanren, met with Yasuoki Takeuchi, President of the Petroleum Association of Japan, many times in order to discuss this issue, Uchida could not persuade Takeuchi to put the regulations regarding the petroleum sector on the deregulation list (*Nihon Keizai Shimbun*, 18 November 1994).
45. Interview, Keidanren, Tokyo, September 1995.
46. *Keidanren Review*, Special Issue, 1993, p.2.
47. *Keidanren Review*, no.148, February 1995, p.4.
48. For example, labour productivity in the manufacturing sector grew 5.8 per cent annually between 1985 and 1992, while that in the non-manufacturing sector increased 3 per cent in the same period (*Nihon Keizai Shimbun*, 18 September 1993).
49. *Gaiko Foramu*, June 1992, pp.14–15.
50. The other players who stand in line with Keidanren are such ministries as the Ministry of Foreign Affairs, MITI, the Economic Planning Agency and the media. For the stance of major players over agricultural liberalization, see George (1990).
51. Interview, Zenchu, Tokyo, September 1995.

52. The food industry produced 24 trillion yen of the total value of goods with 1.14 million employees in 1981, compared with 12 trillion yen with 5.34 million in agriculture. The industry was the third largest manufacturing sector in Japan, with 10.7 per cent of the total value of produced goods.

53. The high price of domestic agricultural materials is pointed out in several of Keidanren's reports. For instance, one report states that '[d]omestically produced rice costs 3.2 times more than imported rice. Likewise, industrial users pay 3.8 times more for domestic wheat, 3.8 times more for soybeans, and 2.5 times more for butter.... The result is that raw material costs add up to 64.4% of the total value of the food processing industry's annual production' (*KKC Brief*, no.11, September 1983). The *White Paper on the Food Industry* issued in December 1986 also stated that one kilogram of sugar costs 58 yen in Melbourne, 118 yen in New York, 90 yen in London and 198 yen in Tokyo, while one kilogram of skim milk costs 138, 287, 254, 545 yen, respectively.

54. In order to draw up the report, the Subcommittee held 16 seminars which involved hearings from the Ministry of Agriculture, Forestry and Fisheries (MAFF), local governments, and other interested organizations, as well as observation tours to obtain first-hand information (*Keidanren Review*, no.103, February 1987, p.2).

55. *The Japan Times*, 28 January 1987.

56. In the first phase, the ratio of rice the government buys from the farmers to the total harvest should be reduced from 60 per cent to 30 per cent, and in the second phase, the volume of government rice should be reduced to a level sufficient for adjusting supply and demand and maintaining stockpiles. The second phase also aimed to remove farm cooperative rice, which is distributed independently by agricultural cooperatives (*nokyo*), from government control, and to promote rational price formation guided by transactions on the rice market (*KKC Brief*, no.41, March 1987).

57. Keidanren organized a top-level meeting with the Central Union of Agricultural Cooperatives (*Zenchu*) on 10 May, two weeks earlier than Keidanren's resolution. Senior executives of Keidanren suggested that liberalization of the rice market should be promoted with policies to mitigate effects attended by its opening (Honjo 1993, pp.300–1).

58. *The Japan Times*, 28 May 1991.

59. *Mainichi Daily News*, 26 May 1991.

60. *The Nikkei Weekly*, 16 November 1991.

61. For example, when tariff reductions on agricultural products were determined in the Action Programme in 1985, the Chairman of *Zenchu* commented that although the government explained the reductions as a response to foreign requests, the agricultural sector was sacrificed to a massive volume of exports of manufacturing products (*Asahi Shimbun*, 26 June 1985). In addition, *Zenchu*'s position paper, *Gatto uruguai raundo nogyo kosho ni kansuru nogyo seisansha no shucho* [The assertion of farmers regarding the GATT Uruguay Round negotiations on agriculture], released in February 1991, states that 'excess exports of Japan's manufacturing products have rapidly expanded under the GATT

free-trade system causing trade friction with importing countries. Closed markets other than agriculture are also criticized by Japan's trading partners, as shown by the Japan–US Structural Impediments Initiative talks. Japan is required to revise its industrial and trade policies by the international community, yet there is an argument to put an excess burden of international responsibility on the agricultural sector in order to delay substantial solutions for these issues. This argument lacks justice, making agriculture a scapegoat' (Zenchu 1991, p.5).

62. Interview, Keidanren, Tokyo, September 1995.
63. *Zenchu* encompasses some 4,300 *nokyo* representing 4.4 million farmers and approximately 12 per cent of all households (Higashi and Lauter 1990, p.162).
64. *Asahi Shimbun*, 21 September 1983.
65. *Asahi Shimbun*, 21 September 1983.
66. *The Japan Economic Journal*, 29 May 1984.
67. Another two firms took a similar approach, and the Federation reached reconciliation with Ajinomoto and Daiei in May and with Sony in July.
68. *Keidanren Jigyo Hokoku*, 1984, p.37. The two Special Committees were transformed into the Special Divisions in 1985.
69. *The Japan Times*, 2 July 1991.
70. *The Daily Yomiuri*, 7 June 1994.
71. The Forum published a paper in January 1992, entitled 'Towards the Success of the GATT Uruguay Round'. This paper emphasized the possibility that the United States and the European Community would move towards the formation of exclusive economic blocs if the Uruguay Round broke down. It also argued that if the rice issue shifted to bilateral Japan–US negotiations as a result of the breakdown of the Uruguay Round, the amount of imports Japan would be compelled to agree to would exceed the minimum access amount required under the GATT negotiations.
72. *Far Eastern Economic Review*, 24 September 1992, p.47.
73. Interview, Keidanren, Tokyo, September 1995.
74. In 1985, for example, the Division on Agriculture and Forestry with 149 members was the largest among 17 LDP's PARC divisions, while the Comprehensive Farm Policy Committee with 216 members was the biggest committee in PARC (Satō and Matsuzaki 1986, pp.256–9).
75. In August 1986, Kazuo Tamaki, Director General of the Management and Coordination Agency, ordered the implementation of administrative inspections on business practices of *nokyo* (*Nihon Keizai Shimbun*, 14 September 1986). The Agency implemented the investigation on 124 *nokyo*, and submitted its final report in June 1988. In September 1986, Tamaki also suggested purchasing American rice by using the official development assistance budget, and sending it to developing countries as official assistance products (*Nihon Keizai Shimbun*, 24 September 1986).
76. In a nationwide poll for the 126 seats of the 252 member Upper House, the LDP won 36 – down from 69 – while the Japan Socialist Party gained 46 – up from 22.
77. The LDP decided to maintain 830,000 hectares of rice planting limits,

although the original plan of MAFF was to expand these limits by 100,000 hectares. The LDP's decision had a high probability of leading to an excess supply of rice (*Asahi Shimbun*, 11 November 1989). The subsidies on acreage cutbacks also increased, to 180 billion yen. MOF's intention to reduce the subsidies was rejected owing to strong pressure from the LDP which was keen to regain support from the agricultural bloc (*Asahi Shimbun*, 16 November 1989).

78. In July 1990, Toshio Yamaguchi, Chairman of the LDP's Special Committee for Economic Coordination, contended that the acceptance of 5 per cent of rice imports in total domestic demand would be inevitable (*Asahi Shimbun*, 14 July 1990). In 1991, quite a few senior leaders of the LDP followed Yamaguchi. Takeo Nishioka, Chairman of LDP's Executive Council, Shin Kanemaru, the former Vice President of the LDP, and Prime Minister Toshiki Kaifu admitted that a partial lifting of the import ban on foreign rice was inevitable (*Mainichi Daily News*, 26 May 1991; *The Nikkei Weekly*, 8 June 1991).

79. *Asahi Shimbun*, 4 June 1990.

80. The Diet passed resolutions against rice market liberalization in April 1980, July 1984, and September 1988.

81. In July 1990, Keidanren resumed its campaign on agricultural liberalization by sending a letter which called on the government to reduce or eliminate regulations imposed on agricultural imports (*The Daily Yomiuri*, 2 July 1990).

82. For example, agriculture and forestry *zoku* successfully dropped the reduction of quotas on agricultural products from the list of the Action Programme in July 1985, in spite of the earnest desire of the Nakasone Cabinet. In the case of the decision on producer rice price in 1986, even the leaders of agriculture and forestry *zoku* were unable to resist pressure from the rice Diet members and junior Diet members. Although the government intended to lower the producer rice price, and the bosses of agriculture and forestry *zoku* agreed to this, the rice Diet members and junior Diet members, who were subject to various pressures from the agricultural group, led the LDP to agree to leave the price at the previous year's level (Inoguchi and Iwai 1987, pp.246–52).

83. Interview, Keidanren, Tokyo, September 1995.

84. Interview, Zenchu, Tokyo, September 1995.

85. Interview, Keidanren, Tokyo, September 1995.

86. Tashiro (1989, p.10), examining the arguments surrounding reform of the food control system, concluded that 'all the turning points for the argument on the food control system were suggested by *zaikai* through the Provisional Council for Administrative Reform and the recommendations of the peak business federations'.

87. *Asahi Shimbun*, 30 May 1991.

88. The Agricultural Policy Advisory Council, established in June 1961, is the most important panel which determines the future course of agricultural policy.

89. These are *Promotion of the Comprehensive Agricultural Policy* (1970), *Expansion of the Comprehensive Food Policy* (1975), *Basic Stance on Agricultural Policy in the 1980s* (1980), *Basic Stance on Agricultural*

Policy for the 21st Century (1986), and *Directions for Agricultural Policy in a New International Climate* (1994).

90. The standards and certification systems mean the administrative system imposing regulations on goods and services with an eye to protecting consumers, ensuring the people's health and security, and unifying industrial standards. The content of the systems is different country by country according to social and economic conditions. However, if the systems consider domestic conditions alone, these impede the entry of foreign products to the domestic market (Kawano 1991, p.50). For overall discussions on trade friction regarding the standards and certification systems in Japan, see Anezaki and Noguchi (1983), and Negishi (1986).

91. Examples are high-cube containers, metal baseball bats, and tulip bulbs. The issue of high-cube containers will be discussed later. Metal baseball bats were classified as 'specified products' subject to the S-mark system under the Consumer Product Safety Law. This classification, aiming to prevent injury to consumers, required foreign suppliers to submit each individual bat for inspection. The US government, which had complained about this system since May 1980, filed it to the GATT in September 1982 as a violation of the Standards Code. MITI removed the special classification in January 1983. As far as tulip bulbs are concerned, Japan adopted cultivation in isolation as a quarantine system for imported tulip bulbs, which caused problems such as an inability of exporters to ship bulbs as finally packaged products through normal sales routes to wholesalers and retailers, and increased costs due to the expense of cultivation in isolation. The Netherlands, the major exporter of tulip bulbs, requested that the Japanese government revise the system on the grounds that cultivation in isolation was an outmoded quarantine method which caused healthy bulbs to become infected with viruses (*KKC Brief*, no.35, September 1986).

92. The first package of the liberalization programme, which was announced in December 1981, included the two-year advanced implementation of tariff reductions agreed on in the Tokyo Round, and the second package in May 1982 attained the elimination and reduction of tariff rates on 215 items and the elimination of import quotas on four farm products.

93. For example, the US government sent requests regarding standards and certification systems to the Headquarters on 26 February, and the European Community took the same action on 10 March (*Toki no horei*, no.1193, 13 October 1983, p.7).

94. This decision contained five principles for revision: the legal and institutional preservation of domestic and external non-discrimination in the process of certification; the maintenance of transparency in standards and regulations; the promotion of standards and certification systems compatible with international norms; the further acceptance of foreign inspection data; and the simplification and speeding-up of certification procedures.

95. *Keidanren Jigyo Hokoku*, 1982, pp.70–1.

96. *KKC Brief*, no.3, January 1983.

97. *Keidanren Jigyo Hokoku*, 1982, pp.71–2.

98. *KKC Brief*, no.35, September 1986.
99. *KKC Brief*, no.35, September 1986.
100. *Keidanren Geppo*, May 1983, pp.55–6.
101. The Committee initiated and coordinated the decisions both of the first package of the liberalization programme in December 1981, and of the second package in May 1982. The establishment of OTO in January 1982 was also realized with a strong commitment of the Committee (*Gekkan Jiyu Minshu*, March 1982, pp.39–40). In respect of import procedures, the Committee called on the government in February 1982 to improve import procedures on 67 of 99 items of which foreign countries complained (Funabashi 1987, p.39). In the revision of standards and certification systems in May 1983, the Committee supervised the actions of ministries towards improving certification and import procedure systems.
102. *Keidanren Jigyo Hokoku*, 1982, p.71.
103. For the background and effects of the Action Programme, see Higashi and Lauter (1990, chap.3).
104. *KKC Brief*, no.26, February 1985.
105. *KKC Brief*, no.35, September 1986.
106. *Asahi Shimbun*, 21 March 1985.
107. *Asahi Shimbun*, 8 April 1985.
108. *KKC Brief*, no.35, September 1986.
109. *KKC Brief*, no.21, July 1984.
110. *Nihon Keizai Shimbun*, 16 July 1982.
111. *Nihon Keizai Shimbun*, 16 July 1982.
112. *Toki no horei*, no.1193, 13 October 1983, p.6.
113. *Keidanren Review*, no.77 October 1982, p.4.
114. For example, see *Toward Strengthening and Preserving the Free Trade System* (27 September 1983); *Toward Rebuilding and Strengthening the Free Trade System* (26 February 1985); and *How Japan Can Contribute to a Healthy World Economy* (25 February 1986).
115. *KKC Brief*, no.27, March 1985.

8   Conclusions

1. This finding is in line with those in previous studies that stress the influence of particular national characteristics on states' policies in the sense that vertical relations influence trade policy through firms' preferences in Japan (Katzenstein (ed.) 1978; Zysman 1983; Hart 1992).
2. MITI, *Kaigai toshi tokei soran* [Statistical Report on Foreign Investment], No.3 (1989), p.10; No.6 (1998), p.38.
3. For the strong state thesis and the bureaucracy-dominant model, see Krasner (1978), Zysman (1983), Vogel (1978), and Pempel (1982) as well.
4. *The Japan Economic Journal*, 9 December 1989.
5. *Nikkei Bijinesu*, 26 March 1990, p.16.

Bibliography

ACCJ (1993) *1993 United States–Japan Trade White Paper*, Tokyo: American Chamber of Commerce in Japan.

Adams, F. G. and Ichimura, S. (1983) 'Industrial Policy in Japan', in F. G. Adams and L. R. Klein (eds), *Industrial Policies for Growth and Competitiveness: An Economic Perspective*, Lexington, Mass.: D.C. Heath.

Aggarwal, V. K., Keohane, R. O. and Yoffie, D. B. (1987) 'The Dynamics of Negotiated Protectionism', *American Political Science Review*, 81, 2, pp.345–66.

Allinson, G. D. (1987) 'Japan's Keidanren and Its New Leadership', *Pacific Affairs*, 60, 3, pp.385–407.

Amaya, N. (1981) 'Sōpu nashonarizumu wo haisu' (Disregard soap opera nationalism), *Bungei shunjū* (July), pp.318–38.

Anchordoguy, M. (1989) *Computers Inc.: Japan's Challenge to IBM*, Cambridge, MA: Council on East Asian Studies, Harvard University.

Anderson, K. and Baldwin, R. E. (1987) 'The Political Market for Protection in Industrial Countries', in A. M. El-Agraa (ed.), *Protection, Cooperation, Integration and Development*, London: Macmillan.

Anezaki, N. and Noguchi, N. (1983) 'Bōeki masatsu ni kansuru rippō sochi' (Legislative measures regarding trade friction), *Jurisuto*, 795 (15 July), pp.38–42.

Asanuma, B. (1989a) 'Nihon ni okeru mēkā to sapuraiyā tono kankei' (The relationships between makers and suppliers in Japan), in M. Tsuchiya and Y. Miwa (eds), *Nihon no chūshō kigyō* (Small and medium-sized companies in Japan), Tokyo: Tokyo Daigaku Shuppankai.

— (1989b) 'Manufacturing–Supplier Relationships in Japan and the Concept of Relation-Specific Skill', *Journal of the Japanese and International Economies*, 3, pp.1–30.

Balassa, B. (1986) 'Japan's Trade Policies', *Weltwirtschaftliches Archiv*, 122, pp.745–90.

Baldwin, R. E. (1985) *The Political Economy of U.S. Import Policy*, Cambridge, Mass.: MIT Press.

Bergsten, C. F. and Noland, M. (1993) *Reconcilable Differences?: United States–Japan Economic Conflict*, Washington D.C.: Institute for International Economics.

Bhagwati, J. N. (1982) 'Directly Unproductive, Profit-Seeking (DUP) Activities', *Journal of Political Economy*, 90, 5, pp.988–1002.

— (1988) *Protectionism*, Cambridge, Mass.: MIT Press.

Bhagwati, J. N. and Srinivasan, T. N. (1980) 'Revenue Seeking: A Generalization of the Theory of Tariffs', *Journal of Political Economy*, 88, 6, pp.1070–87.

Calder, K. E. (1982) 'Opening Japan', *Foreign Policy*, 47, pp.82–97.

— (1988a) *Crisis and Compensation: Public Policy and Political Stability in Japan, 1949–1986*, Princeton, N.J.: Princeton University Press.

Calder, K. E. (1988b) 'Japanese Foreign Economic Policy Formation: Explaining the Reactive State', *World Politics*, 40, 4, pp.517–41.

—— (1989) 'Elites in an Equalizing Role: Ex-Bureaucrats as Coordinators and Intermediaries in the Japanese Government–Business Relationship', *Comparative Politics*, 21, 4, pp.379–403.

—— (1993) *Strategic Capitalism: Private Business and Public Purpose in Japanese Industrial Finance*, Princeton, N.J.: Princeton University Press.

Caves, R. E. (1976) 'Economic Models of Political Choice: Canada's Tariff Structure', *Canadian Journal of Economics*, 9, 2, pp.278–300.

—— (1996) *Multinational Enterprise and Economic Analysis*, 2nd edn, Cambridge: Cambridge University Press.

Chen, E. K. Y. and Drysdale, P. (1995) *Corporate Links and Foreign Direct Investment in Asia and the Pacific*, Pymble, NSW: Harper Educational.

Chen, Y. (1994) 'Nihon no terebi seisan ni okeru kigyōkan kankei' (Interfirm relationships in Japanese TV industry), *Keizai ronsō*, 154, 3, pp.63–84.

Chung, M. J. (1993) 'The Government–Business Relationship of Japan: A Case Study of the Japanese Automobile Industry', Ph.D. diss., The Johns Hopkins University.

Cline, W. R. (1987) *The Future of World Trade in Textiles and Apparel*, Washington D.C.: Institute for International Economics.

Cowhey, P. F. and Aronson, J. D. (1993) *Managing the World Economy: The Consequences of Corporate Alliances*, New York: Council on Foreign Relations Press.

Curtis, G. L. (1975) 'Big Business and Political Influence', in E. F. Vogel (ed.), *Modern Japanese Organization and Decision-Making*, Berkeley: University of California Press.

Dertouzos, M. L., Solow, R. M. and Lester, R. K. (1989) *Made in America: Regaining the Productive Edge*, Cambridge, MA: MIT Press.

Destler, I. M. and Odell, J. S. (1987) *Anti-Protection: Changing Forces in United States Trade Politics*, Washington D.C.: Institute for International Economics.

Dicken, P. (1992) *Global Shift: The Internationalization of Economic Activity*, 2nd edn, New York: Guilford Press.

Dobson, W. (1993) *Japan in East Asia: Trading and Investment Strategies*, Singapore: Institute of Southeast Asian Studies.

Dohlman, P. A. (1993) 'The US–Japan Semiconductor Trade Arrangement: Political Economy, Game Theory, and Welfare Analyses', Ph.D. diss., Duke University.

Doi, M., Hayakawa, S. and Yamaguchi, Y. (1985) 'Gendai nihon ni okeru seiji katei heno apurōchi'(Approaches to the political process in contemporary Japan), *Handai hōgaku*, 136, pp.177–247.

Doi, Y. (1995) 'Seni sangyō bōeiron' (Defending the textile industry), *Voice* (August), pp.198–207.

Dore, R. (1986) *Flexible Rigidities: Industrial Policy and Structural Adjustment in the Japanese Economy, 1970–80*, London: Athlone Press.

Doz, Y., Hamel, G. and Prahalad, C. K. (1986) 'Strategic Partnerships, Success or Surrender?: The Challenge of Competitive Collaboration', paper presented at Joint AIB–EIBA Meeting, London, 20–23 November.

Drysdale, P. (1995) 'The Question of Access to the Japanese Market', *The Economic Record*, 71, 214, pp.271–83.

Dunning, J. H. (1993) *Multinational Enterprises and the Global Economy*, Wokingham: Addison-Wesley Publishing.

EIAJ (1987) 'Views of the Electronic Industries Association of Japan on the US–Japan Semiconductor Trade Issue and Suggestions for the Future', Tokyo: EIAJ (mimeo).

—(1988) Statement on Semiconductors, Tokyo: EIAJ (mimeo).

—(1989) Second Statement on Semiconductors, Tokyo: EIAJ (mimeo).

—(1993a) *Design-in Guide Book*, Tokyo: EIAJ.

—(1993b) *'93 kaigai hōjin risuto* (Register of overseas subsidiaries 1993), Tokyo: EIAJ.

—(1994a) *'94 IC gaido bukku* ('94 IC guide book), Tokyo: EIAJ.

—(1994b) *Handōtai sangyō no genjō to shōrai tenbō chōsa hōkokusho* (Survey report on the present state of and future perspectives in the semiconductor industry), Tokyo: EIAJ.

—(1994c) *Semiconductor Facts 1994*, Tokyo: EIAJ.

—(1995) *Semiconductor Facts 1995*, Tokyo: EIAJ.

Encarnation, D. J. (1986) 'Cross-Investment: A Second Front of Economic Rivalry', in T. K. McCraw (ed.), *America Versus Japan*, Boston: Harvard Business School Press.

Enomoto, S. (1991) 'Hand ōtai sangy ō ni okeru teikei' (Alliances in the semiconductor industry), *Kikan keizai kenkyū*, 14, 2, pp.39–64.

Etō, M. (1994) 'Nihon no kisei kanwa: Naniga mondai nanoka' (Deregulation in Japan: What is the matter?), *Keizai seminā*, 474 (July), pp.6–9.

Fallows, J. (1989) 'Containing Japan', *The Atlantic* (May), pp.40–54.

Ferguson, T. (1984) 'From Normalcy to New Deal: Industrial Structure, Party Competition, and American Public Policy in the Great Depression', *International Organization*, 38, 1, pp.41–94.

Fourin (1991) Nihon jidōsha buhin mēkā kokusai jigyō tenkai no shin kyokumen (New phase in international development of the Japanese auto parts manufacturers), *International Automotive Industry Quarterly Report*, 2, 2, Nagoya: Fourin.

—(1993) Hokubei jidōsha sangyō (The automobile industry in North America), *International Automotive Industry Quarterly Report*, 4, 1, Nagoya: Fourin.

Friedman, D. (1988) *The Misunderstood Miracle: Industrial Development and Political Change in Japan*, Ithaca, N.Y.: Cornell University Press.

Friman, H. R. (1990) *Patchwork Protectionism: Textile Trade Policy in the United States, Japan, and West Germany*, Ithaca, N.Y.: Cornell University Press.

FTC (1993a) *Jidōsha buhin no torihiki ni kansuru jittai chōsa* (Survey of conditions of auto parts deals), Tokyo: Fair Trade Commission.

—(1993b) *Jōyōsha no ryūtsū jittai chōsa* (Survey of actual conditions of car distribution), Tokyo: Fair Trade Commission.

—(1993c) Jigyōsha dantai no katsudō to dokusen kinshi hōjō no shomondai: Yori hirakareta katsudō wo mezashite (Activities of trade associations and various problems with the Antimonopoly Law: Searching for openness), Tokyo: Fair Trade Commission (mimeo).

Fujii, M. (1971) *Nihon seni sangyō keiei shi* (The history of management in the Japanese textile industry), Tokyo: Nihon Hyōronsha.

Fujiwara, M. (1988) 'Nichibei handōtai kyōtei, kore ga mitsuyaku bunsho da' (The Japan–US Semiconductor Arrangement: The secret document), *Bungei shunjū* (May), pp.124–37.

Fukui, H. (1987) 'Too Many Captains in Japan's Internationalization: Travails at the Foreign Ministry', in K. B. Pyle (ed.), *The Trade Crisis: How Will Japan Respond?*, Seattle: University of Washington, Society for Japanese Studies.

Fukushima, M. (1991) 'Nichibei tsūshō seisaku keisei jisshi no kōzu' (Formation and implementation of the Japan–US trade policy), in M. Matsushita *et al.*, *Henyō suru nichibei keizai no hōteki kōzō* (The legal structure of evolving Japan–US economies), Tokyo: Tōyōdō Kikaku.

Funabashi, Y. (1987) *Nichibei keizai masatsu* (Japan–US economic friction), Tokyo: Iwanami Shoten.

George, A. (1990) 'The Politics of Liberalization in Japan: The Case of Rice', *Pacific Economic Papers*, 188, Canberra: Australia–Japan Research Centre.

—— (1991) 'Japan's America Problem: The Japanese Response to U.S. Pressure', *Washington Quarterly*, 14, pp.5–19.

George, A. and Saxon, E. (1986) 'The Politics of Agricultural Protection in Japan', in K. Anderson and Y. Hayami (eds), *The Political Economy of Agricultural Protection: East Asia in International Perspective*, Sydney: Allen & Unwin.

Goodman, J. B., Spar, D. and Yoffie, D. B. (1996) 'Foreign Direct Investment and the Demand for Protection in the United States', *International Organization*, 50, 4, pp.565–91.

Gourevitch, P. (1986) *Politics in Hard Times: Comparative Responses to International Economic Crises*, Ithaca, N.Y.: Cornell University Press.

Graham, E. M. and Krugman, P. R. (1991) *Foreign Direct Investment in the United States*, 2nd edn, Washington D.C.: Institute for International Economics.

Grimwade, N. (1989) *International Trade: New Patterns of Trade, Production and Investment*, London: Routledge.

Haley, J. O. (1986) 'Administrative Guidance Versus Formal Regulation: Resolving the Paradox of Industrial Policy', in G. K. Saxonhouse and K. Yamamura (eds), *Law and Trade Issues of the Japanese Economy: American and Japanese Perspectives*, Seattle: University of Washington Press.

Hamilton, C. B. (1992) 'The New Silk Road to Europe', in K. Anderson (ed.), *New Silk Roads: East Asia and World Textile Markets*, Cambridge: Cambridge University Press.

Hanamura, J. (1994) ' "Zaikai seiji buchō" kaisōroku 1: Keidanren no seiji kenkin assen wa kō kizukareta' (Reminiscences of the 'politics director' of business world: How political donation by Keidanren was built up), *Ekonomisuto* (24 May), pp.88–93.

Hart, J. A. (1992) *Rival Capitalists: International Competitiveness in the United States, Japan, and Western Europe*, Ithaca, N.Y.: Cornell University Press.

Heiwa Keizai Kenkyū Kaigi (1982) *Zaikai: Sei kan tono yuchaku no kōzō*

(Business world: Business and its close relationship with politics and bureaucracy), Tokyo: Ochanomizu Shobō.

Helleiner, G. K. (1981) *Intra-Firm Trade and the Developing Countries*, London: Macmillan.

Higashi, C. (1983) *Japanese Trade Policy Formulation*, New York: Praeger.

Higashi, C. and Lauter, G. P. (1990) *The Internationalization of the Japanese Economy*, 2nd edn, Boston: Kluwer Academic Publishers.

Higashi, N. and Ōkawa, M. (1993) 'Erekutoronikusu gyōkai ni okeru senryaku teikei' (Strategic alliances in the electronics industry), *Zaikai kansoku*, 58, 12, pp.78–105.

Hirai, T. (1991) *Seni gyōkai* (The textile industry), Tokyo: Kyōikusha.

Hiramoto, A. (1994) *Nihon no terebi sangyō: Kyōsō yūi no kōzō* (The TV industry in Japan: The structure of advantage in competition), Kyoto: Mineruba Shobō.

Honjo, J. (1993) *Dokyumento Keidanren* (Document Keidanren), Tokyo: Kōdansha.

Horaguchi, H. (1992) *Nihon kigyō no kaigai chokusetsu tōshi: Ajia heno shin-shutsu to tettai* (Foreign direct investment of Japanese firms: Investment and disinvestment in Asia), Tokyo: Tokyo Daigaku Shuppankai.

Howell, T. R., Bartlett, B. L. and Davis, W. (1992) *Creating Advantage: Semiconductors and Government Industrial Policy in the 1990s*, Santa Clara: Semiconductor Industry Association.

Howell, T. R., Noellert, W. A., MacLaughlin, J. H. and Wolff, A. W. (1988) *The Microelectronics Race: The Impact of Government Policy on International Competition*, Boulder, Colo.: Westview Press.

Ike, B. (1980) 'The Japanese Textile Industry: Structural Adjustment and Government Policy', *Asian Survey*, 20, 5, pp.532–51.

Imai, K. (1990) 'Japanese Business Groups and the Structural Impediments Initiative', in K. Yamamura (ed.), *Japan's Economic Structure: Should It Change?*, Seattle: Society for Japanese Studies.

Inoguchi, T. and Iwai, T. (1987) '*Zoku giin' no kenkyū* (Research on 'tribal Dietmen'), Tokyo: Nihon Keizai Shimbunsha.

Ishibashi, S. (1991) 'Jidōsha ryūtsū shisutemu no nichibei hikaku' (Comparison of the car distribution systems of Japan and the United States), *Shōkei ronsō*, 32, 2, pp.109–57.

Ishii, M. (1990) 'Hokubei ni okeru nikkei jidōsha sangyō no genchika senryaku' (Localization strategy of Japanese-affiliated auto companies in North America), *Kaigai tōshi kenkyūshohō*, 16, 2, pp.1–38.

Ishizawa, Y. (1992) *Gensō no nichibei masatsu: Genba de mita gokai to murikai* (Japan–US friction in an illusion: Misunderstanding and nonunderstanding perceived on the scene), Tokyo: TBS Britanika.

Itoh, M. (1994) 'The Japanese Wool Product Industry', in C. Findlay and M. Itoh (eds), *Wool in Japan: Structural Change in the Textile and Clothing Market*, Pymble, NSW: Harper Educational.

Itoh, M. and Urata, S. (1994) 'Small and Medium Enterprise Support Policies in Japan', paper presented at the public seminar of the Australia–Japan Research Centre, 28 February 1994.

Iwai, T. (1990) '*Seiji shikin' no kenkyū* (Research on 'political donation'), Tokyo: Nihon Keizai Shimbunsha.

JAIC (1993) *Tsūshō mondai shōiinkai gyōkai hiyaringu shiryō* (Report on the hearing at the subcommittee on trade issues) (mimeo).

JAMA (1990) Automotive Distribution in Japan, Tokyo: JAMA (mimeo).

— (1993) U.S. Sales of Auto Parts to Japanese Automakers, Tokyo: JAMA (mimeo).

JAPIA (1992) *Nihon no jidōsha buhin kōgyō, 1992/1993* (The auto parts industry in Japan), Tokyo: Ōto Torēdo Jānarū.

JCFA (1993) Tsūshō mondai shōiinkai gyōkai hiyaringu shiryō (Report on the hearing at the subcommittee on trade issues), (mimeo).

Johnson, C. (1982) *MITI and the Japanese Miracle: The Growth of Industrial Policy, 1925–1975*, Stanford: Stanford University Press.

— (1995) *Japan: Who Governs? The Rise of the Developmental State*, New York: Norton.

JSA (1993) *Tsūshō mondai shōiinkai gyōkai hiyaringu shiryō* (Report on the hearing at the subcommittee on trade issues), (mimeo).

JTIA (1993) *Tsūshō mondai shōiinkai gyōkai hiyaringu shiryō* (Report on the hearing at the subcommittee on trade issues), (mimeo).

Kaplan, E. J. (1972) *Japan: The Government–Business Relationship*, Washington D.C., U.S. Department of Commerce.

Katzenstein, P. J. (1978a) 'Introduction: Domestic and International Forces and Strategies of Foreign Economic Policy', in P. J. Katzenstein (ed.), *Between Power and Plenty: Foreign Economic Policies of Advanced Industrial States*, Madison: University of Wisconsin Press.

— (1978b) 'Conclusion: Domestic Structures and Strategies of Foreign Economic Policy', in P. J. Katzenstein (ed.), *Between Power and Plenty: Foreign Economic Policies of Advanced Industrial States*, Madison: University of Wisconsin Press.

Katzenstein, P. J. (ed.) (1978) *Between Power and Plenty: Foreign Economic Policies of Advanced Industrial States*, Madison: University of Wisconsin Press.

Kawano, K. (1991) 'Waga kuni no kijun ninshō seido' (Standards and certification systems in Japan), *Bōeki to kanzei* (September), pp.50–60; (October), pp.52–9.

Kitayama, T. (1985) 'Nihon ni okeru sangyō seisaku no shikkō katei' (The implementation of industrial policy in Japan), *Hōgaku ronsō*, 117, 5, pp.53–76: 118, 2, pp.76–98.

Kline, J. M. (1985) 'Inter-MNC Arrangements: Shaping the Options for U.S. Trade Policy', *Washington Quarterly*, 8, 4, pp.57–71.

Komine, T. (1986) *Keizai masatsu: Kokusaika to nihon no sentaku* (Economic friction: Internationalization and Japan's choice), Tokyo: Nihon Keizai Shimbunsha.

Komiya, R. (1988) 'Introduction', in R. Komiya, M. Okuno and K. Suzumura (eds), *Industrial Policy of Japan*, Tokyo: Academic Press Japan.

Kotani, H. (1982) *Dai 2 ji nichibei jidōsha sensō* (The second Japan–US auto war), Tokyo: Nikkan Kōgyō Shimbunsha.

Krasner, S. D. (1978) 'United States Commercial and Monetary Policy: Unravelling the Paradox of External Strength and Internal Weakness', in P. J. Katzenstein (ed.), *Between Power and Plenty: Foreign Economic Policies of Advanced Industrial States*, Madison: University of Wisconsin Press.

Krauss, E. S. (1993) 'U.S.–Japan Negotiations on Construction and Semiconductors, 1985–1988: Building Friction and Relation-Chips', in P. B. Evans, H. K. Jacobson and R. D. Putnam (eds), *Double-Edged Diplomacy: International Bargaining and Domestic Politics*, Berkeley: University of California Press.

Krueger, A. O. (1974) 'The Political Economy of the Rent-Seeking Society', *The American Economic Review*, 64, 3, pp.291–303.

Kusano, A. (1983) *Nichibei orenji kōshō* (Japan–US negotiations on oranges), Tokyo: Nihon Keizai Shimbunsha.

—(1992) *Daitenhō: Keizai kisei no kōzō* (The Large-Scale Retail Store Law: Structure of economic regulations), Tokyo: Nihon Keizai Shimbunsha.

Kuwata, Y. (1990) 'Nichibei dōmeika no ryōkoku handōtai kyōsō' (Semiconductor competition under the Japan–US alliance), *Keizai ronsō*, 145, 12, pp.73–99.

Lavergne, R. (1983) *The Political Economy of U.S. Tariffs: An Empirical Analysis*, Toronto: Academic Press.

Lawrence, R. Z. (1991a) 'The Reluctant Giant: Will Japan Take Its Role on the World Stage?', *Brookings Review*, 9, pp.36–9.

—(1991b) 'Efficient or Exclusionist?: The Import Behavior of Japanese Corporate Groups', *Brookings Papers on Economic Activity*, 1, pp.311–41.

Lincoln, E. J. (1986) 'Comment', in T. A. Pugel (ed.), *Fragile Interdependence: Economic Issues in U.S.–Japanese Trade and Investment*, Lexington, Mass.: Lexington Books.

Lynn, L. H. and McKeown, T. J. (1988) *Organizing Business: Trade Associations in America and Japan*, Washington D.C.: American Enterprise Institute for Public Policy Research.

Mainichi Shimbun (1991) *Zaikai to seikai: Saihen heno taidō* (Business world and political world: Indications of reorganization), Tokyo: Aipekku Puresu.

Mair, A. (1994) *Honda's Global Local Corporation*, New York: St. Martin's Press.

Maki, T. (1982) 'Rincho 500 nichi no kiseki' (The 500-day history of Rincho), *Sekai* (September), pp.62–75.

Management and Coordination Agency (1995) *Kisei kanwa suishin no genjō* (The present state of the promotion of deregulation), Tokyo: The Management and Coordination Agency.

Mason, M. (1992) *American Multinationals and Japan: The Political Economy of Japanese Capital Control, 1899–1980*, Cambridge, Mass.: Council on East Asian Studies, Harvard University.

—(1995) 'Japan's Low Levels of Inward Direct Investment: Causes, Consequences and Remedies', in E. K. Y. Chen and P. Drysdale (eds), *Corporate Links and Foreign Direct Investment in Asia and the Pacific*, Pymble, NSW: Harper Educational.

Matsumoto, A. (1993) ' "Keidanren shisutemu" no shūen' (The end of the 'Keidanren system'), *Sekai* (October), pp.78–87.

McKean, M. A. (1993) 'State Strength and the Public Interest', in G. D. Allinson and Y. Sone (eds), *Political Dynamics in Contemporary Japan*, Ithaca, N.Y.: Cornell University Press.

Mikanagi, Y. (1996) *Japan's Trade Policy: Action or Reaction?*, London: Routledge.

Milner, H. V. (1987) 'Resisting the Protectionist Temptation: Industry and the Making of Trade Policy in France and the United States During the 1970s', *International Organization*, 41, 4, pp.639–65.

— (1988) *Resisting Protectionism: Global Industries and the Politics of International Trade*, Princeton, N.J.: Princeton University Press.

Milner, H. V. and Yoffie, D. B. (1989) 'Between Free Trade and Protectionism: Strategic Trade Policy and a Theory of Corporate Trade Demands', *International Organization*, 43, 2, pp.239–72.

MITI (1994a) *Tsūshō hakusho 1994* (White paper on international trade and industry 1994), Tokyo: Ōkurasho Insatsukyoku.

— (1994b) *Dai 27 kai gaishikei kigyō no dōkō* (The 27th survey on foreign-affiliated companies), Tokyo: Ōkurasho Insatsukyoku.

— (1994c) *Sekai seni sangyō jijō* (Report on the world textile industry), Tokyo: Tsushō Sangyō Chōsakai.

— (1995a) *Shin seni bijon* (New textile report), Tokyo: Gyōsei.

— (1995b) Tainichi tōshi sokushin saku ni tuite (Measures to promote inward investment in Japan), Tokyo: MITI (mimeo).

Morita, A. (1992) ' "Nihongata keiei" ga abunai' ('Japanese-style management' in critical moment), *Bungei shunjū* (February), pp.94–103.

— (1993) 'Renewing the Global Free-Market Framework', *Japan Echo*, 20, 2, pp.48–54.

Mukaiyama, M. (1989) 'Ryūtsū kōzō no henkaku to chūshō kigyō' (The reform of distribution structure of small and medium-sized companies), *Shōkō kinyū*, 39, 6, pp.18–35.

Muramatsu, M. (1993) 'Industry's Flexible Friend', *Look Japan* (March), pp.14–15.

Nakatani, I. and Ōta, H. (1994) *Keizai kaikaku no bijon: 'Hiraiwa repōto' wo koete* (Perspectives for economic reform: Beyond the 'Hiraiwa Report'), Tokyo: Tōyō Keizai Shimpōsha.

Namura, A. (1991) 'Nihon kigyō no kokusai senryaku ni kansuru kenkyū' (Research on global strategies of Japanese firms), *Kokusai Kankeigaku Kenkyū*, 4, pp.65–78.

National Research Council (1992) *U.S.–Japan Strategic Alliances in the Semiconductor Industry: Technology Transfer, Competition, and Public Policy*, Washington D.C.: National Academy Press.

Negishi, A. (1986) 'Bōeki masatsu to kijun ninshō seido' (Trade friction and standards and certification systems), *Jurisuto*, 873 (1 November), pp.10–15.

Nihon Keizai Shimbunsha (ed.) (1990) *Zemināru: gendai kigyō nyūmon* (Seminar: Introduction to contemporary enterprises), Tokyo: Nihon Keizai Shimbunsha.

Niihanda, H. and Mishima, B. (1991) 'Ryūtsū keiretsuka no tenkai: Katei denki' (The development of distribution keiretsu: Home electrical appliances), in Y. Miwa and K. Nishimura (eds), *Nihon no ryūtsū* (Distribution in Japan), Tokyo: Tokyo Daigaku Shuppankai.

Nikkei Ryūtsū Shimbun (ed.) (1993) *Kaden ryūtsū saihen heno chōsen* (Challenge to the reform of distribution in home electrical appliances), Tokyo: Nihon Keizai Shimbunsha.

NIRA (National Institute for Research Advancement) (1989) *Nichi bei ō no keizai masatsu wo meguru seiji katei* (Political processes surrounding economic friction among Japan, the United States and Europe), Tokyo: NIRA.

Noble, G. W. (1989) 'The Japanese Industrial Policy Debate', in S. Haggard and C. Moon (eds), *Pacific Dynamics: The International Politics of Industrial Change*, Inchon: Center for International Studies, Inha University; Boulder, Colo.: Westview Press.

OECD (1993) *Intra-Firm Trade*, Paris: OECD.

—(1994) *International Direct Investment Statistics Yearbook*, Paris: OECD.

Okamoto, Y. (1988) 'Takokuseki kigyō to nihon kigyō no takokusekika (2)' (Multinational corporations and the multinationalization of Japanese firms II), *Keizaigaku ronshū*, 53, 3, pp.67–92.

Okimoto, D. I. (1984) 'Political Context', in D. I. Okimoto, T. Sugano and F. B. Weinstein (eds), *Competitive Edge: The Semiconductor Industry in the U.S. and Japan*, Stanford: Stanford University Press.

—(1988) 'Political Inclusivity: The Domestic Structure of Trade', in T. Inoguchi and D. I. Okimoto (eds), *The Political Economy of Japan, Vol 2: The Changing International Context*, Stanford: Stanford University Press.

—(1989) *Between MITI and the Market: Japanese Industrial Policy for High Technology*, Stanford: Stanford University Press.

Olson, M. (1965) *The Logic of Collective Action*, Cambridge, Mass.: Harvard University Press.

Ostry, S. and Nelson, R. R. (1995) *Techno-Nationalism and Techno-Globalism: Conflict and Cooperation*, Washington D.C.: The Brookings Institution.

OTA (US Congress, Office of Technology Assessment) (1993) *Multinationals and the National Interest: Playing by Different Rules*, Washington D.C.: US Government Printing Office.

Ōtake, H. (1979) *Gendai nihon no seiji kenryoku keizai kenryoku* (Political and economic power in contemporary Japan), Tokyo: Sanichi Shobō.

Ōtani, K. (1989) *Nihon ga beikoku wo kaeru* (Japan changes the United States), Tokyo: Nihon Keizai Shimbunsha.

Ōuchi, A. (1987) 'Onwo adade kaerareta yōna kimochi' (Evil returned for good), *Bungei shunjū* (June), pp.97–100.

Ouchi, W. G. (1984) *The M-Form Society: How American Teamwork Can Recapture the Competitive Edge*, Reading, Mass.: Addison-Wesley.

Ōyama, K. (1989) 'Gendai nihon ni okeru gyōsei shidō no seiji kōzō' (The political structure of administrative guidance in contemporary Japan), *Shakai kagaku kenkyū*, 40, 6, pp.1–134.

—(1996) *Gyōsei shidō no seiji keizai gaku: Sangyō seisaku no keisei to jisshi* (Political economy of administrative guidance: The formation and implementation of industrial policy), Tokyo; Yūhikaku.

Ōyane, S. (1992) 'Kokusai rezīmu to taigai seisaku katei: GATT, MFA rezīmu wo meguru nihon no seni seisaku katei' (International regimes and the external policy-making process: Japanese policy making in textiles at the GATT, MFA regime), *Kokusaihō gaikō zasshi*, 90, 6, pp.32–66.

—(1997) 'Nichibei handōai masatsu ni okeru "suchi mokuhyō" keisei katei' (The formation process of 'numerical target' in the Japan–US semiconductor friction), *Nenpō seijigaku 1997*, pp.155–75.

Ozawa, T. (1991) 'Japan in a New Phase of Multinationalism and Industrial Upgrading: Functional Integration of Trade, Growth and FDI', *Journal of World Trade*, 25, 1,2, pp.43–60.

Park, Y. and Anderson, K. (1992) 'The Experience of Japan in Historical and International Perspective', in K. Anderson (ed.), *New Silk Roads: East Asia and World Textile Markets*, Cambridge: Cambridge University Press.

Patrick, H. and Rosovsky, H. (1976) 'Japan's Economic Performance: An Overview', in H. Patrick and H. Rosovsky (eds), *Asia's New Giant: How the Japanese Economy Works*, Washington D.C.: Brookings Institution.

Pempel, T. J. (1982) *Policy and Politics in Japan: Creative Conservatism*, Philadelphia: Temple University Press.

PFC (People's Finance Corporation) (1990) *Nihon no chūshō seni kōgyō*, 2nd edn (The small and medium-scale textile industry in Japan), Tokyo: Chūshō Kigyō Risāchi Sentā.

Phongpaichit, P. (1990) *The New Wave of Japanese Investment in ASEAN*, Singapore: Institute of Southeast Asian Studies.

Pincus, J. J. (1975) 'Pressure Groups and the Pattern of Tariffs', *Journal of Political Economy*, 83, 4, pp.757–78.

Prestowitz, C. V. (1988) *Trading Places: How We Allowed Japan to Take the Lead*, New York: Basic Books.

Pugel, T. A. and Walter, I. (1985) 'U.S. Corporate Interests and the Political Economy of Trade Policy', *Review of Economics and Statistics*, 67, pp.465–73.

Ray, E. (1981) 'Determinants of Tariff and Nontariff Trade Restrictions in the United States', *Journal of Political Economy*, 89, pp.105–21.

Ripley, R. B. and Franklin, G. A. (1984) *Congress, the Bureaucracy, and Public Policy*, 3rd edn, Homewood, Ill.: The Dorsey Press.

Rogowski, R. (1989) *Commerce and Coalitions: How Trade Affects Domestic Political Alignments*, Princeton, N.J.: Princeton University Press.

Rosenbluth, F. M. (1989) *Financial Politics in Contemporary Japan*, Ithaca, N.Y.: Cornell University Press.

Ryū, K. (1995) 'Shōchō no gaikaku dantai, gyōkai dantai, shimon kikan' (Extra-governmental organizations, industrial associations, and advisory councils), in M. Nishio and T. Muramatsu (eds), *Kōza gyōseigaku dai 4 kan: Seisaku to kanri* (Public administration seminar vol.4, policy and control), Tokyo: Yūhikaku.

Sakakibara, E. (1991) 'The Japanese Politico-Economic System and the Public Sector', in S. Kernell (ed.), *Parallel Politics: Economic Policymaking in the United States and Japan*, Washington D.C.: Brookings Institution.

—— (1996) *Shinpo syugi kara no ketubetu* (A departure from progressivism), Tokyo: Yomiuri shinbunsha.

Sakura Research Institute (1995) 'Gōsen gyōkai no takakuka senryaku: Genjō to tenbō' (Diversified management strategies in the synthetic fibre sector: Present situation and perspectives), *Keizai repōto*, 29, pp.1–17.

Samuels, R. J. (1983) 'The Industrial Destructuring of the Japanese Aluminium Industry', *Pacific Affairs*, 56, 3, pp.495–509.

—— (1987) *The Business of the Japanese State: Energy Markets in Comparative and Historical Perspective*, Ithaca, N.Y.: Cornell University Press.

Samuels, R. J. (1996) *Rich Nation, Strong Army: National Security and the Technological Transformation of Japan*, Ithaca, N.Y.: Cornell University Press.

Satō, H. (1991) *Nichibei keizai masatsu, 1945–1990 nen* (Japan–US economic friction, 1945–1990), Tokyo: Heibonsha.

Satō, S. and Matsuzaki, T. (1986) *Jimintō seiken* (LDP power), Tokyo: Chūō Kō ronsha.

Schoppa, L. J. (1993) 'Two-Level Games and Bargaining Outcomes: Why *Gaiatsu* Succeeds in Japan in Some Cases But Not Others', *International Organization*, 47, 3, pp.353–86.

Schwartz, F. (1993) 'Of Fairy Cloaks and Familiar Talks: The Politics of Consultation', in G. D. Allinson and Y. Sone (eds), *Political Dynamics in Contemporary Japan*, Ithaca, N.Y.: Cornell University Press.

Sei, S. (1987) 'Jidōsha wo meguru keizai masatsu' (Economic friction over automobiles), in S. Satō (ed.), *Nichibei keizai masatsu no kōzū* (The structure of Japan–US economic friction), Tokyo: Yūhikaku.

Sheard, P. (1993) '*Keiretsu*, and Closedness of the Japanese Market: An Economic Appraisal', Working Paper Series 93–5, Centre for Japanese Economic Studies, Macquarie University (April).

Shimokawa, K. (1987) 'Nichibei jidōsha sangyō no ryūtsū hanbai shisutemu no kokusai hikaku to kongo no jidōsha ryūtsū no kakushin' (International comparison of the distribution and sales systems between the Japanese and US auto industry and innovations in the future car distribution), *Keiei shirin*, 24, 2, pp.1–13.

—— (1993) 'Making it Work: The Real Challenge of Globalization for Japan's Automobile Industry', *Keiei shirin*, 30, 2, pp.25–52.

Shimura, Y. (1992) *2000 nen no handōtai sangyō* (The semiconductor industry in 2000), Tokyo: Nihon Nōritsu Kyōkai Manejimento Sentā.

—— (1993) 'Handōtai sensō: Amerika no gotsugō shugi' (Semiconductor war: US opportunism), *Bungei shunjū* (May), pp.284–90.

Shindō, M. (1992) *Gyōsei shidō* (Administrative guidance), Tokyo: Iwanami Shoten.

Shioji, H. (1991) 'Jidōsha hanbai ni okeru nijū no "keiretsu" mondai' (Double 'keiretsu' problem in car sales), *Shōkei ronsō*, 32, 1, pp.189–226.

—— (1992) 'Nichibei jidōsha masatsu no teiryū wo tsuku' (Focus on the undercurrents in Japan–US auto friction), *Keizai*, 343, pp.179–93.

SIA (1990) 'A Deal is a Deal: Four Years of Experience under the U.S.–Japan Semiconductor Agreement', Santa Clara: Semiconductor Industry Association (mimeo).

Soete, L. (1991) 'National Support Policies for Strategic Industries: The International Implications', in OECD (ed.), *Strategic Industries in a Global Economy: Policy Issues for the 1990s*, Paris: OECD.

Sone, Y. (1993) 'Conclusion: Structuring Political Bargains: Government, Gyokai, and Markets', in G. D. Allinson and Y. Sone (eds), *Political Dynamics in Contemporary Japan*, Ithaca, N.Y.: Cornell University Press.

Starr, M. K. (1991) *Global Corporate Alliances and the Competitive Edge: Strategies and Tactics for Management*, New York: Quorum Books.

Stevens, B. (1991) 'Support Policies for Strategic Industries: An Assessment and Some Policy Recommendations', in OECD (ed.), *Strategic Industries in a Global Economy: Policy Issues for the 1990s*, Paris: OECD.

Takeda, S. (1992) *Kokusai senryaku teikei* (International strategic alliances), Tokyo: Dobunkan.

Takenaka, H. and Miyoshi, M. (1995) 'Kisei kanwa ha naze susumanainoka' (Why it takes time to promote deregulation), *Keizai seminā*, 480, (January), pp.38–46.

Takeuchi, K. (1994) 'Kaden sangyō' (The home electrical industry), in Japan Commission on Industrial Performance (ed.), *Meido in Japan* (Made in Japan), Tokyo: Daiyamondosha.

Tanaka, A. (1989) 'Nihon gaikō to kokunai seiji no renkan' (The relations between Japanese diplomacy and domestic politics), *Kokusai mondai*, 348, pp.23–36.

Tanaka, Y. (1979) 'The World of *Zaikai*', in H. Murakami and H. Johannes (eds), *Politics and Economics in Contemporary Japan*, Tokyo: Japan Culture Institute.

Tashiro, Y. (1989) 'Kome mondai' (The rice issue), *Nōgyō to keizai* (May), pp.6–13.

Terada, T. (1994) 'Political Economy of the Large-Scale Retail Store Law: Transforming "Impediments" to Entering the Japanese Retail Industry', *Pacific Economic Papers*, 237, Australia–Japan Research Centre.

Teranishi, K. and Yamasaki, M. (1995) 'Ajia wo kakuni kōzō henkaku ga kasoku suru erekutoronikusu sangyō' (The electronics industry accelerating structural reform around Asia), *Zaikai kansoku*, 60, 5, pp.52–95.

Thomsen, S. and Nicolaides, P. (1991) *The Evolution of Japanese Direct Investment in Europe: Death of a Transistor Salesman*, New York: Harvester Wheatsheaf.

Toray (1977) *Tōre 50 nen shi: 1926–1976* (The 50-year history of Toray: 1926–1976), Tokyo: Toray Industries.

Toyne, B. *et al.* (1984) *The Global Textile Industry*, London: George Allen & Unwin.

Trezise, P. H. (1983) 'Industrial Policy Is Not the Major Reason for Japan's Success', *The Brookings Review*, 1, 3, pp.13–18.

Tsuchiya, M. (1989) 'Nissan jidōsha' (Nissan Motors), *Will* (December), pp.52–8.

Tsujinaka, U. (1988) *Rieki shūdan* (Interest groups), Tokyo: Tokyo Daigaku Shuppankai.

Tsurumi, Y. (1976) *The Japanese Are Coming: A Multinational Interaction of Firms and Politics*, Cambridge, Mass.: Ballinger Publishing.

Tsuruta, T. (1992) 'Kigyō shūdan, keiretsu no mondaiten to kyōsō seisaku' (Problems of corporate groups and *keiretsu* with competition policy), *Kōsei torihiki*, 496, pp.4–9.

Tyson, L. D. (1992) *Who's Bashing Whom?: Trade Conflict in High-Technology Industries*, Washington D.C.: Institute for International Economics.

Tyson, L. D. and Yoffie, D. B. (1993) 'Semiconductors: From Manipulated to Managed Trade', in D. B. Yoffie (ed.), *Beyond Free Trade: Firms, Governments, and Global Competition*, Boston: Harvard Business School Press.

Uchihashi, K. (1994) 'Nichibei "ketsuretsu" no shinin' (The true cause for the Japan–US breakdown), *Sekai* (April), pp.60–71.

UCOM (1993) *Gaikokukei handōtai yūzā kyōgikai 5 nenkan no ayumi* (The five-year history of the Users Committee of Foreign Semiconductors), Tokyo: Users Committee of Foreign Semiconductors.

Uekusa, M. and Nanbu, T. (1973) 'Gōsei seni' (Synthetic fibre), in H. Kumagai (ed), *Nihon no sangyo soshiki II* (Japanese industrial structure II), Tokyo: Chūō Koronsha.

Ueno, H. and Atsuya, J. (1977) 'Jigyōsha dantai bunseki no wakugumi' (An analytical framework for industrial associations), *Keizai Seminā*, 265, 2, pp.19–25: 266, 3, pp.67–74.

Urata, S. (1992) 'Japanese Foreign Direct Investment and Its Impact on Foreign Trade in Asia' (mimeo).

——(1993) 'Electronics Industry' (mimeo).

Uriu, R. M. (1996) *Troubled Industries: Confronting Economic Change in Japan*, Ithaca, N.Y.: Cornell University Press.

Uryū, F. (1990) *Industrial Adjustment in Japan and the U.S.: The Case of the Textile Industry*, Cambridge, Mass.: Program on U.S.–Japan Relations, Harvard University.

US Senate (1991) Renewal of the United States–Japan Semiconductor Agreement, Hearing before the Subcommittee on International Trade, Washington D.C.: US Government Printing Office.

van Wolferen, K. (1989) *The Enigma of Japanese Power: People and Politics in a Stateless Nation*, London: Macmillan.

Vogel, E. (1978) 'Guided Free Enterprise in Japan', *Harvard Business Review*, 56, pp.161–70.

Wada, T. (1990) 'Jigyōsha dantai no kinō (The functions of industrial associations), *Jurisuto*, 950 (February 15), pp.57–62.

Watanabe, Y. (1992) *Toyota ga nihon wo kaeru* (Toyota changes Japan), Tokyo: Nikkan Shobō.

Whalley, J. (1992) 'The Multi-Fibre Arrangement and China's Growth Prospects', in K. Anderson (ed.), *New Silk Roads: East Asia and World Textile Markets*, Cambridge: Cambridge University Press.

Wu, D. (1991) 'Nihon no seizōgyō ni okeru kigyōkan bungyō kankei' (Division of labour practices among firms in Japanese manufacturing industry), *Keizai ronsō, bessatsu chōsa to kenkyū*, 1, pp.62–80.

Yaginuma, H. (1992) 'Keiretsu mondai no rironteki apurōchi' (Theoretical approach to the keiretsu issue), in T. Kiyonari and K. Shimokawa (eds), *Gendai no keiretsu* (Contemporary keiretsu), Tokyo: Nihon Keizai Hyōronsha.

Yamakawa, K. (1984) 'Zaikai dantai to seiji' (Peak business organizations and politics), *Hōgaku seminā*, 3396, Tokushū: Korekara no nihon no seiji (Special issue: The future of Japanese politics), pp.107–16.

Yamamura, K. (1994) 'The Deliberate Emergence of a Free Trader: The Japanese Political Economy in Transition', in C. Garby and M. B. Bullock (eds), *Japan: A New Kind of Superpower?*, Washington D.C.: Woodrow Wilson Center Press.

Yamamura, K. and Vandenberg, J. (1986) 'Japan's Rapid-Growth Policy on Trial: The Television Case', in G. K. Saxonhouse and K. Yamamura (eds), *Law and Trade Issues of the Japanese Economy: American and Japanese Perspectives*, Seattle: University of Washington Press.

Yamawaki, H. (1992) 'International Competition and Japan's Domestic

Adjustments', in K. Anderson (ed.), *New Silk Roads: East Asia and World Textile Markets*, Cambridge: Cambridge University Press.

Yamazawa, I. (1980) 'Increasing Imports and Structural Adjustment of the Japanese Textile Industry', *The Developing Economies*, 18, pp.441–62.

—(1988) 'The Textile Industry', in R. Komiya, M. Okuno and K. Suzumura (eds), *Industrial Policy of Japan*, Tokyo: Academic Press.

Yanaga, C. (1968) *Big Business in Japanese Politics*, New Haven, Conn.: Yale University Press.

Yoffie, D. B. (1988) 'How an Industry Builds Political Advantage', *Harvard Business Review*, 66, 3, pp.82–9.

Yonekura, S. (1993) 'Gyōkai dantai no kinō (The function of industrial associations), in T. Okazaki and M. Okuno (eds), *Gendai nihon keizai sisutemu no genryū* (The origin of contemporary economic system in Japan), Tokyo: Nihon keizai shimbunsha.

Yoshihara, K. (1978) *Japanese Investment in Southeast Asia*, Honolulu: University Press of Hawaii.

Young, S., Hamill, J., Wheeler, C. and Davies, J. R. (1989) *International Market Entry and Development*, Englewood Cliffs, N.J.: Prentice Hall.

Young, M. K. (1984) 'Judicial Review of Administrative Guidance: Governmentally Encouraged Consensual Dispute Resolution in Japan', *Columbia Law Review*, 84, 4, pp.923–83.

Zenchu (1991) Gatto uruguai raundo nōgyō kōshō ni kansuru nōgyō seisansha no shuchō (The assertion of farmers regarding the GATT Uruguay Round negotiations on agriculture), Tokyo: Zenchū (mimeo).

Zhao, Q. (1993) *Japanese Policymaking: The Politics behind Politics, Informal Mechanisms and the Making of China Policy*, Westport, Conn.: Praeger.

Zysman, J. (1983) *Governments, Markets, and Growth: Financial Systems and the Politics of Industrial Change*, Ithaca, N.Y.: Cornell University Press.

Index